Routledge Library Editions

ECONOMIC PHENOMENA BEFORE & AFTER WAR

ECONOMICS

Routledge Library Editions – Economics

ECONOMIC HISTORY
In 4 Volumes

I	A Short Economic History of Modern Japan	*Allen*
II	Depression and Protectionism	*Capie*
III	Enterprise and Trade in Victorian Britain	*McCloskey*
IV	Economic Phenomena Before & After War	*Šećerov*

ECONOMIC PHENOMENA BEFORE & AFTER WAR

A Statistical Theory of Modern Wars

SLAVKO ŠEĆEROV

Routledge
Taylor & Francis Group
LONDON AND NEW YORK

First published in 1919

Reprinted in 2003 by
Routledge
2 Park Square, Milton Park, Abingdon, Oxon, OX14 4RN
or
270 Madison Avenue, New York, NY 10016

First issued in paperback 2010

Routledge is an imprint of the Taylor & Francis Group

British Library Cataloguing in Publication Data
A CIP catalogue record for this book
is available from the British Library

Economic Phenomena Before & After War
ISBN 978-0-415-31306-3 (hbk)
ISBN 978-0-415-60706-3 (pbk)
ISBN 978-0-415-31302-5 (set)

Miniset: Economic History

Series: Routledge Library Editions – Economics

ECONOMIC PHENOMENA BEFORE & AFTER WAR

A Statistical Theory of Modern Wars

By

SLAVKO ŠEĆEROV

PH.D., M.SC. (ECON.) (LONDON), F.S.S.

Routledge
Taylor & Francis Group
LONDON AND NEW YORK

Thesis approved for the Degree of Master of Science (Economics) in the University of London

PREFACE

THE " Economic Phenomena before and after War " embodies the result of the author's search for a scientific, synthetic explanation of modern wars, by means of economic statistical data, as far as they exist, in the statistics of consumption, production, and natural growth of population in the several countries investigated.

It is partly an ordered and critical assemblage and exposition of existing data with regard to this synthetic explanation of modern wars, and partly a record of original research of economic phenomena and their measurement by means of statistical methods.

The author attempted to measure the growth of consumption in the chief countries by means of index numbers with a similar base, so as to render a comparison possible. Further, the author endeavoured to measure the growth of production of primary and secondary goods by production index numbers, computed with a similar base for like commodities for the whole world, for longer and shorter periods.

The theory the author propounds, assumes that a state of war in the modern communities is dependent on the general economic equilibrium, which becomes more and more unstable as industrialization progresses. The economic equilibrium of the modern communities is a resultant of the growth of population and consumption and of the state of production and distribution. In order that the economic equilibrium of modern communities should be stable, there has to be a certain proportion in the growth of population and consumption and the state of production and distribution. The forces affecting the growth of population, consumption, and production, and the state of distribution have to run in parallel direction, if the proportion and economic equilibrium be stable.

The pre-war unstable state of economic equilibrium is indicated by a situation where the actions of the forces become more and more of antagonistic nature. The natural growth of population is in a declining phase, while the consumption per head is in an ascending phase. Yet although the short pre-war period of consumption is in ascending phase, the average of this period is lower than that of the preceding equal period ; that is termed the pressure on consumption.

The state of pre-war production is characterized by a disproportionate rate of increase in the production of primary and secondary goods, the former including the necessaries of life and raw materials connected with them, the latter the industrial and commercial products of modern communities. The rate of increase in the production of secondary goods is twice as great as that of the production of primary ones.

A state of war indicates a turning point in the action of balancing forces; it moves the economic forces in an opposite direction, and therefore it is a means to stabilize the general economic equilibrium.

After war, the rate of natural growth is in an ascending phase and the consumption is in a declining one; the production of secondary goods is either supplemented by areas of production of primary ones, under very different political formulas, by the countries winning the war, or the production is directed to an intensive cultivation of primary goods in the countries losing it.

The state of distribution, although of fundamental importance, is not yet investigated; yet it is the author's idea, that the ultimate cause of modern wars is dependent on the action of distributive forces, effecting a continuous accumulation of capital, and therefore creating a demand for investment and employment, and that is done in industrial processes; thereby the disproportion in the production of primary and secondary goods is continuously pushed forward. Yet the function of war in regard to this accumulated capital is partly to destroy it and partly to bind it in the shape of government debts and therefore depressing its action. These, although obvious phenomena, have not been statistically investigated here.

S. S.

CONTENTS

ECONOMIC PHENOMENA BEFORE AND AFTER WAR

"As the level of welfare rises, the struggle for existence will change, but not diminish; it will become a struggle, not for life itself, but for the comforts of life, and there is no reason to believe that the latter struggle will be less severe. It will be a struggle like that in which, already now, we may see the banker engaged when he does not want to be forestalled by his fellow-bankers; or the manufacturer, who wants to attain a high standing in his trade; or the shopkeeper or dealer, who wants to compete successfully.

"If we were to assume that, with advancing welfare, wants would remain stationary, we should not be right in saying what we have said. But as welfare increases, wants increase even more rapidly as a rule."

—N. G. PIERSON, *Principles of Economy*, vol. 2, p. 124.

"The increase of population in Europe is having one of Malthus' positive checks, administered with very great sharpness."

—PROF. E. CANNAN, *Economic Journal*, vol. 26, p. 219. 1916.

I

INTRODUCTION

THE aim of this essay is to find out a possible numerical or statistical connexion between the economic phenomena of a community and a state of war.

Whatever the cause of a war may have been, the effect is always a readjustment of political power, in accordance with the success or defeat resulting from the war, accompanied by a territorial readjustment of boundaries. The former arrangement, existing previous to the war, was not in harmony with the actual political forces, and the war effects a rearrangement, according to the actual political forces, as shown in the course of the war. We could state the same idea by saying that war is a restoration of balance or equilibrium of political forces by means of violent and rather primitive methods of killing people, and also by great destruction of wealth, actual and potential. But besides the actual loss of human life a war affects the economic phenomena of production and consumption of goods too, and if the readjustment of political power is effected by means of the death of people (killing, diseases, etc.), there is reason to believe and to suppose, that the actual number of people living in a given territory may not be in accordance with the economic situation, the production and consumption of goods at the moment. In other words, population, whether we take the actual numbers or the growth and the proportionate increase of consumption and production of goods, may show some definite characteristics, indicating an approaching state of war. The idea of readjustment supposes a balancing of economic and political forces, and that assumes a kind of unstable equilibrium.

This kind of economic situation where the rate of the growth of the population and the rate of increase of consumption and the state of production have some definite features, which indicate an approaching war, we shall call shortly a war-equilibrium. A war-equilibrium indicates an approaching state of war inasmuch as there the violent rupture by means of war always comes in, provided no other means of political and economic readjustment are applied to prevent it.

As to the causal relation between the economic conditions of a community and a state of war, the investigation may be carried out under the following assumptions.

Firstly, the pre-war economic condition is the cause of war, as, for instance, in an agricultural community a failure of the harvest causes a famine, and the community, to avoid complete destruction through famine, tries to seize means of living in a neighbouring community.

Secondly, the pre-war economic conditions are one among the causes of war. The causes may be of political, economic and dynastical natures. This assumption could be considered as more approaching to the reality of the complex social and economic phenomena of modern times, as it is impossible to think that a war is caused by only one economic condition, at least in a more developed community, such as ours.

Thirdly, war is a function of economic conditions; this does not suppose a direct causation by economic phenomena, but it affirms a looser dependence on them.

The impossibility of observing the economic phenomena as direct causes of a war, in strict logical manner, makes the view more suitable to statistical research. From this assumption it follows that the economic situation or conditions must have some definite relations of dependence to a war, and must show definite features before and after war. These features, characterizing the pre-war, war, and post-war economic situations, are the subject of the inquiry.

The pre-war and post-war economic phenomena are tending to act in opposite directions and to balance the action of each other, and the balancing action assumes a kind of dynamic equilibrium.

But, in order to make clear the idea of equilibrium, and to connect it with the economic balancing of forces before and after war, I shall try in the following chapter to gain some clear conception of the idea of equilibrium by consideration of the meaning attached to the term in physics, chemistry, and economics, without any use of mathematics.

II

EQUILIBRIUM

Physics.

IF we draw [1] a straight line and fix on any point O in it, we may suppose a force acting on the point O, along the line AB, either towards A or B; then O is called the point of application of the force, AB its line of action. If it acts towards A, its direction is OA, if towards B, its direction is OB. It is not necessary, therefore, to distinguish between the line of action and direction of force. If a force acts from O to A and another from O to B, the directions may be indicated by positive and negative signs, as for instance $+ P$ or $- P$. Now if the force OA contains the same units as OB but of opposite direction, the whole system will be in equilibrium, because the action of the force OA balances the action of the force OB.

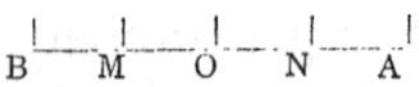

Fig. 1.

If these units be P and Q, and their equivalent force of opposite direction R, then putting this relation into an equation as follows, we get

$$R = P + Q.$$

Expressing the relation numerically, we may say, that if the system be in equilibrium, the forces of three and four units, acting on O in the direction of OA require an action of a single force of seven units, acting in opposite direction. This single force is called resultant, and if the forces are in equilibrium,

[1] Ganot's *Physics*, 18th ed., 1910.

the forces have the tendency to move the point O in opposite directions.

A good illustration of the principle is a pulley. Suppose that two equal masses are balanced on a pulley with fixed axle. Now if the masses are of equal weight, and if therefore both weights of equal magnitude are tending to move the pulley but in opposite directions, the system will be in equilibrium, and the forces, that is the weights, balance each other.

But if the system is in equilibrium and an additional mass is placed on the one side, the system will move in this direction. To balance the action of this mass, a mass of equal weight must be placed on the other side, which will act in the opposite direction and therefore equalize the action of the first mass. The result is an equilibrium of a system.

If there is an action of several forces, then a material point is in equilibrium if any one of the forces is capable of neutralizing the combined effects of all the others. The parallelogram of forces and the triangles of forces are only special cases of this principle. The forces whose effect is equivalent to the combined effects of several others is called their resultant, and the other forces are termed components with respect to the resultant.

Applying the principle of virtual velocity,[1] on the idea of equilibrium, we may say that a material system, whose relative motives are unresisted by friction, is in equilibrium in any particular configuration if the work done by the applied forces is equal to the potential energy gained in any possible infinitely small displacement from that configuration.

To comprehend this proposition we have to think that the system cannot possibly move away from any configuration except by work being done upon it by the forces to which it is subject, and it is therefore in equilibrium if the work of the applied forces is

[1] W. Thompson and P. G. Tait, *Treatise on Natural Philosophy*, vol. I p. 265 and following pages.

equivalent to the potential energy gained. That this condition can secure the equilibrium, we have to consider a system having only one degree of *freedom to move.* Whatever forces act on the whole system, we may always hold it in equilibrium by a single force applied to any one point of the system in its line of motion, opposite to the direction in which it tends to move, and of such magnitude that in any infinitely small motion in either direction it resists and does as much work as the other forces, applied or internal, all together do or resist. Now by the principle of superposition of forces in equilibrium, we might, without altering their effect, apply to any one point of the system such a force as would hold the system in equilibrium and another force equal and opposite to it.

The theory of energy gives a clearer and simpler test for distinguishing the character or determining whether the equilibrium is neutral, stable or unstable. If there is just as much work resisted as performed by the applied and internal forces in any possible displacement, the equilibrium is neutral. If in every possible infinitely small displacement from a position of equilibrium, they do less work among them than they resist, the equilibrium is thoroughly stable. If in any or in every infinitely small displacement from a position of equilibrium, they do more work than they resist, the equilibrium is *un*stable.

It follows from this, that if the system is influenced only by internal forces, or if the applied forces follow the law of doing always the same amount of work upon the system, passing from one configuration to another by all possible paths, the whole potential energy must be constant in all positions, for neutral equilibrium ; it must be a minimum for the position of thoroughly stable equilibrium and it must be either an absolute maximum or a maximum for some displacements and a minimum for others, when there is unstable equilibrium.

Chemistry.

The chemical equilibrium [1] can be illustrated best by an example. N_2O_4 dissociates into NO_2, and if the gas is contained in a closed vessel, the dissociation does not go on indefinitely but until a certain proportion of the gas has been dissociated, after which no further change takes place in the gas if the temperature and pressure remain constant. A more general case of chemical equilibrium is when solutions of sulphuric and nitric acids and nitrate and sulphate of sodium are mixed together; chemical changes will go on until a state is reached in which there is a certain relation between the masses of the four substances present; after this no further change will take place in the constitution of the mixture. It is worth while to consider the differences between statical and chemical equilibrium.

All chemical systems seem to reach a steady state, while it is only under exceptional circumstances that frictionless dynamical systems do so. Further, so far as our knowledge extends, a chemical system gradually approaches the state of equilibrium, and when it has once reached it, remains in it; nothing corresponding to the oscillations of a dynamical system about its position of equilibrium seems to have been observed. The dynamical systems whose behaviour most closely resembles that of chemical systems are those in which the friction is very large or the inertia very small.

The difference between partial and complete chemical equilibrium may be expressed as follows: when a system is in partial equilibrium, the quantities of some of the constituents may be altered without any change in the others, while in complete equilibrium a change in the quantity of one of the constituents involves a change in the quantities of some or all of the others. The introduction of an infinitely small amount of a third substance, or the communication of an infinitely

[1] Watts' *Dictionary of Chemistry*, vol. 2, p. 434.

small quantity of energy to a system in complete equilibrium, will only produce an infinitely small change in the state of equilibrium, while the state of a system in partial equilibrium may be profoundly modified by the same measure. The reason of partial chemical equilibrium is that the system has no chemical freedom and must stay in whatever chemical state it was placed initially. In complete equilibrium the quantities of any substance can both increase and decrease, or they are reversible.

A good example of partial chemical equilibrium is the relation between hydrogen and oxygen at low temperature. We may have given quantities of hydrogen and oxygen at low temperature in equilibrium when arranged in an infinite number of ways, for since steam, hydrogen and oxygen do not combine at such temperatures, we may divide the hydrogen and oxygen in any proportion between H_2O, O_2 and H_2 and yet still have equilibrium. That is because the system has no chemical freedom and must stay in whatever state it was placed initially. This example is an extreme one as no chemical action goes on at all; there are cases in which some of the quantities may change, but only in one way, as for instance they can increase but not decrease, and vice versa. Thus, at low temperatures HI can be decomposed by light, while H and I cannot combine so that the action is irreversible, and when a mixture of HI, H and I is exposed to the action of light, the decomposition of HI goes on indefinitely. (Experiment of Lemoine.)

The statical as well as the complete and partial chemical equilibrium have their analogies in economics. We shall consider the economic analogies with statical equilibrium later on. The economic phenomena of the whole industrial world before war could be compared with a partial chemical equilibrium. For the introduction of an infinitely small amount of a third substance, or the communication of an infinitely small quantity of energy, to a system in complete equilibrium, will only produce an infinitely small change in the state of equilibrium ; the state of a system in partial equilibrium may be profoundly modified by the same means ; so the economic phenomena before war have the possibility of future profound changes through war, and the state after war is similar to complete chemical equilibrium, because the additional economic changes do not produce profound modification. Yet this resemblance of economic phenomena before war with partial chemical equilibrium is only an expression of instability or neutrality if compared with a statical equilibrium, and the resemblance of economic phenomena after war with a complete chemical equilibrium has its pendant in the stable state of statical equilibrium.

In each case, whether we take the analogies with statical or chemical equilibrium, one should remember that economic phenomena before and after war are in a state of continuous movement and change and the analogies have their value only if limited to fixed periods.

When we consider the economic phenomena in a limited period, the fluctuations may be due to changes of short or long periods and in treating the economic phenomena before war and their action in bringing about a war, we have to consider the twofold effects of these short and long period fluctuations, and of their balancing action through war.

Economics.

The term equilibrium is used now very often in connexion with the terms supply and demand, but besides this, there exist cases of simpler relation as between a desire and an effort to satisfy it.

The simplest case of equilibrium,[1] the balancing action between desire and effort (in this case also demand and supply), is found when a person satisfies

[1] A. Marshall, *Principles of Economics*, 6th ed., p. 331,

one of his wants by his own direct work. So, when a boy picks blackberries for his own eating, the action of picking is probably itself pleasurable for a while; and for some time longer the pleasure of eating is more than enough to repay the trouble of picking. But after he has eaten a good deal, the desire for more diminishes, while the task of picking begins to cause weariness. Equilibrium is reached when at last his eagerness to play and his disinclination for the work of picking counterbalance the desire of eating. The satisfaction which he can get from picking fruit has arrived at its maximum.

In a barter there is seldom an equilibrium of supply and demand, because it is always possible that one side will be willing to give something besides the article given in exchange.

In a true exchange, when the amount produced is such that the demand price is greater than the supply price, then sellers receive more than is sufficient to make it worth their while to bring goods to market to that amount, and there is at work an active force tending to increase the amount brought forward for sale. On the other hand, when the amount produced is such that the demand price is less than the supply price, sellers receive less than is sufficient to make it worth their while to bring goods to market on that scale; so that those who were just on the margin of doubt as to whether to go on producing are decided not to do so, and there is an active force at work tending to diminish the amount brought forward for sale. When the demand price is equal to the supply price, the amount produced has no tendency either to be increased or to be diminished: it is in equilibrium.

When demand and supply are in equilibrium, the amount of the commodity, which is being produced in a unit of time, is called by Professor Marshall the *equilibrium amount*, and the price at which it is being sold the *equilibrium price*.

Such an equilibrium is stable, that is, the price, if displaced a little from it, will tend to return. It is a characteristic of stable equilibria that in them the demand price is greater than the supply price for amounts just less than the equilibrium amount. When the demand price is greater than the supply price, the amount produced tends to increase. Therefore, if the demand price is greater than the supply price for amounts just less than the equilibrium amount, then if the scale of production is temporarily diminished somewhat, below the equilibrium amount, it will tend to return. If the demand price is greater than the supply price for amounts just less than the equilibrium amount, it is sure to be less than the supply price for amounts just greater: and therefore, if the scale of production is somewhat increased beyond the equilibrium position, it will tend to return.

When demand and supply are in stable equilibrium, if any accident should move the scale of production from its equilibrium position, there will be instantly brought into play forces tending to push it back to that position.

Jevons considered equilibrium as cardinal conception in the abstract science.[1] He explains the use of the term equilibrium by the following reasoning. The real condition of industry is one of perpetual motion and change. Commodities are being continually manufactured and exchanged and consumed. If we wish to have a complete solution of the problem in all its natural complexity, we should have to treat it as a problem of motion—a problem of dynamics. But it would surely be absurd to attempt the more difficult question when the easier one is yet so imperfectly within our power. It is only as a purely statical problem that one can venture to treat the action of exchange. Holders of commodities will be regarded, not as continuously passing on these commodities

[1] R. H. I. Palgrave, *Dictionary of Political Economy*, p. 149, *act.* equilibrium. W. S. Jevons, *The Theory of Political Economy*, 4th ed., 1911, London.

in streams of trade, but as possessing certain fixed amounts which they exchange until they come to equilibrium.

Basing his reasoning on the proposition that the ratio of exchange of any two commodities will be reciprocals of the ratio of the final degree of utility of the quantities of the commodity available for consumption, after the exchange is completed, he concludes that exchange will go on until each party has obtained all the benefit that is possible, and loss of utility would result if more were exchanged, and that therefore both parties rest in satisfaction and equilibrium when the degrees of utility have come to the level, as it were. This point of equilibrium will be known by the criterion that an infinitely small amount of commodity exchanged in addition, at the same rate, will bring neither gain nor loss of utility. In other words, if increments of commodities are exchanged at the established ratio, their utilities will be equal for both parties.

Let dx denote a small increment of a commodity and dy a small increment of another commodity, exchanged for the first, and let x be the whole quantity of the first commodity given for y, the whole quantity of the second commodity, received; then dy must have the same ratio to dx as y to x if the Law of Indifference is effective in the market. So we have

$$\frac{dy}{dx} = \frac{y}{x} \text{ or } dy = \frac{y}{x}\, dx.$$

In a state of equilibrium, the utilities of these increments must be equal in the case of each party, in order that neither more nor less exchange would be desirable.

Now the increment dy is $\frac{y}{x}$ times as great as the increment dx, so that in order that their utilities shall be equal, the degree of utility of dy must be $\frac{x}{y}$ times as great as the degree of utility of dx. Or the degrees of utility of commodities exchanged will be in the inverse proportion of the magnitude of the increments exchanged.

Let $f^1\ (a - x)$ denote the final degree of utility of dx to A, and f'^1y denote the final degree of utility of dy to A, then A is going to be satisfied exchanging one commodity for another if

$$f^1(a - x)dx = f'^1y\ dy$$

or

$$\frac{f'^1(a - x)}{f'^1y} = \frac{dy}{dx}.$$

Substituting $\frac{dy}{dx}$ for $\frac{y}{x}$, we have the equation:

$$\frac{f^1(a - x)}{f'^1y} = \frac{y}{x}.$$

Thus expressing the principle that the degrees of utility of commodities exchanged will be in the inverse proportion of the magnitudes of the increments exchanged.

This equation expresses the exchange only from the standpoint of A; expressing it also for B, it would look as follows:

$$\frac{f^2x}{f'^2(b - y)} = \frac{y}{x}.$$

Or the exchange is going to be determined by two equations, written together:

$$\frac{f^1(a - x)}{f'^1y} = \frac{y}{x} = \frac{f^2x}{f'^2(b - y)}.$$

Jevons remarks on the curious fact, that when we take the theory of the lever treated according to the principle of virtual velocities, we get equations exactly similar in form to those of the theory of value. The general principle of virtual velocities is to the effect that, if any number of forces be in equilibrium at one or more points of a rigid body, and if this body receives an infinitely small displacement, the algebraic sum of the products of each force into its displacement is equal to zero. In the case of a lever of the first order, this amounts to saying that one force multiplied into its displacement will be neutralized by the other force multiplied into its *negative* displacement. But inasmuch as the displacements are exactly proportional to the length of the arms of the lever, we obtain a derivative equation, that the forces multiplied each by its own arm are equal to each other.

Or if P be the force applied to A, and W the force exerted or resistance overcome or weight raised at B, then

$$\text{P} \times \text{AA}' \text{ (arch)} = \text{W} \times \text{BB}'$$

or

$$\text{P} \times \text{AC} = \text{W} \times \text{BC}$$

or

$$\text{P} \times \text{its arm} = \text{W} \times \text{its arm}$$

or

$$\frac{\text{W}}{\text{P}} = \frac{\text{AA}'}{\text{BB}'} = \frac{\text{AC}}{\text{BC}}.$$

This equation has a visible analogy to the equation above referred to, and puts it into form as follows:

$$\frac{f^1(x)}{f'^1(y)} = \frac{dy}{dx} = \frac{y}{x}.$$

Professor Marshall,[1] besides the application referred to above, has a broader biological conception of economic equilibrium too.

He uses it to express the growth and decay of a business firm. A business firm grows and attains great strength and afterwards perhaps stagnates and decays: at the turning point there is a balancing or equilibrium of the forces of life and decay. As with the growth of trees, so is it with the growth of business. As each kind of tree has its normal life in which it attains its normal height, so the length of life during

[1] A. Marshall, *Principles of Economics*, vol. 1, 5th ed., 1907.

which a business of any kind is likely to retain full vigour is limited by the laws of nature, combined with the circumstances of place and time and the character and stage of development of the particular trade in which it lies. The laws of nature press upon it by limiting the length of the life of its original founders, and by limiting even more narrowly that part of their lives in which their faculties retain full vigour. And so after a while the guidance of the business falls into the hands of people with less energy and less creative genius; and so either it decays altogether or it may be carried on with more or less wisdom and ability by a public company. But it is almost sure that it will lose much of its elasticity and of its progressive force; the advantages are no longer exclusively on its side in its competition with younger and smaller rivals, and if it be in some exceptional trades, it can no longer obtain from every increase in its scale of production the means of reducing considerably the price at which it sells its goods or its services. Although there are some firms rising or falling, the growth of wealth and population is not very much affected by this ascending or descending phase of individual firms, because in times of average prosperity decay in one direction is sure to be more than balanced by growth in another. The representative firm will generally increase in size if there is an increase in the aggregate volume of production of anything: that is, the internal economies possessed by the representative firm will increase as the external economies increase to which the firm has an access; this will thus enable it to manufacture at a less proportionate cost of labour and sacrifice.

And so the part which man plays shows a tendency to an increasing return, but the part which nature plays shows a tendency to diminishing return.

Therefore, in those industries which are not engaged in raising raw produce, an increase of capital and labour generally gives a return increased more than in proportion; and further, the improved organization tends to diminish or even override any increased resistance which nature may offer to raising increased amounts of raw produce. If the actions of the laws of increasing and diminishing return are balanced, we have the law of constant return, and an increased produce is obtained by labour and sacrifice increased just in proportion. The two tendencies towards increasing and diminishing return press constantly against each other, and in the production of some commodities the latter tendency prevails, in another the former, and sometimes they just neutralize each other.[1]

[1] See the historical development and Pareto's conception of economic equilibrium in V. Furlan's Wirtschaftsgleichgewicht, *Handwört der Staatswiss.* VIII, p. 825–31, and Pareto's *Manuale di Econ. Polit.*

III

RELATION BETWEEN ECONOMICS AND WAR IN HISTORY[1]

IN the Introduction I argued that it is best to treat the relations between war and economic conditions as functionally dependent upon each other, and this view is the most suitable for statistical investigation. But the historical conception of the relations of economics and war is that of cause and effect, and I shall try to show the usual historical conception between war and economics during the development of the human race.

Hunting Stage.

During the hunting stage of human civilization the tribes existed on the products furnished spontaneously by nature. War was nearly the normal condition of life. The reason was mainly economic ; the scarcity and precariousness of the food supply rendered much land necessary to the support of each family. Unless climatic conditions absolutely prevented an increase of population, the hunting grounds of the several tribes were of necessity extended until they overlapped, and so arose a war of extermination, whose issue was the destruction of the less efficient social organization and the restoration of the equilibrium

[1] E. van Dyke Robinson, pp. 134–174, in Th. N. Carver's *Sociology and Social Progress*, 1905. See also E. R. Seligman, *The Economic Interpretation of History*, 1902. This chapter is based on E. van Dyke Robinson's article.

between population and food supply. At this stage of economic development war is not only a business enterprise but the only conceivable business enterprise; that is the only means by which a vigorous tribe may procure for itself an increased food supply.

Pastoral and Agricultural Stage.

Whether the next stage in human history shall be pastoral or agricultural, depends on environment. In an open country where there are animals suitable for domestication, the tribe will become pastoral; without such animals or in a broken forest land, it becomes agricultural. Other things being equal, the change to pastoral life is more easy and natural. The food supply obtainable from a given area being greatly increased, the population is multiplied, but not in like proportion. And whereas the hunting existence scatters the population, the pastoral life lends to greater concentration, through need of mutual protection for the herds and to social and political consolidation through the development of a patriarchal organization. For this reason, while hunting tribes are limited to guerilla warfare, the numbers, discipline, mobility and stored-up food supply of pastoral peoples enable them to undertake distant expeditions and to make conquests on a large scale. These things are, moreover, forced upon them by the economic limitations inherent in their mode of life. War is eventually as much an economic necessity for pastoral as for hunting tribes. Population depends upon herds and herds upon accessible pasturage. But owing to the rapid increase of population, due to the greater regularity and comfort of their life as compared with hunting tribes, *the limit of safety is soon passed.* In this condition the least failure of pasturage, from drought or other cause, drives them forth into distant lands with the suddenness and violence of a tidal wave.

As for pastoral nations war is an economic necessity,

so it is not less true that war is an economic necessity for agricultural nations. For the time comes when foreign lands must be drawn upon to feed the people, and in the absence of international division of labour, the only possible means to this end is war. The development of commerce on a grand scale and the use of a money economy do not remove all the causes tending to war, but they offer the possibility of a peaceful expansion. This was neither possible nor conceivable in a natural economy such as characterized the Orient, and this fact explains the predominance of conquest in the ancient world.

Greeks.

The early Greeks were a rude race, half pastoral, half agricultural, and still partially nomadic, who waged war ceaselessly for herds, slaves, and fertile lands. War was for them strictly a business enterprise and it existed as if by nature; peace required to be established by special treaty.

In the later stages and through all the changes of advancing civilization, war, and even private war, continued in the eyes of people to constitute an honourable mode of acquisition or getting of a means of living.

Romans.

They were originally a pastoral people and as such necessarily dependent on war to enlarge their pasture lands. The same conditions confronted them during and after their transition to agriculture. War was, therefore, the normal condition of getting a means of living: peace the exceptional state of welfare. Even after the transition to a money economy, marked by the social crisis in the fourth and fifth centuries, the policy of conquest underwent no change. The first reason was the inland position of the city, which prevented commerce on a large scale and thus made war the only possible form of national expansion;

besides this, and forming a no less important reason, was the force of habit and the power of tradition.

The death and agony of the Roman Empire had a simple economic cause, that is, consumption exceeded production, mainly due to two chief causes, viz., slavery and the absence of industry.

Middle Ages.

The wars in the Middle Ages, after the close of the great migrations of nations, may be divided into four classes: (1) Defensive wars against new invaders. (2) Feudal or territorial wars. (3) The Crusades. (4) Commercial wars. It is fairly evident that three of these belong to the economic wars, and the fourth class, the Crusades, are by no means exempted from economic influence.

A Theory of the Origin of Modern Wars.

Van Dyke Robinson gives us the following explanation of the origin of modern wars.[1]

The conception of the natural and necessary harmony of interest of all nations is just as false as that of their natural and necessary antagonism. The conception is true as long as each nation has a natural monopoly in some one line in industry. While competition is absent, commerce is a bond of peace between those who buy and those who sell. But the moment that two nations try extensively in the same line of industry, that moment commerce becomes a sword, dividing and setting at enmity those who are rivals for the same markets. No profit can be made by one except to the damage of another. The increase of one is the decrease of the other; the prosperity of one is the other's destruction.

The rivalry of the nation is more and more strengthened by the fundamental fact of economics, that is the law of diminishing returns. It is the source of

[1] Van Dyke Robinson, pp. 170–174.

the origin and development of civilization ; for without pressure of population on subsistence man would never have risen above the lowest savagery. But it is at the same time and for the same reason the source of poverty and war. To equalize population and subsistence there are four possible means, two operating to check the population, two to increase the available food supply. These are : (1) Natural limitation of the population as in India, by disease and famine, or artificial limitation, as in France ; (2) emigration ; (3) conquest ; (4) commerce. By conquest nations have obtained from other lands wealth not produced at home, without rendering an equivalent service; by commerce nations set the laws of constant and increasing against that of diminishing returns, exchanging manufactured articles for food to feed their surplus population, which could not be fed from their own soil. The superiority of commerce to conquest as an economic measure arises from the fact that it stimulates, whereas conquest for purposes of exploitation checks production on both sides. Commerce is thus capable of indefinite expansion. But, nevertheless, it does not altogether escape the law of diminishing returns. In order that people may buy, they must have something to sell, and to this end they must produce more of some articles than is absolutely necessary to their own consumption. Not only so but the marginal cost of producing this quantity must be less than the marginal utility of the imported article. The pain of production, derived from labour, must be smaller compared with the pleasure of consumption, or people will not continue to produce. Obviously this is a standard which varies from place to place. Throughout the tropical and sub-tropical regions, where the indisposition to work is great and the pain of labour consequently high, it is this subjective limit which causes vast resources to lie undeveloped, checks population, keeps back commerce, and drives landowners either to adopt some form of forced labour or to abandon in despair the attempt to exploit the natural resources of the country.

On the other hand, in regions where the pain of labour is not held so great, production is pursued on a more intensive plan. This explains the anomalous fact that the countries having the largest production are often countries not having the greatest natural wealth. But inasmuch as every increase of agricultural production means a larger proportional increase of labour, there is always a point at which it ceases to pay. This is then the fixed or objective limit of production, and consequently to commerce. Its population increases: it therefore becomes progressively more difficult and finally impossible to create a surplus of agricultural products for purposes of exchange. When this point is reached, the country ceases to offer a market for manufactured goods, for the reason that there is nothing wherewith to pay for them; and the people are confronted with the old dilemma: starvation, emigration, war, or manufacturing. In this way the number of manufacturing nations is constantly increasing, and that of agricultural decreasing: the hunters multiplying while the game diminishes. The result is a rivalry for markets, that is for means to employ and feed the people, which grows fiercer day by day.

The cause of war is as permanent as hunger itself, since both spring from the same source, the law of diminishing returns. So long as that persists, war must remain in the last analysis a national business undertaking, designed to procure or preserve foreign markets, that is the means of continued growth and prosperity.

The origin of war is, according to this theory, in the rivalry for markets, or the extension of commerce, which itself cannot escape the influence of the law of diminishing returns.

This point of view does not seem to me to represent satisfactorily the facts and the economic source of wars. It is a fact that people, in order to buy, must have something to sell and therefore they must produce more of some article than is absolutely necessary to their consumption. But that the pain of production, derived from labour, on which the exchange is founded, must be smaller compared with the pleasure of consumption, is rather doubtful.

There is no clear reason why every increase of agricultural production should mean a larger proportional increase of labour, and why there should be a point at which the agricultural production ceases to create a surplus of agricultural products for purposes of exchange, and why that should not be applied to industrial labour too.

According to this reasoning, modern wars have their origin when the agricultural communities reach the point at which they cease to create a surplus of agricultural products for purposes of exchange, because the pain of agricultural labour is becoming equal or greater than the pleasure of consumption. In consequence, the agricultural communities seem to try to evade the economic exchange, and they begin to manufacture themselves.

Now the connexion is completely reversed; the agricultural communities are not those who are bound to live upon an exchange of products, but the industrial, manufacturing countries. The agricultural communities were and are more self-supporting, chiefly on account of the lower standard of living; the manufacturing communities try to open them to exchange for manufactured articles, food and raw material, either by a peaceful commercial penetration or by some economic pressure or by a war. Professor Marshall reverses the situation when he says that after all the chief cause of the modern prosperity of new countries lies in the markets that the old world offers, not for goods delivered on the spot, but for promises to deliver goods at a distant date.[1] The old, or manu-

[1] *Principles of Economics*, p. 669.

facturing countries do not at all offer their goods only *for promises* but for *real food* and raw material, but as they are stronger in bargaining they offer their goods on better terms, and the delivery of goods at a distant date by the new countries is a surplus of exchange value effected by mortgaging of the properties of new countries by old ones in consequence of a good bargain. The continuous economic prosperity of the old industrial countries depends on the new countries or markets, firstly because all the food and raw material of old countries are not sufficient to support their population, and therefore their imports are slowly growing and they are coming from the new countries; and secondly, because all the surplus goods and capital are employed in the new countries.

The origin of modern wars is in the economic situation of industrial communities. Deficiency of agricultural products and raw material and surplus of capital and manufactured goods drive to commercial extension and also to territorial aggrandisement.

Supposing the industrial communities were producing agricultural products by increasing the productivity of land and applying all scientific means to raise the productivity in the same proportion as the population and the manufactured goods are growing, and that this proportion were permanent, then they would not be obliged to seek for a continuous extension of markets, but they could be self-supporting. The cause of the continuous extension of markets is the action of the economic distributive forces in the industrial communities, which effect a continuous accumulation of capital, wanting an investment. The creation of this surplus capital is the chief reason why the industrial communities are continuing to search for a new field for investment, and why the rivalry for markets between them is so effective. Besides this continuous growth of surplus capital, there is a continuous increase of population in the industrial communities, the wants of which cannot be satisfied, because they also are continuously increasing and because the standard of living is continuously rising.

So we see the effects of industrialization, in the disproportionate growth of production of manufactured goods and a corresponding decrease of agricultural production, but at the same time a continuous rising of the consumption of the population, which is getting more and more difficult to satisfy.

The origin of war is in the surplus capital, which creates a demand for labour and thereby gives opportunity to a growth of population, and drives the same to manufacturing, which creates values for exchange for food and raw material. Surplus capital neglects the agricultural production, since the investment of capital in the latter is or seems to be rather limited.

The effect of accumulating capital in industrial communities is not only to create a tendency to extend the markets, but at the same time to transform the agricultural communities into industrial ones. It is a rather curious point of view to suppose that reaching the point at which an increase of agricultural production and labour ceases to pay is able to transform an agricultural community into an industrial one. Supposing this point reached, the effect would be only that the agricultural community would produce only as much as is necessary for its own needs, and not for exchange, and the agricultural production would be stationary, and therefore the population stationary, or the standard of living proportionately decreasing, and the population increasing. But an agricultural community would never be able to transform itself, at least at this stage of economic development, and in the direction of modern industrial production, without the assistance of industrial communities, that is, without the aid of capital. So capital is effectively accelerating an industrialization of agricultural communities, and therewith effecting a still greater disproportion between the production of agricultural and manufactured goods.

Growth of population, continuous growth of industrialization, the disproportionate production of agricultural and manufactured commodities and the continuous growth of capital, waiting for investment, and the continuous growth of consumption, are the forces leading to a war: they may be partially checked by natural limitation of the population, by emigration, or commerce in time of peace, but they are checked effectively by war. A war effects an actual diminution of population, a lowering of the standard of living or of consumption, a proportionate increase of agricultural production in industrial communities, a territorial readjustment in the interest of stronger industrial communities, and at last a destruction of fixed capital and a binding of floating capital in the shape of State war debts.

These points will be treated in the light of the idea of equilibrium in the next chapter.

IV

GENERAL THEORY OF WAR EQUILIBRIUM

THE economic equilibrium of a community (or a social group) depends on the following factors: 1. Growth of population; 2. Consumptive capacity of the community; 3. Productive capacity, firstly of means of subsistence and secondly of means connected with the standard of life and their production, as, e.g., capital goods; 4. The state of distribution of economic goods.

Growth of the population consists in the excess of births over deaths in the community, not taking into account the possible gain or loss caused by immigration or emigration, that is, the natural increase of the population. This phenomenon is the most significant of vital statistical phenomena, more significant than emigration or immigration, for judging the state of the community. It is perhaps the most complex of vital statistical phenomena as it is influenced by the marriage rate, birth rate, and death rate at the same time. Besides, it is closely bound with economic conditions, and it may be taken as indicating the state of economic equilibrium of the community. As production is the basis of consumption, so consumption influences through the standard of life the above three vital phenomena, and the rate of natural increase may run parallel with consumptive capacity, or the consumptive capacity may reach a point where a proportionate increase of the rate of natural increase cannot go on without endangering the standard of life of the community. So the growth of population is closely bound with the state of consumption, and therefore production and the balancing tendencies are continuously interacting.

The terms demand and supply are not used, on account of their being associated with the use of solitary commodities or groups of commodities, and the terms consumptive and productive capacity are substituted for them.

Consumptive capacity extends to the means of subsistence, the necessaries of life, connected with the preservation of primary physiological functions, as food, shelter and clothing, and to the means, connected with the satisfaction of wants having their origin in the standard of life. Commodities satisfying the first needs should be called primary economic goods, and commodities satisfying the secondary wants of the standard of life, secondary economic goods. Nitti [1] has a broader conception of means of subsistence, saying that by means of subsistence we mean what is closely bound up with the needs of civilization. But I hope to justify the distinction later on as it clears many interactions and relations of agriculture and the manufacturing power of a community.

It is of advantage to distinguish between primary and secondary economic goods while treating their production, and also to have in mind capital goods, as means of production aiming at the serial production of goods.

The consumptive capacity of a community may be high or low if compared with others. It is high in the case of civilized nations. Now it is evident that it may be well satisfied if growth of population and the trend of production are running in parallel directions with it. The economic equilibrium of the community is stable if the consumption is balanced by production, and the population is growing proportionately to the standard of life. If the standard of

[1] F. S. Nitti, *Population and Social System*, pp. 98–101. London, 1894.

life is very high and the consumptive capacity great, the growth of population must be proportionately lowered. In other words, there is a limit of the rising standard of life, after which it can continue to rise only if the growth of population decreases, and the forces, at the beginning running parallel, become antagonistic and check and balance each other. But besides the direct connexion of growth of population with the standard of life, the consumptive capacity and therefore the maintenance of the standard of living depends on the productive capacity of the community. As a community produces more goods connected with the standard of living and their means of production, and less goods of primary importance, their position is more and more dependent on the general possibility of exchange of secondary economic and capital goods for primary ones. And as a community gives more and more secondary economic goods in exchange for primary economic ones, it stimulates the rise of the standard of living in other communities also, and while raising the standard of living, it reacts on the methods of production in the same community, which begins more and more to produce secondary economic goods and less of primary ones.

Now this point of changing of production methods in a community from primary economic goods to secondary ones is still more accelerated· by the latter community, in consequence of the distributive forces, acting in these communities. As there the accumulation of capital wanting employment is continuously going on in consequence of the favourable exchange conditions, their use is [1] getting less profitable in their original countries and capital goods begin to be exported in the former ones. So the agricultural communities and the agricultural production are slowly transformed into industrial and manufacturing ones. This tendency to transformation is continuously

[1] See Hobson, *Export of Capital.*

going on, and therefore the production of primary economic goods proportionately decreases, while that of secondary and capital goods increases. But the consumptive capacity of the community for primary goods is increasing on account of the rising standard of life of large masses, and the same is the case with secondary economic goods. The consumptive capacity of industrial communities for primary and secondary goods cannot be satisfied at the same rate, and they can therefore do this only if finding communities supplementing them with food and raw material and taking in exchange the secondary economic or capital goods.

Therefore, the economic equilibrium of the industrial communities is growing more complex, but at the same time it loses its stability.

Besides this, the production of secondary goods produces, at least to-day, a large number of growing non-productive people, living on the earnings of ancestors or on capital: persons not engaged either in direct production but only in consumption of goods. These people become a class, and though usually not directly concerned with production, yet their consumptive capacity is highest, and they therefore induce the population to produce for them commodities, and the work spent on the production of goods for them is, from the standpoint of the community, lost. Nitti says:[1] "We can assert that a country, which in the actual form of economic constitution is capable of sustaining a certain number of individuals, could sustain a much greater number, when the economic form is changed in the direction of a wider distribution of wealth produced." And further: "Thus in our state of society the term, means of subsistence, has come to express not only the total of natural needs, but a total of artificial needs originated by given economic surroundings, and hence very change-

[1] Nitti, p. 102, pp. 103–4.

able needs, and such as will change in passing from a strictly individualistic economic phase to a phase of ordered and intelligent social co-operation. Now a large part of these industrial efforts are originated by the need of providing, not the necessaries of life, but its superfluities, and often what is simply evil."

That is because demand [1] implies a want on the part of the person demanding not only an effort to satisfy a want, but a power and willingness to give something in exchange, or to pay. The distributive forces therefore favour the demand of a relatively small part of society, and their influence on production is disproportionately great in comparison with the demand of the larger part of the community. The economic structure of the society is therefore acting powerfully on production, and on the general economic equilibrium of the community too. Now this action may be cumulative and the visible effect not so clear; in the long run it tends to press the population to increase the production of secondary goods connected with the standard of life, and to seek outlets for market goods produced by their capital on the one side, and to induce other communities to exchange the primary economic goods for the produced secondary ones. The exchange, as has been mentioned, effects a raising of the standard of life in communities producing primary economic goods, and at the same time induces the latter community after a while to a proportionate lowering of the production of primary and raising of secondary goods.

Another influence of distributive forces, acting in the community, effects, when a pressure upon production of secondary economic goods is existing, a lowering of real wages paid to workmen.

These are the main points indicating the forces acting on the economic equilibrium of modern communities. Some of the mentioned notions have a similarity to Malthusianism. Malthus and Malthu-

[1] E. Cannan, *Wealth*, pp. 106–117.

sianism assert that there is a relation between growth of population and means of subsistence, and that population cannot grow above a limit of available and at the time disposable means of subsistence without being checked by some positive checks, as vice, misery, war, or some prudential checks as preventive means or restraint upon marriage. So W. S. Thompson [1] expounds Malthusianism as follows: "There are two main points to Malthus' thesis: the first relates to the tendency of population to increase in numbers with the increase in production of food, the second relates to the effect of this increase upon lower classes of the population, where the burden falls. The first part may be stated in another way, viz., that the supply of labour tends to increase faster than the demand for it, except under unusual conditions. . . .

"If the supply of labour is tending to increase faster than the demand for it, there would not be sufficient of the necessaries of life to go round, and the result would be a lower class which would be always suffering for lack of them." In his investigation Thompson stated that population increases in individual countries, except France, when food increases, and that the determining factor in the size of families is the pressure upon the means of subsistence in the Western world.

This connexion between the means of subsistence and the growth of population is acknowledged even by Levasseur: "En tout temps et en tout lieu, les subsistances produites sur le sol national ou acquises par échange, limite la population."[2] He says further: "Cette formule n'est pas contestable." Although these ideas as expounded by Thompson seem to me to be quite plausible, yet they do not emphasize the connexion of the growth of population with the consumptive capacity of a modern community, and also

[1] W. S. Thompson, "Population," *Studies in History, Economic and Public Law*, vol. 63, p. 15. Columbia Univ., New York, 1915.

[2] *La Population Française*, Tom. 3, p. 14. Paris, 1899.

they neglect the ties between the production of primary and secondary goods and their interactions in different communities. According to Malthus a war is just a positive check, in consequence of pressure upon the means of subsistence, or as Professor E. Cannan says about the war of to-day: "The increase of population in Europe is having one of Malthus' 'positive checks' administered with very great sharpness."

Although there is a pressure upon the consumption, as we shall see later on, there is no real pressure upon the means of subsistence in Malthus' sense.

War is checking the increase of population, but it has relation to other economic phenomena too, for example, consumption and production.

If war is a positive check to the growth of population, it is pre-eminently a struggle for means of subsistence, but now and at the same time it is a struggle for standard of living. N. G. Pierson puts this point clearly in the already quoted sentences:[1] "As the level of welfare rises, the struggle for existence will change, but not diminish; it will become a struggle, not for life itself, but for the comforts of life, and there is no reason to believe that this latter struggle will be less severe. It will be a struggle like that in which, already now, we may see the banker engaged when he does not want to be forestalled by his fellow-bankers; or the manufacturer who wants to attain a high standing in his trade; or the shopkeeper or dealer who wants to compete successfully. If we were to assume, that, with advancing welfare, wants would remain stationary, we should not be right in saying what we have said. But as welfare increases, wants increase, even more rapidly as a rule."

This is just the point Malthusianism forgets to treat according to its importance. Modern communities struggle for their standard of living, and we can judge the standard of living from the consumptive capacity, measured by the consumption of commodities per

[1] N. G. Pierson, *Principles of Economics*, vol. 2, p. 124.

head of population. Now this consumption per head does not remain unchanged, but shows a constant tendency to increase, and this increase can be explained only on the assumption that there is a law (or an economic tendency) at work in every community, acting in the direction of increase of consumption, and that is the law of increasing wants. We could express it in a general form that human wants increase in intensity and quantity. Supplementing it by the law of variety and the law of substitution, we could say that human wants in a progressive society increase not only quantitively in intensity to a point of satiety, but by the action of the law of substitution and variety numerically in diversity.

Therefore the *per capita* consumption of all the commodities shows a tendency to increase in quantity, and there is no one of staple commodities the consumption of which could not be raised above the level of to-day's consumption. Only in the United Kingdom the consumption of beverages is diminishing; in the United States, tea, in Germany, tobacco; all the other commodities are rising with the usual fluctuations.

The law of increasing wants, which is the most powerful factor in determining the consumptive capacity of a community, tends to be balanced by the law of diminishing returns. The law of diminishing returns could be expressed as follows: [1] If one or more of the industrial agents, the co-operation of which is necessary for the production of any commodity, be increased, the others remaining unaltered, and the increase of product be in a less proportion than the increase of the industrial agents considered, there we express the fact by saying that in this case the product obeys the law of diminishing returns. Marshall [2] says about the effect of the law of diminishing returns, that although an improvement in the arts of agriculture may raise the rate of return which

[1] Palgrave's *Dictionary of Political Economy*, vol. 1, p. 583.

[2] *Principles of Economy*, p. 153.

land generally affords to any given amount of capital and labour, and that although the capital and labour already applied to any piece of land may have been so inadequate for the development of its full power that some further expenditure on it even with the existing arts of agriculture would give a more than proportionate return, yet these conditions are rare in an old country; and except when they are present, the application of increased capital and labour to land will add a less than proportionate amount to the produce raised, unless there be meanwhile an increase in the skill of the individual cultivator. Secondly, it must be remembered that whatever may be the future developments of the arts of agriculture, a continued increase in the application of capital and labour to land must ultimately result in a diminution of the extra produce, which can be obtained by a given extra amount of capital and labour.

Supposing the law of diminishing returns acting, the economic equilibrium of the community would be influenced in the sense that the consumptive capacity is lowered, or the consumption per head diminished, or, as Mr. Thompson pointed out, when the available food influences the size of the family, so it effects a pressure on the rate of natural increase by depressing it.

It does not seem to me that the action of the law of diminishing returns sufficiently explains the economic phenomena before and after war.

There is no statistical evidence on the action of the law of diminishing returns in agriculture and manufacture, and it indicates only the theoretically possible case that at any given time increase of labour, up to a certain point, is attended by increasing proportionate returns, and beyond that point increase of labour is attended by diminishing proportionate returns. If we call this fixed point the point of maximum return, with Professor Cannan, then we may state that there is no proof that the point of maximum return in agriculture has been reached in any modern communities; the best evidence is the still increasing yields of cereals per acre.

Not the law of diminishing returns, but the disproportionate production of primary and secondary goods is of importance. The disproportions between agriculture and manufacture tend to influence the economic equilibrium of a modern community more than the law of diminishing returns. Although one country may exist without producing any primary economic goods, yet the trend of transformation of production of primary economic goods to secondary and capital goods cannot go on in many countries without disturbing the economic equilibrium of production between primary and secondary goods, and therefore without endangering in the long run the general economic equilibrium of the communities.

The disproportionate production of primary economic goods in industrial communities, if compared with that of secondary ones, can be explained only by the action of capital. The consumptive capacity of people having capital is directed to demand for secondary goods. Therefore capital induces people to produce those commodities demanded by capitalists, without much regard for the wants of other people who have not the ability to pay for the satisfaction of their wants, and they therefore have to be without them. The origin and the source of the relative rise of demand for secondary goods is therefore capital.

But besides originating the production and consumption of secondary economic goods, capital is directed to such use as to bring interest. The interest and profits are continuously increasing the capital available for employment, and the periodical crises are not able to destroy the fixed capital nor to bind it effectively. Therefore capital is accumulating and wanting employment in order to bring interest. The capitalists therefore try and induce people to produce any kind of secondary economic goods by giving the labourers higher wages than they would have for primary economic goods.

The cause of agricultural depopulation is not only capital, but the form of landownership. It is self-evident that depopulation is favoured by large estates and checked by small farms, as in the case of Ireland in recent times.

We could also say that primary economic goods are produced just as much as they are wanted; if the supply is above the demand, that is due to the action of accidental natural forces, e.g., in the case of good harvests. Therefore we are not exaggerating in saying that the production and supply of primary economic goods is at the margin of demand. But the supply and the production of secondary goods is not governed by demand only, but by the available capital wanting employment. That this is the case is proved by periodical crises, with regular intervals. Supposing that demand governed the production of secondary goods, and the law of supply and demand were effective, there would never be crises in industries. Now, the crises are due mostly to over-production, and over-production to employment of surplus of capital, and it is therefore justifiable to say that production of secondary goods is governed by the supply of capital, although not limited in J. S. Mill's sense. We may therefore say that the production of secondary goods is at the margin of supply.

Capital absorbs all available labour and induces agricultural labour to change this kind of labour for an industrial one. But besides this it creates a possibility to a continuous growth of population, as long as there are supplementing communities.

The vertical competition between agricultural and industrial production is decided in the favour of the latter by capital, probably chiefly because the employment of capital is more remunerative in this kind of production, and because the use of capital in agricultural production seems to be limited. But capital favours industrial production not only in one community, but also in horizontal competition between different countries; seeking employment, it goes to other countries and stimulates industrial production, proportionately decreasing agricultural production.

Therefore the supply of secondary goods is not in conformity with internal and external demand, and that is the source of the need for extension of markets supplementing the over-populated industrial communities with primary economic goods.

Similarly, applying the same ideas to consumption, we could say that the consumption of primary goods is at the margin of supply, while that of secondary goods is at the margin of demand, and disproportionately risen, compared with primary ones. This is again due to the action of capital, helping to produce them in large quantities *en masse,* and inducing the people to buy them by lowering the prices.

Therefore the consumption of primary goods increases, but not at the same rate as the secondary goods, which as solitary commodities or as groups of commodities grow more rapidly than the former ones.

Considering the effect of time in connexion with these tendencies, it is noticeable that, as the primary goods are approaching the margin of supply, their prices are rising; on the contrary, the prices of secondary goods are falling, not only on account of serial production and more application of machinery in industrial processes, but because this kind of production is approaching, through application of surplus capital, the limit or margin of demand, and to induce their sale the producers must lower the prices.

The best proof is the method of "dumping," when by lowering the prices in foreign markets, the producers try to induce the foreign customers to buy them, yet the same products are sold at higher prices in the home markets.

It is therefore evident that the standard of living

rises, but proportionately more in consumption of secondary goods than in that of primary ones. A rather significant phenomenon is the pre-war pressure on consumption, manifesting itself chiefly in the lowered average consumption of primary commodities in the pre-war short period of years.

Although in consequence of the action of the law of increasing wants, consumption is generally rising, yet the change of consumption is not easy, and once it has taken place, it is conservative.[1] Consumptive capacity is not only increasing in consumed quantities of particular commodities and in the number of commodities, but it is conservative, and therefore the pressure is visible just on the averages of the few years before the war, while the years immediately after are generally in a rising state.

Shortly, we may state, that as long as the increased consumptive capacity of the community is balanced by its productive ability, there cannot be a disturbance of the economic equilibrium, except by the influence of the natural growth of population, which, perhaps on account of biological peculiarities of race, may not keep pace with production. But as the substitution of production of primary goods by secondary ones progresses, or as the industrialization of communities is going on, the production of secondary goods very soon overtakes the demand of a limited area, and therefore there is a need for supplementing the community by new areas producing primary economic goods, or the restoration of the economic equilibrium of the community.

To re-establish the economic equilibrium it is necessary to lower the consumption, that is, the standard of living, or to increase proportionately the production of primary economic goods, or to lower the increase of population, or to look for supplementary territories providing the necessary primary economic goods and

[1] I. S. N. Patten, *The Consumption of Wealth*, p. 64, Publ. of Univ. of Pennsylvania, Philadelphia, 1889.

offering a market for secondary goods. Now of these four possibilities, two are effective before war, that is the consumption is lowered and the rate of natural increase is depressed. But the equilibrium is effectively re-established by war. War effects an actual diminution of population (killing, diseases), it lowers still more the consumption and the standard of living; it raises proportionately the production of primary economic goods in communities, particularly in industrial ones; it gives an opportunity to acquire new supplementary territories by a successful war, and it destroys or binds the capital wanting employment.

The disturbed state of equilibrium manifests itself before the actual outbreak of war, for the effects of the pre-war economic situation are cumulative. Therefore we may note the following phenomena before the war: 1. A decline of the rate of natural increase of population. 2. A rise of consumption per head of population, indicating a slight pressure of consumption in the years immediately preceding war. 3. The disproportionate production of primary as compared with secondary economic goods, and in consequence a rise of prices of primary goods (see Fig. 2).

If the idea of war-equilibrium is correct, war is a turning point, and after war the balancing of forces tends to restore the economic equilibrium, and therefore the phenomena of post-war economic equilibrium are acting in opposite directions; so we notice:

1. A decline of consumption and lowering of the standard of life.

2. A rise of the rate of natural increase of the population.

3. A proportionate rise in the production of primary economic goods and decline of secondary in consequence of the lowered standard of life.

I shall try to find the pre-war and after-war antagonistic tendencies in different communities in different wars.

But while examining the statistics of different

countries in the light of the war-equilibrium theory, one has to remember that there are two parties in each war, one the aggressor and another the defender, and one cannot expect to find the same phenomena in both parties. It is likely that the aggressor will show the more characteristic features of war equilibrium, and we may therefore state that in each war some countries are more representative than others. They are representative in the sense that the economic equilibrium is approaching more to the theory, and in some respects, we may say, it is riper for war. As there are more representative communities, so there are more or less representative wars, approaching the above phenomena. As the wars are made by diplomacy, they could be arranged without any economic consideration whatever. Usually economic phenomena coincide with the diplomatic and political events, although they are not bound to do so. As the political actions are carried out with a consideration of the psychological disposition of the crowd (public opinion); and as the politicians and diplomatists may be more or less good psychologists, so they may understand and act upon the advice of public opinion, maintained by economic interests and therefore be influenced by economic causes, but they are not bound to found all their actions on economic considerations, and still less to treat them as primarily important in making a war. Therefore a war may not show features according to the theory of war equilibrium. The last remark I have to make is that the theory of war equilibrium is only applicable to modern, more or less industrial communities.

I shall consider in the next two chapters the economic dependence of the rate of natural increase, and then the statistical phenomena of the rate of natural increase in the light of the war-equilibrium theory.

V

NATURAL INCREASE OF POPULATION

SOME previous authors [1] have already noticed some features of the rate of natural increase of population in accordance with the war-equilibrium theory, and its being influenced by war. So Nitti says,[2] in the essay already quoted, that "we may almost say that death calls for life and that there is something unconscious and fatal in this vicissitude of things. Wars, famines and epidemics are generally succeeded by years of a very high birth-rate. In France in the two years preceding 1870, the birth-rate was only 20·5 per 1,000, but after the very high death-rate produced by war and smallpox in 1870–1871, the birth-rate rose in 1872 and for some years following remained at 26·7. In Prussia while for two years preceding 1870 the birth-rate was 39, it increased and remained at 41·5 for the three succeeding years."

A. B. Wolfe, in a recent publication,[3] describes the birth-rate phenomena after war more clearly still: "It is a well-known fact that a war of any great intensity or duration checks both the marriage-rate and the birth-rate, and that *after the close of hostilities and the demobilization of troops comes a year or two of recovery and sometimes of extreme rebound in marriages and births.* This fact has been evidenced by practically every important war since the beginning

[1] R. Mayo-Smith, *Statistics and Sociology*, 1895, p. 137.

[2] *Population and Social System*, p. 96.

[3] "Economic Conditions and Birth-rate after War," *The Journal of Political Economy*, vol. 25, June, 1917, pp. 521–41.

of the publication of reliable vital statistics. War temporarily checks marriage and reproduction; war kills off its thousands or millions of men, but experience shows that in the past, with the possible exception of the extremely destructive Thirty Years' War, these ravages in the population have been quickly made good."

As the rate of natural increase is a resultant of the following component forces: (1) marriage-rate, (2) birth-rate, and (3) death-rate; so it is evident that the rebound of the marriage- and birth-rate is going to influence favourably the rate of natural increase too, and therefore to act in the direction of the restoration of the economic equilibrium of the community.

The natural increase of population is the excess of births over deaths. As a quantity, it may be positive, negative, or zero. In the first case, the population is progressive; in the second, retrogressive; and in the third, stationary.

The progressive rate of natural increase is caused by a surplus of births over deaths; the retrogressive rate by a surplus of deaths over births, and the stationary one [1] either by proportionate increase of the birth- and death rates or by their proportionate decrease.

If we accept Malthus' terminology, then if marriage- and birth-rates diminish, we may speak of the pressure of a population on means of subsistence, and in this sense the diminished rate of natural increase would be caused by inadequacy of economic conditions to satisfy the individual wants of the population, so that the procreative wants cannot have a full satisfaction. Now, it is a well-known fact that poorer people have proportionately more children, and that the rate of natural increase does not increase only by an increase of birth-rate, but by a decrease of death-rate. The decrease of the death-rate is caused by improvement in knowledge and in sanitary con-

[1] See A. Newsholme, *Vital Statistics*, 1888, pp. 74–75.

ditions. So Porter[1] says: "The steady decline in the death-rate from 1801–1851 may be assigned, among other causes, to the less crowded state of dwellings, the command of better kinds of food, the superiority and cheapness of clothing, more temperate habits and greater personal cleanliness. One influential cause of diminished mortality among children, was the introduction of vaccination."

The improvement in knowledge may have a very slight effect on the improvement of hygienic conditions, if the average man is not economically able to carry out the hygienic presumptions, and therefore the death-rate is ultimately connected with the economic conditions of the community, that is, with its well-being.

It is perhaps best not to speak of cause, but of dependency. This view is expressed in the laws of G. Cauderlier,[2] according to which the number of marriages in a population is an index of the facility of getting means of living. ("Le nombre de mariages dans une population déterminée est un indice certain de la facilité, dont jouit cette population de se procurer les resources nécessaire à la vie.") It increases when the facility of getting means of living increases, it diminishes if this facility diminishes, other things being equal, such as legislation, which may limit it. It is in accordance with this view that the marriage-rate may increase in England as the price of wheat rises, but the price of wheat is not the only determining factor in making marriage easier, and therefore the marriage-rate is more dependent on the amount of wages, as it expresses the demand for labour, and therewith on the possibility of exporting goods and exchanging them for material and food and all the necessaries of the standard of living.[3] Consequently the marriage-rate fluctuates with the

[1] Porter-Hirst, *The Progress of Nation*, p. 9.
[2] *Les Lois de la Population.* Bruxelles, 1900.
[3] Newsholme, *Vital Statistics*, p. 45.

exports of British goods rather than with the cheapness of food. But the economic connexion of the marriage-rate with the export of goods is more valid in purely industrial countries ; the export of goods is a sign of facility in getting means of living, but as the standard of living is lower, the determining factor is more the price of food, particularly of wheat. Cauderlier also approaches the notion of equilibrium, while saying, " the general economic development determines the marriage-curve of each nation, and *this curve tends to recover its irregularities after some great disturbance, as epidemics, war, etc.*"

According to Cauderlier, the birth-rate (legitimate) is constant if the age, customs, and duration of marriage do not vary ; it increases if economic conditions improve, and if the average age of marriage diminishes, and if the average duration diminishes, and if the proportion of urban to rural population diminishes.

Now, considering the legitimate birth-rate in the light of the corrected birth-rate,[1] based on a standard rate (Sweden, 1891) which takes into account both the ages and the number of the wives, Newsholme and Stephenson state a decline from 1880–1 to 1901–4 as follows :

Countries.	Decline in Corrected Birth-rate. Corrected Birth-rate in 1880–1.	1901–4.	Decline per cent.
German Empire	40·37	35·34	12
Austria	39·04	38·50	1
Italy	36·89	33·71	9
England and Wales	34·65	28·41	18
Belgium	40·76	31·01	24
France	25·06	21·63	14

This decline in the legitimate birth-rate might be due either to an increased number of sterile marriages or to smaller families. French, Danish, Swedish, Australian and other statistics agree in showing that

[1] A. Newsholme and T. H. C. Stephenson, " The Decline of Human Fertility in the United Kingdom and Other Countries," *Jour. R.S.S.*, vol. 69, 1906, pp. 34–87.

it is the smaller size of families which affects the decline in the corrected birth-rate.

This decline is not affected by a decrease of fecundity, because, if the decline was due to physical degeneration, affecting the reproductive powers, the decrease of fecundity would increase the number of sterile marriages, which is not the case. In England, Germany and other countries the birth-rate declined with a general raising of the standard of life or social comfort, and therefore is dependent on consumption and the development of the consumptive capacity of the community. Messrs. Newsholme and Stephenson say that "it is not unlikely that, up to a certain point, improvement in prosperity favours fertility, though beyond this it may act, to a limited extent, in the opposite direction."

The decline of the birth-rate is associated therefore with a general raising of the standard of comfort, and it is an expression of the determination of the people to secure an increased comfort and consumptive capacity, and it is therefore dependent on the economic conditions of the community and on its general economic equilibrium.

It is by no means satisfactorily explained, and still less proved, by W. Willcox,[1] that the spread in the volitional control of the birth-rate is the true cause of the falling off in it. If we conceive "cause" as an event immediately preceding another event, this could be considered as a satisfactory representation of the phenomena, but as the "cause" is connected with other events, as is the case here, the volitional control of natural increase of births is dependent on the standard of living and consumptive capacity of people, and therefore on economic conditions. It approaches the reality far better to say that birth-rate is a function of the standard of living and economic equilibrium, than that it is caused by volitional

[1] *The Nature and Significance of the Changes in the Birth-rate and Death-rate.* Amer. Stat. Assoc., vol. 15, 1916, pp. 1–15.

control. Even Brentano [1] has no such narrow conception of the causation of the decline in the birth-rate, but he considers as its causes, (1) the diseases of sex, (2) mental diseases, and as a principal cause the diminution of the desire for reproduction. He quotes Mr. Sidney Webb as pointing out that the protective measures which prohibit the factory woman from returning to work for a definite number of weeks after child-birth, deprive her of the means of subsistence, and she naturally seeks to avoid the recurrence of such a stoppage of supplies. "With this we enter into the domain of economic causes, which are especially responsible for the decline in the desire for reproduction in the case of man. . . . The most potent check is the consideration how far, if he were to call a great number of children into existence, the increased demand thus made on his resources would cut him off from other satisfactions." This again proves that the falling off in the birth-rate, and therefore the rate of natural increase, has to be considered as connected and dependent on the economic conditions of the community.

In what way are the economic factors influencing the marriage- and birth-rates and therewith the rate of natural increase? Mr. Hooker [2] and Mr. Yule tried to solve the problem, and their answer seems to be satisfactory.

The explanation is that the economic factors influence the marriage-rate, so that if the economic factors are favourable, the marriage-rate varies directly as the rate of change in favourable economic factors, and inversely as the rate of change in unfavourable factors. The unfavourable economic factors act by postponing the marriages of the given year, but the postponement does not depend only on that year,

[1] "The Doctrine of Malthus and the Increase of Population during the Last Decades," *Econ. Jour.*, vol. 20, pp. 371–393.

[2] Hooker, *Transact. Manch. Stat. Soc.*, 1898. "Is the Birth-rate Still Falling?"

but on the values of the factors for the preceding years too.

Mr. Yule[1] represents the theory of postponement and the influence of economic factors as follows.

If the highest possible marriage-rate M_0 is maintained steadily for a number of years, and if in year n unfavourable circumstances occur causing a postponement rate (on population), p_n, then for the marriage-rate M_n we have:

$$M_n = M_0 - p_n \quad (1)$$

For $\overline{n+1}$ we have:

$$M_{n+1} = M_0 + p_n - p_{n+1}(1 + a_1 p_n)$$

$a_1 p_{n+1}$ being the residuum of p_n, repostponing the marriage, or generally

$$M_m = M_0 + p_{m-1}(1 + a_1 p_{m-2} + a_1 a_2 p_{m-2} p_{m-3} + \ldots) - p_m(1 + a_1 p_{m-1} + a_1 a_2 p_{m-1} p_{m-2} + \ldots)$$

or neglecting the terms of second order:

$$M_m = M_0 + p_{m-1} - p_m$$

The relation between the postponement p_m of year m and any economic factor such as trade or unemployment f_m, we may assume the just approximation:

$$p_m = a \pm b f_m$$

a and b being constants and the positive sign being taken for a factor unfavourable to marriage.

Therefore:

$$M_n = M_0 \pm b(f_{m-1} - f_m)$$

That is to say, the marriage-rate varies directly as the rate of change in favourable economic factors, inversely as the rate of change in unfavourable factors. But the postponement in any one year does not depend on the economic factors of that year only, but on the values of the factors for the preceding half-period or even more. Therefore, for instance,

[1] "On the Changes in the Marriage- and Birth-rates, etc.," *Journ. R. Stat. Soc.*, vol. 69, p. 93.

the postponements in a given year are assumed to depend, not on the state of employment for that year alone, but on the cumulative effect of the state of employment for several years preceding.

Hence the postponement in year m varies directly as the average economic factors during year m and the preceding years r, and we have for the new relation between p_m and f's in the following equation :

$$p_m = a' \pm b'(f_m + f_{m-1} + \ldots + f_{m-r})$$

or

$$M_m = M_o \pm b'(f_{m-r-1} - f_m)$$

To illustrate this theory by an actual case, Mr. Yule worked out the values of $f_{m-5} - f_m$ for the deviation from the eleven year means of Mr. Hartley's unemployment index, and $f_{m-6} - f_m$ for deviations from eleven year means of Sauerbeck's index numbers for prices. The correlations are as follows :

Marriage-rate oscillations and price differences :

(6 year) = 0·813.

Marriage-rate oscillations and unemployment differences :

(5 year) = 0·921.

We have to find some direct index of postponement, and according to Mr. Hooker the average age at marriage is an index of the postponement rate, if we assume that the average age of those who postpone, in any one year, is identical approximately with the average age of those who marry.

Sauerbeck's index numbers of prices are the best suitable factor indicating a similarity with fluctuations of marriage-rate and to which the postponements would be approximately related. They exhibit a maximum in 1874–5, and from 1875 a steady and continuous fall to 1899 inclusive. Mr. Yule is of the opinion that the price movements have been directly or indirectly a predominant factor during the period

[1] Manchester Stat. Soc., 1898.

1865–1900, or at least so closely related to a predominant factor that they serve as an accurate index to its changes; but besides that some other cause has to be taken into account as a second predominant factor during the last fifteen or twenty years (1880–1885–1900).

Mr. Yule finds a close relationship between the course of prices and increase of population, that is the birth-rate and death-rate, although he speaks only about the influence on the birth-rate (p. 129).

TABLE I

1 Period.	2 Percentage Increase of Population, E. and W.	3 Period.	4 Average Index Number.[1]	5 Period.	6 Average Index Number.
1801–11	14·0	1797–1807	156	1791–1801	142
1811–22	18·1	1807–17	156	1801–11	165
1821–31	15·8	1817–27	124	1811–21	142
1831–41	14·9	1827–37	101	1821–31	108
1841–51	12·9	1837–47	96	1831–41	103
1851–61	11·9	1847–57	89	1841–51	86
1861–71	13·2	1857–67	99	1851–61	94
1871–81	14·4	1867–77	100	1861–71	100
1881–91	11·7	1877–87	81	1871–81	95
1891–1901	12·2	1887–97	61	1881–91	75

The birth-rate of any year being dependent on the average price level of several years preceding, and therefore lagging behind the price movement, Mr. Yule worked out, for comparison with the increase rates, the averages of these index numbers for the eleven year periods (1797–1807, 1807–1817). They exhibit an agreement which is certainly fairly close.

[1] Index numbers based on Jevons' and Sauerbeck's numbers; the former reduced to Sauerbeck's on the basis of the overlapping years, 1846–65.

As the increase rates fell from 18·1 per cent. in 1811–21 to 11·9 in 1851–61, the average price index numbers fell from 156 to 89; as the increase rate then rose from 11·9 to 14·4, the index numbers rose from 89 to 100; finally as the increase rate fell from 14·4 to 11·7 and 12·2 (the latter unduly large owing to the low death-rate, and the former unduly low owing to high emigration) the index numbers fell from 100 to 61. In column 6 are given the average index numbers for the eleven years preceding each census decade, and these exhibit a still closer correspondence, though this may be partly accidental.

The course of prices, either directly by its influence on consumptive power and on profits, indirectly by effects on trade, or more directly as an index to the course of some other variable, has been through the past century the factor of most outstanding importance in the rate of reproduction of the race.

This does not exclude the presence of other factors, but merely ranks their importance somewhat lower in the scale.

The course of prices cannot have such a direct influence on the rate of natural increase or on the rate of reproduction through some undetermined efforts of trade, but the only reasonable supposition, as determined by Mr. Yule too, is that the rate of reproduction and therefore the rate of natural growth also, is dependent on the course of prices through the influence on consumptive power, or in using the terms of this essay, on consumptive capacity.

We may therefore conclude that the standard of living of people influences the consumptive capacity, and therefore the marriage- and birth-rate too. We are approaching more the real phenomena of life if we use these terms and do not speak of means of subsistence.

As human evolution surpassed the organic evolution, so the human wants in a progressive society surpassed the minimum of means of existence, that is, the physiological limit of maintenance of life, at least in industrial communities. But whatever becomes an integral part of consumptive capacity in the progressive communities through the standard of living, the struggle for it is a struggle for the maintenance of life, as it is, and in this sense the term means of subsistence is justified. The interdependence of the phenomena is as follows: the marriage-rate of a given standard of living depends on the economic facility of getting means of living; birth-rate depends on natural fertility of race, and again on facility to provide children with means of living under a given standard of life; the death-rate depends on the general knowledge of hygiene, and on the economic ability of individuals as well as of the community to realize the hygienic measures for a healthy life.

Economic conditions raise or lower marriage-, birth- and death-rates, and therefore the rate of natural increase.

The differences of the marriage-rate in successive years are due to economic pressure on consumptive capacity, and the differences of birth-rate in successive years are again due to economic pressure on consumptive capacity, as Newsholme and Stephenson stated that the size of families is diminishing and not the natural fecundity of race.[1] Therefore, the differences of the rate of natural increase in successive years represent an expression of functional dependency on economic conditions, and among the latter we may take the general course of prices, or, perhaps better for some countries, the course of prices of primary economic goods.

We can represent the connexion between the rate of natural increase and other vital and economic phenomena in the following manner:

[1] Cauderlier is in agreement with the above statement too. " La fécondité légitime des femmes est une constante, pourvu que les conditions économiques ainsi que les circonstances d'âge sont les mêmes." The normal curve of marriage tends to retain the same shape after great fluctuations.

Rate of Natural Increase.

Birth-rate	Death-rate
Marriage-rate	General knowledge of hygiene
Standard of living	Economic condition of individuals
Economic conditions	and community.

To sum up: the rate of natural increase in a community is dependent on the birth-rate and death-rate; the former on the marriage-rate and the latter on general knowledge of hygiene; the marriage-rate on standard of living, and this on economic conditions; so the general knowledge of hygiene can be carried out only if there is economic ability, and therefore the death-rate is dependent on economic conditions too. The economic conditions include mostly the conditions of the consumptive capacity of the community, its developments and its fluctuations.

VI

THE RATE OF NATURAL INCREASE AND WAR-EQUILIBRIUM THEORY

BESIDES the pre-war and post-war phenomena of the rate of natural increase in a population, actually connected with war equilibrium, there is another, the trend of the growth of population, dependent on the causes acting for longer periods. So, examining the recent growth of population in Western Europe,[1] we find that during thirty years, 1880–1909, the population grew at a moderate rate or that the rate of natural increase slackened; the period, until towards its end, was interrupted by considerable emigration, which was reduced later except in one or two cases. In the United Kingdom the marriage rate, measured crudely by the total population, declined 8 per cent. from 1870 to 1905; measured more accurately by the marriageable part of the population (15–45 age), it has declined 19 per cent. The birth-rate, measured crudely, has fallen 23 per cent. in thirty-five years; measured by the female population of ages from 15 to 45, it has fallen 29 per cent. Illegitimate births declined nearly 52 per cent., and legitimate 24 per cent.[2] The decline of the birth-rate is explained in some small part by the diminished illegitimacy, in larger part by the diminished proportion of the married to the unmarried, and about three-fourths by limitation of the size of families.

[1] Sir J. A. Baines, "The Recent Growth of Population." *Journ. R. Stat. Soc.*, vol. 72, 1909, pp. 685–701.

[2] Palgrave, *Dictionary of Political Economy*, Appendix.

The phenomenon of the general slackening of growth of population depends mostly, as in the case of the United Kingdom, three-fourths, *on the limitation* of the size of families, and this is an effect of the rising standard of living and of consumptive capacity, the growth of which I shall consider in the next chapter. They could be considered as representing the pressure and outgrowth of population, which is temporarily relieved by emigration, and I do not doubt that their relations to the war situation could be worked out.

But although they affect the general state of economic equilibrium, they are not significant for periods just preceding a war.

I argued in the fourth chapter that the pre-war phenomena of war equilibrium, in respect of the rate of natural increase, is an exhibition of a declining period, effected by a continuous rise of consumption and standard of living, and its post-war phenomenon is an ascending period, effected by greater facility of getting means of living and of lowered standard of living.

War effects a continuous lowering of the rate of natural increase, by the absence of married people, or by checking the marriage-rate, and it is therefore an organic continuation of declining period. But through the actual loss of human life it makes it easier for the survivors to get means of living and to marry proportionately more, and renders the maintenance of families easier, therefore checking the limitation of the size of families.

The phenomena of the war-equilibrium rate of natural increase are more significant in industrial communities than in agricultural ones, for the former are steadily raising the standard of living, and it is their consumptive capacity which affects and presses upon the size of families and upon the rate of natural increase. The violent fluctuations of the rate of natural increase are partly due to incomplete and incorrect statistics, but partly to their dependence on the harvests; during good harvests the people marry more, and the births in the subsequent years are therefore more abundant. During bad harvests the people marry less, and therefore the birth-rate falls. The agricultural communities are dependent on nature, and their reactions and actions are similar to the natural discontinuous phenomena, while the industrial communities are characterized by steadiness of progress in declining or ascending.

I shall treat the rate of natural increase of some countries during the following wars:

(1) Franco-Prussian War, 1870–1.
(2) American Civil War, 1861–5.
(3) Serbo-Bulgarian War, 1885.
(4) South African War, 1899–1902.
(5) Russo-Japanese War, 1904–5.
(6) Balkan Wars, 1912–13.
(7) The Great World War, 1914.

(1) *The Franco-Prussian War*, 1870–1.

The pre-war declining period of the rate of natural increase in Prussia extends from 1865 to 1869; the actual numbers are, measured per 1,000 inhabitants:

1865 . .	12·1	
1866 . .	5·2	(exceptional on account of Asiatic cholera)
1867 . .	12·7	
1868 . .	9·5	
1869 . .	11·8	

The recovery of the year 1867 is above the year 1865, and it is due to the influence of the prevailing epidemic in the previous year. Therefore it should be below 12·1; or averaging the years 1866 and 1867, we get 8·95. The following years 1868 and 1869 are irregular, either on account of the more violent fluctuation of the agricultural population, which formed the chief part of the inhabitants of Prussia, or it is due to the disturbing influence of cholera.

The war period is pronouncedly regular; the rate

of natural increase was in 1870, 11·1, and in 1871, 5·0. The ascending post-war period in Prussia is again in conformity with the war-equilibrium theory; the rates were in 1872, 10·4; in 1873, 11·6; in 1874, 14·3; 14·1 in 1875, and 15·2 in 1876.

The stationary population of France shows shorter periods; so the pre-war declining period lasts from 1867–9, with following rates per 1,000: 3·7 in 1867, 1·6 in 1868, and 2·2 in 1869. The war period shows an actual diminution of the population; the rates were − 2·9 in 1870 and − 12·2 in 1871. The post-war ascending phase of the rate of natural increase shows some remarkably large figures for France. So the rate of natural increase was in 1872, 4·7, a quite exceptionally high figure; 2·7 in 1873, and 4·8 in 1874, again exceptionally high. The two rates cannot be found in France after 1861.

Taking the average annual increase of the population of some years, preceding and succeeding war, we see clearly the position of balance of forces by war.

Average Increase of Population in France and Prussia per 1,000 Inhabitants.[1]

Year.	Prussia.	France.
1865–6	9·9	3·6
1870–1	5·8	1·8
1875–6	9·2	5·4
1880–1	11·4	4·1

It seems that the winning country exhibits a longer ascending period of the rate of natural increase than the losing one.

(2) *The American Civil War*, 1861–5.

There are no statistics available on the rate of the natural increase, to illustrate the theory of war equilibrium. Yet the elements of the rate of natural increase indicate an ascending and declining phase after and during the war.

[1] *Stat. Int. du Mouvement de la Population jusqu'en* 1905, p. 39.

The following table[1] shows the declining war and ascending post-war periods of marriage and births in Massachussetts.

Marriage- and Birth-rates in Massachussetts per 1,000 Inhabitants.

1860	20·15	29·28	Declining Phase.
1861	17·72	28·63	
1862	17·68	25·92	
1863	17·36	24·20	
1864	19·86	24·17	
1865	20·60	23·87	
1866	22·15	26·16	Ascending Phase.

Whereas the birth-rate has a regular declining war period and a sudden ascending phase from 1866, the marriage-rate is irregular from 1864, that is increasing, due probably to the prospect of soon ending the war.

(3) *The Serbo-Bulgarian War*, 1885.

Although passing to small modern communities, as Serbia and Bulgaria are, we cannot expect them to exhibit as clearly the pre-war and post-war economic phenomena of war equilibrium as the great industrial or semi-industrial communities do. We have to assume the declining and ascending periods to be much shorter, and, as in agricultural communities in general, more irregular, and under this assumption the periods can be traced with sufficient clearness to harmonize with the theory.

Rate of Natural Increase in Serbia and Bulgaria, per 1,000.

1883	Declining.	24·2	18·7
1884		22·6	21·3
1885		19·7	20·9
1886	Ascending.	12·4	13·4
1887		21·4	20·2
1888		21·3	19·5

[1] *Journal of Political Economy*, vol. 25, 1917, Wolfe, p. 527.

The war happened to be in the month of November, and therefore the decline is visible in 1886 more than in the war year 1885. Serbia was the aggressor and is more representative. The year 1884 is exceptional for Bulgaria, when she annexed Roumelia, and therefore the high figure.

(4) *The South African War,* 1899–1902.

Although Sir R. Giffen [1] says that the broad conclusion regarding the effects of this war is "that although the war has caused a great disturbance of local industry, greater in proportion to the industry of localities which are the seat of war, than any similar disturbance upon record, yet the war altogether has not caused any great disturbance, because it has really been small in proportion to the resources of the British Empire," yet we trace the pre-war and post-war phenomena of the rate of natural increase, in accordance with the theory of war equilibrium.

The declining pre-war period of the rate of natural increase lasted from 1896 to 1899, and the rates are as follows: 12·5 in 1896, 12·2 in 1897, 11·8 in 1898, and 10·9 in 1899. The war ended in 1902, and curiously enough, the ascending period began during war in 1901; the war rates are as follows: 10·7 in 1900, 11·6 in 1901, 12·2 in 1902, and 13·0 in 1903; the rates being those of England and Wales.

(5) *The Russo-Japanese War,* 1904–5.

Japan, which was at the same time the aggressor, is the more representative country (see Fig. 5).

The declining period of the rate of natural increase lasted from 1901 to 1903; the rates are: 12·8 in 1901; 12·0 in 1902, and 12·0 in 1903, per 1,000 of population.

The war period shows a marked further decrease in the rates: 9·4 in 1904, and 8·7 in 1905.

The post-war slowly ascending phase lasted from

[1] "Some Economic Aspects of the War." *Econ. Journ.*, vol. 9, pp. 195–207.

1906 to 1911. The rates are: 9·3 in 1906; 12·2 in 1907; 12·8 in 1908; 12·3 in 1909; 12·8 in 1910; and 13·7 in 1911.

Russia is less significant in her bearing to this phenomena; the periods are shorter.

The declining pre-war period is marked just for 1902–3, with the rates 17·6 in 1902 and 17·7 in 1903.

The war period is characterized by an increase of the rate of natural increase in the first year of war, 18·6 in 1904, and by a sudden decrease to 13·5 in 1905. The years 1906 and 1907 have a tendency to an increased ascending phase of the rate of natural increase, with the rates 17·0 in 1906 and 18·5 in 1907, per 1,000 of inhabitants.

(6) *The Balkan Wars*, 1912–13.

In these wars Serbia, Greece, Bulgaria and Turkey actually fought; Roumania did not fight, but she marched into Bulgaria after the battle already fought out by Serbs and Greeks against the Bulgars.

There is a pronounced tendency to the depression of the rate of natural increase in Serbia, beginning from 1906 to 1911. The rates were as follows:[1] 17·5 in 1906; 17·6 in 1907; 13·1 in 1908, and 19·4 in 1909; 16·6 in 1910; 14·5 in 1911, and 16·9 in 1912. The year 1908 is exceptional, for Serbia mobilized in connexion with Austria's declaration of annexation of the Serbian provinces, Bosnia and Herzegovina; but taking the average, we get the numbers 16·25 and 16·25, which is just below the next year's rate, 16·6.

Roumania shows also a tendency to depression of the rate of natural increase from 1906 onwards. The rates are 16·0 in 1906; 15·0 in 1907; 13·0 in 1908; 13·9 in 1909; and 14·6 in 1910; but the years 1911 and 1912 have high rates, 17·3 and 20·5. This is probably due to good harvests, and to the general

[1] The average rates being: 1906–7, 17·55; 1908–9, 16·25; 1910–12, 13·3.

conditions of agricultural communities, which have more violent fluctuations.

Bulgaria too shows a tendency to decline in the rate of natural increase from 1906 onwards: the rates being 21·7 in 1906; 21·3 in 1907; 16·4 in 1908; 14·0 in 1909; and again a relative rise to 18·5 in 1910 and 18·8 in 1911.

There are no statistics for other countries nor for other periods.

(7) *The Great World War*, 1914.

Besides the decline of the rate of natural increase, immediately preceding the war, which will be treated separately for each country, there was a more or less general depression of the natural growth from 1896 onwards, connected with the general slackening of the growth of population in Western Europe during the recent thirty-five years.

The latest period of this decline of the natural growth is visible in the following table, giving the average rate of the natural increase in quinquennial periods from 1896–1900.

TABLE IA.

Average Rate of Natural Increase in Quinquennial Periods per 1,000 Inhabitants.

Country.	1896–1900	1901–1905	1906–1910	1911–1913
United Kingdom . .	10·7	11·4	10·8	9·7*
England and Wales .	11·4	12·1	11·5	10·1
Germany	14·7	14·5	14·1	12·1*
France	1·1	1·6	1·1	1·3
Italy	11·1	10·6	11·5	12·6
Austria	11·5	11·4	11·3	10·1*
Hungary	11·3	11·0	11·6	11·4*
Belgium	10·8	10·8	8·7	8·1
Russia	17·0	16·7	16·7	—
Serbia	15·2	12·2	16·8	15·7*
Bulgaria	13·0	18·1	18·2	—

* Only 1911–12.

The steadiest slackening is noticeable in the case of Germany and Austria, the two aggressive countries *par excellence* in this war; then in Belgium, the most industrialized of the countries, with comparatively small outlets; and in Russia, shut off from all the seas. The United Kingdom, as well as England and Wales, shows a steady decline from 1901-1905 onwards; this period has a higher rate of natural increase than the previous quinquennium, probably effected by the South African War, which, as all wars, caused a rise in the post-war rates.

France's rates of natural growth are, as usual in French economic phenomena, in disaccordance with the other countries. Hungary's natural growth was stationary. Italy's was rising from 1901–5, and Bulgaria's from 1896–1900. Serbia's natural growth fluctuated violently, and it declined in the period immediately preceding the war.

Altogether, the natural growth was declining or stationary. The case of Italy does not count as she was already engaged in a war (1912, Tripolis), and the growth of Bulgaria has too small weight compared with the other belligerent countries.

Germany is the most representative country in this war, and it is therefore perhaps not accidentally that Germany is conducting a war of conquest (see Fig. 2).

We find the following numbers, indicating quite clearly a declining period of the growth of the rate of natural increase from 1906 to 1913.

TABLE 2.

The Declining Period of the Growth of the Rate of Natural Increase in Germany per 1,000 of Population.

1906	14·9
1907	14·2
1908	14·0
1909	13·8
1910	13·6
1911	11·3
1912	12·7
1913	12·5[1]

Except the year 1911, the movement of the rate of natural increase is from 1906 continuously downward. The sharp decline of 1911 is due probably to some other cause.

[1] *Stat. Internat. du Mouvement de la Population*, 1905, Paris.

In England and Wales, as well as in the United Kingdom, the fluctuations of the rate of natural increase are more irregular, as is shown in the following table (see Fig. 2).

TABLE 2A.

Table showing the Growth of Natural Increase per 1,000 of Population in England and Wales and United Kingdom.

Year.	England and Wales.	United Kingdom.
1905	12·0	11·5
1906	11·7	11·3
1907	11·4	10·8
1908	11·9	11·3
1909	11·1	10·7
1910	11·6	11·0
1911	9·8	9·6
1912	10·5	10·2
1913	10·2	
1914	9·7	

But taking the averages of three years, we see a clear and pronounced tendency to decline.

Rate of Natural Increase per 1,000 of Population.

Average of Years.	England and Wales.	United Kingdom.
1905–1907	11·7	11·2
1908–1910	11·4	11·0
1911–1913	10·2	9·9 (two years)

1914, of the war period, already shows a sharp movement downward; "the excess of births over deaths in 1914, however, 362,352, having amounted to 9·8 per 1,000, the lowest rate then on record except that of 1911 (9·7, in my table 9·8), it may be inferred that the excess of 25,336 in 1915 would correspond to a rate of about 6·8 per 1,000" (*78th Ann. Rep. of Registrar-General*, 1915, p. 16).

France.—The growth of the rate of natural increase in France is stationary, and the fluctuations are relatively small.

I give the numbers from 1905 per 1,000 inhabitants.

1905	1·0	1910	1·8
1906	·6	1911	1·1
1907	1·5	1912	1·5
1908	1·2	1913	1·3
1909	·4		

The declining period is noticeable from 1910, although interrupted slightly in 1911. Taking the three-yearly averages, we get:

1905–7	1·0
1908–10	1·1
1911–13	1·3

This result is not at all surprising, if we remember that France is not an industrial country *par excellence*, and that usage of preventive means checks and gives another direction to births than in other countries.

The growth of the rate of natural increase in France does not indicate a significant economic situation, for the rates are comparatively small; yet the decline from 1·5 in 1912 to 1·3 in 1913 may be taken as significant for forces affecting equilibrium.

Austria is an industrial country, or at least on the way to industrialization, and it is no exaggeration to say that the state of the economic situation in Austria led to this war as much as Germany's lust for expansion and world-power (see Fig. 2).

The rate of natural increase diminished considerably from 1906 to 1912; we find the number 12·5 in 1906 and 10·8 in 1912, per 1,000 of population.

The following table shows the actual course of growth in the rate of natural increase in Austria per 1,000 inhabitants.

Table showing Growth of Rate of Natural Increase in Austria per 1,000 Inhabitants.

1906	12·5	1910	11·3
1907	11·4	1911	9·5
1908	11·2	1912	10·8
1909	10·5		

In 1908 Austria partially mobilized against Serbia, and we have therefore the sharp decline in 1909 to

10·5, and consequently a sharp recovery in 1910 to 11·3. Averaging them we get for 1909–10, 10·9 and 10·9, which makes the decline smoother to 1911 with 9·5.

The year 1913 is not available. Taking two-yearly averages we notice a pronounced tendency to decline.

1906–7	11·9
1908–9	10·8
1910–11	10·4

It is unlikely that the rate of natural increase in the year 1913 is below the average of 1910–11, that is, below 10·4.

Hungary is an agricultural country, and as such she shows sharp up and down movements in the growth of the rate of natural increase. Willcox's [1] statement that the sharp up and down movements in the curves of birth- and death-rates are undergoing important modifications, and succeeded by a steady progressive downward movement, cannot be applied, at least in respect of the marriage- and birth-rates, to agricultural countries, such as Hungary, Russia, Serbia, etc., where a bountiful harvest still has a great influence on marriage- and birth-rates, and therefore on the rate of natural increase too. But having regard to the possible incorrectness of the figure 13·0 in 1912, yet still the average of the years 1911–12 is below the average of 1909–10, 12·1 and 11·4 being the actual numbers. If we take three-yearly averages of the periods 1907–9 and 1910–12, we get a more stationary state of growth of the rate of natural increase, that is 11·6 and 11·7, which, for an agricultural community, may be taken as significant.

The rate of natural increase fluctuated from 1906 in Hungary as follows, per 1,000 of inhabitants:

1906	11·4	1910	12·1
1907	11·0	1911	9·9
1908	11·7	1912	13·0
1909	12·1	1913	No data.

[1] *The Nature and Significance, etc.* Amer. Stat. Assoc., vol. 15, 1916.

For Russia I have the numbers to 1909,[1] and the fluctuations are from 1907, pronouncedly steadily declining, as is seen from the following numbers, representing the rate of natural increase per 1,000.

1906	17·0	1908	16·3
1907	18·5	1909	15·1

The years 1906 and 1907 represent the ascending period after the Russo-Japanese War, and the pressure on the rate of natural increase seems to be very soon operating again.

In Italy the declining period of the rate of natural increase before the Great War extends to three years, actually known, that is from 1912 to 1914; the rates are: 14·2 in 1912, 13·5 in 1913 and 13·2 in 1914. But it is curious to note the sudden change after 1910 in the growth of the rate; from 1906 to 1911 the rate fluctuated between 11·6 to 10·6, while after 1911 the rate rose above 14·0.

The rates of natural increase in Italy per 1,000 are as follows:

1906	11·1	1911	10·1
1907	10·6	1912	14·2
1908	10·8	1913	13·5
1909	11·6	1914	13·2
1910	13·3		

Serbia is an agricultural country, and the fluctuations of the rate of natural increase are not very significant.

The rates were, per 1,000 inhabitants:

1909	19·4	1911	14·6
1910	16·6	1912	16·9

The last number is probably not correct, as it falls already in a war period (see Balkan Wars, 1912–13), and it does not seem to me probable that the rate rose in 1912, when the Serbo-Turkish War was already in operation.

[1] From 1863–1913, *Recueil Jubilaire du Comité Central de Statistique du Ministère de l'Intérieur de Russie*, 1913.

Belgium.—The declining period of the rate of natural increase is very significant for Belgium. It is continuous from 1901 to 1906; in 1907 it rose slightly and was falling to 1909; the following year it rose again, then fell still more to 1913 (see Fig. 2).

1901	12·3	1907	9·5
1902	11·1	1908	8·4
1903	10·5	1909	7·9
1904	10·3	1910	8·5
1905	9·7	1911	8·5
1906	9·3	1912	7·8

Sir B. Mallet [1] gives in his recent publication the following calculated details of the decline of births in the United Kingdom, Germany, and Hungary (calculated up to the end of June, 1915), as affected by the war.

The United Kingdom lost 500,000 potential lives, or approximately 10,000 per million of the population; Germany lost 2,600,000, or approximately 40,000 per million, and Hungary 1,500,000, or 70,000 per million. It is therefore quite natural that these losses should lower the rate of natural increase, but it is to be expected that the rate, being in decline during the war period, will rise immediately after the conclusion of peace.

To conclude: There are two sharp tendencies, balancing each other and antagonistic, in action before and after a war in the growth of the rate of natural increase. These tendencies create a pre-war declining period in the growth of the rate of natural increase and a post-war ascending phase.

The actual war period is an organic continuation in decline of the rate of natural increase, and the opposite forces tend to balance the loss through deaths or through postponement of marriages and births only after the war. The ascending period of the post-war

[1] "Vital Statistics as Affected by the War." *Journ. R. Stat. Soc.*, vol. 81, 1918.

growth of the rate of natural increase therefore re-establishes the equilibrium of the community, disturbed by actual warfare, as indicated by the pre-war state of neutral or unstable equilibrium, but it may be noticed that the winning party is progressive, the losing stationary or retrogressive. The periods may be longer or shorter as the economic significance of the war is more or less pronounced, and as the actual organization of consumption and production of the country is more industrial and less agricultural.

The agricultural countries have more irregularities in their movements of the rate of natural increase than the industrial ones. The movements are sharply up and down, though the declining and ascending periods may be distinguished. These sharp fluctuations are due more to the fluctuations of marriage- and birth-rates than to that of the death-rate, as will be clear from the table, representing the marriage-, birth-, and death-rates of Russia, Hungary, Serbia, and Bulgaria from 1900.

TABLE 3.

Marriage-, Birth-, and Death-rates per 1,000 Inhabitants.

	Russia.			Hungary.			Serbia.			Bulgaria.		
	Mar.	Bth.	Dth.	Mar.	Bth.	Dth.	Mar.	Bth.	Dth.	Mar.	Bth.	Dth.
1900	—	—	—	—	—	—	—	—	—	—	—	—
1901	8·6	47·9	32·1	8·8	37·8	25·4	8·3	38·0	21·0	8·7	37·5	23·1
1902	8·6	49·1	31·5	8·7	38·9	27·1	10·3	38·1	22·3	9·4	38·8	23·8
1903	8·9	48·1	30·0	8·1	36·9	26·2	9·5	40·9	23·5	9·4	41·0	22·7
1904	7·6	48·5	29·9	9·2	37·4	25·0	11·6	39·8	21·4	11·3	42·4	21·2
1905	7·6	44·8	31·1	8·5	36·1	28·1	9·9	37·3	24·8	10·8	43·5	21·8
1906	9·6	46·8	29·8	8·8	36·5	25·1	10·4	43·0	24·5	9·5	44·0	22·3
1907	8·8	46·6	28·1	9·9	36·6	25·6	10·6	40·0	22·4	9·9	43·6	22·3
1908	7·9	44·3	28·0	9·2	37·0	25·3	9·0	36·8	23·7	8·8	40·4	24·3
1909	7·9	44·0	28·9	8·7	37·7	25·6	9·4	38·7	29·3	9·2	40·6	26·6
1910	—	—	—	8·6	37·7	23·6	10·4	39·0	22·4	—	—	—
1911	—	—	—	9·2	35·0	25·1	10·3	36·3	21·8	—	—	—
1912	—	—	—	8·6	36·3	23·3	10·4	—	—	—	—	—
1913	—	—	—	—	—	—	—	—	—	—	—	

The average of the differences of the successive years in Russia is: of marriage-rate 0·6, of birth-rate 0·9, of death-rate 0·4; in Serbia, of marriage-rate 0·19, of birth-rate 0·27, of death-rate 0·02; in Hungary, of marriage-rate 0, of birth-rate 0·2, of death-rate 1; in Bulgaria, of marriage-rate 0·08, of birth-rate 0·3, of death-rate 0·5.

Mr. Yule, in the already quoted essay,[1] gives an explanation of the depression of the birth-rate, which is in accordance with the war-equilibrium theory. The adjustment of a population to the optimum or best possible number, supposing that one can under any given circumstances say that there is an optimum, does not appear to have been hitherto fully considered. In the modern human industrial state, the direct provision of necessaries is not in question; the procuring of employment and the standard of living is in question. Given employment, subsistence follows. If a population be above the optimum, the supply of labour being in excess, the birth-rate will be depressed and will stay depressed until the reaction begins to have some effect on the labour market. But this effect will not even commence for fifteen or twenty years, and the labour supply may not be adjusted to the demand for, say, thirty years. The birth-rate may now have risen again to normal, but the labour supply will continue to fall owing to the low birth-rates formerly prevalent. The birth-rate will therefore rise above normal and continue above normal so long as the labour supply is in defect; and so matters will go on, the population swinging about the optimum value during a long period of perhaps fifty to a hundred years, and the birth-rate following suit. This will tend to produce corresponding alterations of long periods in the labour market, superposed on the short cycle of trade, and they will probably be even more difficult to deal with and hardly

[1] Udny Yule, "On Changes in the Marriage- and Birth-rates," etc. *Journ. R. Stat. Soc.*, vol. 69, 1906, p. 131.

subject to control. It seems likely that we may regard ourselves as being at present, and having been for some years, near the maximum of such periods of excess in the supply of labour.

If optimum be a stable position of economic equilibrium, then an excess of supply of labour must manifest itself by depressing the marriage- and birth-rates and therefore also the rate of natural increase. The declining period of the rate of natural increase indicates such a state of depression and of an excess of supply of labour; but, here is the difference between the war-equilibrium and the optimum theory, the decline is not effected by an excess of "labour supply," but by the action of forces affecting consumption and production, and most of all the distribution. Consumption is growing by the action of the law of increasing wants; production of primary and secondary goods is getting more disproportionate, and by the action of the distributive forces a relatively small part of the community is appropriating the greatest part of the national income, and of the means of production, that is capital goods and the land. That is the source of the excess of the "supply of labour."

VII

THE LAW OF INCREASING WANTS

HUMAN wants are primarily concerned with the preservation of life, and are therefore of physiological nature. But as some biological peculiarities have been modified, as, for instance, the gradual disappearance of hair, a need arose to cover the body artificially, and to seek a shelter. Food, clothes, and shelter remain, for the greater part of humanity, still the chief source of wants, and therefore the basis of economic consumption. We have seen in the previous (fifth) chapter how economic factors influence the marriage-, birth-, and death-rates, and the two first phenomena form another biological feature of human life, aiming at preservation of race. Preservation of life and preservation of race are both founded on the supply of economic means to satisfy them, and we have seen in the chapter " Economics and War " the variety of economic means and the consequent difference in the struggle for existence at the different stages of the progress of humanity.

It has been asserted that as people advance in civilization, the desire for reproduction diminishes, or as L. Brentano[1] says: " With increasing prosperity, mankind generally rises above the state of blindly giving way to its animal instincts, and so parents become more and more conscious of their responsibility, both for the character and number of the human beings whom they bring into the world. This

[1] " The Doctrine of Malthus," etc. *Econ. Journ.*, vol. 20, pp. 371–393.

leads many weakly people to refrain from giving life to children to whom they might transfer their diseases. In other cases parents will rather strive to ensure to the children whom they have already brought into the world a good education and a larger patrimony so as to equip them better for the modern struggle of life" (p. 386).

I do not find any proof of a diminution of desire of reproduction; the words refer to pathological cases or to the economic consideration of people concerning limitation of the size of families. As the preservation of life is more secured, the tendency to preserve the race and desire for reproduction do not diminish; for the wants having their source in the preservation of life, and those having their source in the preservation of race, are not antagonistic. The physiological wants have to be satisfied first, in order that the reproductive and sexual impulses may appear. A starving man does not have any impulse for reproduction. There is always a limit, a minimum grade of satisfaction of the primary wants, below which reproductive impulses cannot appear. But this limit does not represent any antagonistic tendency between the primary and reproductive wants. The antagonistic tendency appears when the primary wants are joined by secondary ones, and they form the union of the standard of living, or we may say when the primary wants differentiate in primary and secondary ones in the course of a progressive state of humanity. The point where the antagonistic tendency between standard of living and reproductive impulses is reached, is when the law of increasing wants begins to operate in both directions, increasing the variety and intensity of consumption. But the antagonistic tendency is based on the difficulties of satisfying the primary and secondary wants, and also the reproductive impulses, with an inadequate supply of economic means, or shortly, by difficulties of economic production.

The demand of primary wants is firstly to satisfy the appetite, and then by differentiation of wants it leads to the need of covering the human body and obtaining shelter. The wants of food were satisfied by a uniform food, animal or vegetable, and in the progress of human wants the uniformity was substituted by diversity. But as the differentiation of primary wants or necessaries went on, it was accelerated still more by the development of secondary wants, connected with the standard of living; the primary wants and the secondary ones having their origin in the diversity of primary ones, form the standard of living, and all wants drive at the optimum [1] of satisfaction, by which we mean the conditions most favourable to the processes of mankind.

Whatever may be the sense of the law of diminishing utility of successive increments in economic consideration of an individual, it is quite certain that the consumption of very few commodities has no tendency to increase beyond quantities already consumed, and that shows that the optimal limit of very few commodities is reached.

But although the optimal limit of few commodities is reached, yet the higher wants are appearing, but the satisfaction of every lower want does not create a desire for higher (Banfield), and " it would appear to be more correct to say that the lower wants are not absolutely satisfied, but that when their satisfaction has proceeded to a certain point the desire to satisfy higher wants is more urgent than the desire to afford increased satisfaction to the lower wants. While noting, however, that frequently the power of affording satisfaction by increasing the consumption of a given commodity is not exhausted, when such increase ceases and consumption of an entirely different nature is substituted, it is not asserted that instances do not occur, where *further instalments* can produce

[1] H. S. Jennings, *Behaviour of the Lower Organisms*, p. 295. Columbia Univ. Press, New York, 1916.

no further satisfaction" (Palgrave, *Dict. of Pol. Econ.*, vol. 1, p. 583).

The substitution of one commodity for another may happen only, and in a limited sense, if the satisfaction of more urgent primary wants attained this "certain point," that is, the minimum of satisfaction.

The minimum point of satisfaction of commodities is soon reached, and therefore the possibility of the substitution of one commodity for another and the increase of numbers of commodities in consumption.

This is one side of the action of the law of increasing wants; the other side is the increase of the quantity of the commodity concerned. I expressed the law of increasing wants by saying that human wants increase in intensity and variety. The increase of intensity is in the direction of reaching the optimum of satisfaction of each commodity, and the effect of this is visible in increase of consumption *per capita* in each country. The increase of human wants in variety and numbers is visible in the multiplication of commodities in consumption, but it is quite possible that besides the tendency to variety, acting in the direction of increasing the numbers of commodities in consumption, there is always a compensating action between the consumption of supplementary commodities. So we find the consumption of beer, wine and spirits in the United Kingdom diminishing but that of tea and cocoa increasing, or the consumption of coffee in the United States increasing and that of tea decreasing. Patten's[1] assertion that "the progress of society consists not in increasing the consumption of the articles in use, but in substituting new articles with a large sum of pleasure for articles out of harmony with the remaining commodities consumed," is not correct, if we consider the statistical results of consumption of commodities.

The progress of society, at least for large masses,

[1] S. Patten, *Dynamic Economics*. Publ. of Univ. of Pennsylvania, 1891, p. 44.

consists in increasing the consumption of the articles in use, and also—for very few—in substituting or adding new commodities for old ones. Whether the change from one commodity to another also revives and increases the marginal utility of each commodity,[1] I leave without definite answer. But I doubt that Marshall's statement that, "as, however, man rises in civilization, as his mind becomes developed and even his animal passions begin to associate themselves with mental activities, his wants become rapidly more subtle and more various, and in the minor details of life he begins to desire change for the sake of change, long before he has consciously escaped from the yoke of custom," is applicable to the greatest number of humanity. People do not want a change for the sake of change, at least in the consumption of commodities, as long as the minimal limit of consumption of commodities is not reached, and then, if the change happens, the law of increasing wants again pushes the consumption to intensity (optimal limit) of both consumed commodities, afterwards to variety, adding again new commodities for consumption.

The law of increasing wants has been clearly formulated in Palgrave's *Dictionary of Political Economy*, vol. I, p. 394: "It is the growth in the intensity and variety of the demands of consumers which is the mainspring of the increase of the production, and thus of employment of labour."

I shall examine the action of the law of increasing wants as shown by the growth of consumption of commodities per head of population in the United Kingdom, France, Germany, the United States, Italy, and partly Russia and other countries in the next chapter.

[1] S. Patten, *Dynamic Economics*, pp. 40–45.

VIII

GROWTH OF CONSUMPTION

ALTHOUGH consumption per head does not express the real consumed *per capita* quantities in the population, yet there is good reason to assume that if the consumption is distributed according to the normal curve of the law of error, it represents the mode of curve, that is, the amount actually enjoyed by the greatest number of persons.

The growth of consumption can be measured also by relating the subsequent absolute quantities of the totals of consumed commodities in successive years to a fixed quantity. And lastly, the index numbers of consumption are a reliable measure of the relative growth of consumption; in this case an average amount of consumed commodities in a definite period of years is taken as a fixed point (= 100), and the subsequent quantities are expressed as percentages of this base.

United Kingdom.

The fourth table shows the consumption of the principal imported articles retained for home consumption per head of population in the United Kingdom in the years 1840, 1881, and 1913. If we put the amount of the year 1840 as 100, and express the others as percentages of that year, we see the enormous increase in some commodities. So rice increased from 100 in 1840 to 1,679; cocoa increased to 1,425; sugar to 626; tea to 548; tobacco to 243; and currants and raisins to 339 in 1913.

Sir R. Giffen,[1] who stated the increase for the year 1881, says:

TABLE 4.[2]

Quantities of the Principal Imported and Excisable Articles retained for Home Consumption, per head of the Total Population in United Kingdom.

Article.		1840.	1881.	1913.	1840.	1881.	1913.
Currants, raisins	lb.	1·42	4·34	4·82	100	223	339
Rice	,,	0·90	16·32	15·11	100	1,813	1,679
Cocoa	,,	0·08	0·31	1·14 (raw)	100	187	1,425
Coffee	,,	1·08	0·89	0·61	100	82	56
Raw sugar	,,	15·20	58·92	95·13	100	387	626
Refined sugar	,,	—	8·44	83·10	100	100	985
Tea	,,	1·22	4·58	6·68	100	375	548
Tobacco	,,	0·86	1·41	2·10	100	164	243
Wine	galls.	0·25	0·45	0·25	100	160	100

"The articles are not such that the *increased consumption by the rich could have made much difference.* It is consumption emphatically of the mass which is here in question."

But although the increase is steady for all articles except coffee from 1840 to 1881, some commodities show a decrease from 1885 to 1913; so cheese decreases from 649 to 592, wine from 160 to 100, and spirits from 114 to 74, probably due to a change of custom in consumption and to the compensatory substitution of other articles.

But a more reliable measure of the growth of consumption are the index numbers of consumption, indicating not only the relative growth in time, but a comparability between different commodities. It is to be regretted that they have not been worked

[1] *Essays in Finance*, p, 388,

[2] Sir R. Giffen, *Essays in Finance*, 1890, p. 388. Porter-Hirst, *The Progress of the Nation*, p. 170. Stat. Abst. for U.K., 1901–15. Cd. 8448, p. 170, 1913 calculated.

out for all the countries with the same base as was done for the United Kingdom by Mr. Wood, and I shall try to complete them partly.

Taking the average of the years 1870–9 as 100, the quinquennial averages show the following progress in consumption (Table XII, Appendix).

The general level of consumption of the commodities was in 1865–9, 11 p.c.; in 1870–4, 27 p.c.; in 1875–9, 35 p.c.; in 1880–4, 37 p.c.; in 1885–9, 37 p.c.; in 1890–4, 46 p.c.; in 1895–9, 58 p.c.; in 1900–4, 60 p.c.; and in 1905–9, 66 p.c. above the level of 1860–4. Although the real consumption may be a little less or more in the case of some commodities, on account of not having excluded the consumption of animals, the general level itself is not affected.

The consumption of primary commodities, as wheat, advanced about 11 p.c.; meat, 18 p.c.; sugar, 48 p.c.; cotton, 12 p.c.; and wool, 6 p.c., from the level of 1870–9 in the quinquennium of 1905–9. Of the semi-luxuries, cocoa rose 197 and tea 45 p.c., but they were compensated by a decline of 22 p.c. in coffee, 48 p.c. in wine, 27 p.c. in spirits, and 12 p.c. in malt and beer.

Subtracting the percentages of increase from the percentages of decrease in these commodities, we get the percentage 33 as the number indicating the level of increase of consumption of semi-luxuries in the period 1905–9, compared with the years 1870–9. Tobacco, which belongs to the same group of commodities, shows a little higher increase than this percentage of 33, that is, 36 p.c.; currants and raisins increased only 9 p.c., similar to the primary commodities, and they should therefore be calculated in this group. The decennial averages are represented in Table 5.

The commodities increased from 1870–9 to 1900–9: Wheat, 9 p.c.; meat, 18 p.c.; currants, 3 p.c.; sugar, 49 p.c.; wool, 4 p.c., and cotton, 5 p.c.; rice declined 21 p.c.; semi-luxuries increased: tea, 43 p.c.; cocoa,

286 p.c.; coffee declined 30 p.c.; wine and spirits declined 41 and 20 p.c. respectively; malt increased 3 p.c., and tobacco, 33 p.c.

Bringing the table up to date to 1913, and comparing the average numbers of the four years 1910–13 with the average index numbers of 1870–9, the increase was 11 p.c. for wheat, 15 p.c. for cotton, 8 p.c. for currants and raisins, 13 p.c. for meat, 24 p.c. for rice, 50 p.c. for sugar, and 31 p.c. for wool; of the semi-luxuries, 431 p.c. for cocoa, 50 p.c. for wine, 43 p.c. for spirits, and 3 p.c. for beer. It should be noted that the average level of meat consumption in 1910–13 is 5 p.c. below the level of 1900–9.

TABLE 5.

Index Numbers of Consumption of Commodities in United Kingdom, showing the Decennial Average Level of Consumption, 1870–9 = 100, from Wood.[1]

Article.	1860–9.	1870–9.	1880–9.	1890–9.	1900–9.	1910–13.
Wheat	98	100	104	109	109	111
Cocoa	50	100	147	238	386	531
Coffee	114	100	89	73	70	63
Cotton	67	100	107	104	105	115
Currants, raisins	89	100	97	110	103	108
Meat	—	100	100	114	118	113
Rice	56	100	110	81	79	124
Sugar	69	100	126	143	149	150
Tea	73	100	113	130	143	151
Tobacco	91	100	102	117	133	142
Wool	89	100	102	117	104	131
Wine	75	100	77	75	59	50
Spirits	80	100	85	84	80	57
Malt and beer	87	100	99	109	103	97
Average unweighted	80	100	104	115	124	138

[1] G. H. Wood, "Some Statistics Relating to Working Class Progress since 1860." *Journ. of R. Stat. Soc.*, vol. 62, 1899, p. 663. From 1900 completed by figures given to me by Professor Bowley.

The general level of consumption fluctuated year by year from 1860 as follows (Table 6). The general average in 1913 was 24 p.c. higher than the level of 1870–9.

TABLE 6

Consumption Index Numbers in United Kingdom.[1]

Commodities included: Wheat and flour, cocoa, coffee, cotton, currants and raisins, meat, rice, sugar, tea, tobacco, wool, wine, spirits, malt and beer. Weighted system, No. 4.

Year.	Index No.	Year.	Index No.
1860	84	1888	104½
1862	78	1889	110
1864	87	**1890**	112
1865	84	1891	117
1866	89	1892	115
1867	85	1893	108
1868	90	1894	113
1869	92	1895	116
1870	94	1896	117
1871	96	1897	114
1872	97	1898	122
1873	101½	1899	119
1874	101	**1900**	118
1875	103	1901	121
1876	102	1902	117
1877	102	1903	116
1878	104	1904	117
1879	101½	1905	118
1880	102	1906	119
1881	101	1907	122
1882	104	1908	117
1883	106	1909	119
1884	104	**1910**	119
1885	103½	1911	123
1886	103	1912	126
1887	104	1913	124

General Conclusions.

The average level of consumption of commodities in the United Kingdom rose in fifty years, from 1860–4 to 1905–9, 66 p.c.; it rose from 1870–9 to 1910–13, 38 p.c. (unweighted average), or in the year 1913, 24 p.c. (weighted, according to System 4).

[1] Mr. G. H. Wood. *Statistical Journal*, 1899. Brought up to the date 1913.

The relative proportions of the growth of commodities were as in the table shown.

Table showing the Growth of Consumption of Groups of Commodities.[1]

Average percentage increase over the level of 1870–9 in the periods 1905–9 and 1910–13.

Groups of Commodities.	1905–9.	1910–13.
Currants and raisins	9	8
Wheat and meat	14·5	12
Rice	—16	24
Wool and cotton	9	24
Sugar	48	50
Semi-luxuries (tea, coffee, cocoa, wine, beer, spirits, tobacco)	38	56

The growth of semi-luxuries is unduly raised by the phenomenal growth of cocoa consumption, and the relative growth of primary to secondary goods cannot be estimated on the basis of this figure. The proportion is probably not greater than 2 to 1; but still it should be noted that the average consumption of wheat and meat decreased from the period of 1905–9 to the period of 1910–13, due entirely to decrease in meat consumption, while wheat consumption was stationary. Currants and raisins have in some respects the level of consumption of necessaries, for their growth is below the level of the growth of wheat and meat consumption.

I cannot agree with the statement of K. Apelt,[2] that " Bei einer allgemeinen Zunahme des Volkswohlstandes werden daher in erster Linie die besseren Nahrungsmittel und Luxusartikel in Verbrauch steigen. Die unbedingt notwendiger Verbrauchsgegenstande werden dagegen nur bis einem gewissen Punkten diese Steigerung mit erfahren. War dieses Sättigungspunkt zuvor bereits überschritten, so wird sich bei ihnen eine Abnahme bemerken machen." There is no point

[1] Table published by kind permission of Professor Bowley.

[2] K. Apelt, *Die Konsumption*, p. 84.

of satiety to be found in the growth of consumption of the absolute necessaries; on the contrary the decline of consumption is to be found in semi-luxuries as coffee, and rice, which is not a staple food article, wine, spirits, and beer.

The point of satiety in consumption of necessaries is not likely to be reached, and the general optimum is not reached either; the rise in consumption is proportionately smaller, not because the wants are not there, but because they cannot be satisfied on account of difficulties in production.

Mr. Wood [1] tells us the same in connexion with the decline of consumption, that usually the semi-luxuries, as tea, currants, raisins, tobacco, beer, spirits, with clothing, suffer first, but when meat cannot be bought, bread must. 1877–80, for instance, cocoa, cotton, currants, raisins, tobacco, wool, spirits, and beer declined, while tea increased by only 1 p.c.

1888–91, which period may be termed the nearest approach to an inflated period for nearly twenty years (to 1899), cotton, currants, raisins, meat, sugar, tea, tobacco, spirits, beer, and even wine increased at a rapid rate, clearly showing that when the power to procure these commodities is increased, the desire to consume more exists, or in other words, the demand schedule of the working classes has not yet reached its final limit.

Ballod [2] expresses himself in similar manner: "Der Bedarf ist bisher fast bei allen Gütern höher als der Konsum. Die Produktion richtet sich weder nach dem Bedarf, noch nach dem tätsachlichen Konsum, sondern nach dem Preise, und ist bald höher, bald niedriger als der Konsum."

France.

The growth of consumption can be measured not only by calculating index numbers of consumption,

[1] H. G. Wood, *Journ. R. Stat. Soc.*, 1899, p. 661.
[2] *Statistik in Deutschland*, vol. 2, 1911, p. 606.

but also by relating the absolute quantities without any reference to consumption per head of population. Levasseur formed a table of this kind (Table 7), putting the average population and the average total consumed quantities of the years 1820–2 as = 100, and relating the subsequent quantities to this fixed point. Although a table of this kind is not representative for the consumption per head, it indicates clearly the parallel growth of population and consumed goods, and, taking the ratio of the totals of consumed quantities by population, we get a number indicating consumption per head. Levasseur's table (Table 7) reaches the period 1885–7, and the subsequent years are shown in the general table of consumption per head from 1830–1913 (see Appendix, Tables V and VI), or more clearly in Table 9, of Index Numbers of consumption, calculated similarly to that of Mr. Wood for the United Kingdom.

TABLE 7.

The Growth of Consumption in France from 1820–87.[1]

The Average of Total Consumed Quantities in 1820–2 = 100.

Period.	Population.	Potatoes.	Wheat.	Beef.[2]	Veal.	Mutton.	Sugar.	Coffee.	Tea.	Wine
1820–2	100	100	100	100	100	100	100	100	100	—
1825–7	100	100	115	162	125	79	126	106	147	100
1830–2	109	137	124	100	125	80	171	117	141	100
1835–7	112	189	129	28	87	92	240	137	153	151
1840–2	114	250	142	113	150	71	154	173	164	169
1845–7	118	250	150	52	162	55	300	185	179	143
1850–2	119	167	157	52	137	37	285	230	192	195
1855–7	121	222	167	457	325	223	392	320	275	98
1860–2	125	239	169	357	412	359	585	451	412	185
1865–7	127	255	155	386	287	567	614	559	447	297
1870–2	120	276	167	552	450	872	566	543	391	274
1875–7	123	291	175	348	337	1,050	626	612	442	382
1880–2	126	307	213	314	500	1,462	861	735	567	257
1885–7	127	274	197	161	344	1,113	1,028	662	677	251

[1] E. Levasseur, *La Population Française*, vol. 3. Paris, 1892, pp. 32–40.

[2] Beef, veal, mutton, pork, sugar, coffee, cocoa, tea, according to the imports.

Looking at the figures of Levasseur, some of them seem enormously increased in comparison with the figures of the United Kingdom; so the consumption of wheat is 97 p.c. higher in 1885–7 than the average of 1820–2; that of potatoes, 174 p.c.; beef, 61 p.c.; veal, 244 p.c.; mutton, 1,013 p.c.; coffee, 562 p.c.; tea, 577 p.c.; and wine 151 p.c. higher. But we have to consider that the figures do not represent the consumption per head, but the growth of total consumption, mostly of imports. Taking the ratio of population and the respective commodities, we get an increase of 55 p.c. for wheat, which is not so far from the figure representing the increase in the United Kingdom, particularly if we take into account that the years 1820–2 were not economically prosperous, and that the poverty which was the effect of the Napoleonic wars still showed its influence. The ratio for meat shows an increase of 100 p.c.; for sugar, 709 p.c.; for coffee, 421 p.c.; for tea, 433 p.c.; and for wine about 100 p.c.

It should be noted that the beef, veal, mutton, and pork consumption was calculated according to the imports, and these figures are not very significant, as the home produce formed the greatest part of the supply. But cocoa, coffee, and tea, although only imported, represent the total consumed quantities, and their growth is fully significant.

Table 8 shows the quantities of meat produced by slaughter.

TABLE 8.[1]

Production of Meat in France (in millions of Kgs.).

Years.	Cattle.	Sheep.	Swine.	Total.
1812	197	66	241	504
1840	310	82	290	682
1862	480	115	377	972
1882	685	168	387	1,240

The table proves that the supply of meat by slaugh-

[1] Levasseur, vol. 3, p. 39.

ter, and therefore the consumption, doubled from 1812 to 1882. Putting the amount of 1840 as 100, we get the result shown in the following table.

Growth of Meat Supply from 1840. The Year 1840 = 100.

1840	100	100	100	100
1862	155	142	130	143
1882	221	205	133	182

The total supply of 1882 is 82 p.c. above the amount of 1840. Levasseur [1] concludes with the following remark about the general growth of consumption: "Pain, viande, denrée accessoire, boisson, tous ou presque tous les aliments ont augmenté dans une progression beaucoup plus rapide que la population. Nous n'osérions pas fixer d'une manière précise les termes du rapport, mais nous croyons ne pas exagérer en disant qu'ils ont au moins double pendant que le nombre des consommateurs s'accroissait á peine d'un tiers ou d'un quart, et que par conséquent, les Français consomment environ une fois et demie autant d'aliments, qu'en consommaient leurs grandspères sous la Restauration."

Looking at the figures of consumption *per capita* in France from 1830 (for wheat 1827) to 1913,[2] we may state that the consumption of wheat increased in eighty-six years, from 1827–1913, 90 p.c.; potatoes in eighty-three years increased 229 p.c.; the consumption of sugar is 630 p.c. higher in 1913 than in 1827; the consumption of wine, spirits, and beer is 186, 250, and 252 p.c. respectively higher in 1913 than in 1830; the consumption of sugar, coffee, and cocoa was 900, 1,050 and 3,400 per cent. higher in 1913 than in 1831.

Speaking generally, the people of France consumed nearly double as much wheat in 1913 as in 1827, and more than three times as much of potatoes; seven times more of sugar; a little less than three times of wine, three and a half times more of spirits and beer,

[1] Levasseur, vol. 3, pp. 50, 51. [2] See Appendix, Tables V and VI.

eleven and a half times more of coffee, and thirty-five times more of cocoa in 1913 than in 1830 or 1831, and ten times more of tea.

France's consumption *per capita* is supplemented in Table 9 by index numbers of consumption. The average consumption per head in 1870–9 was taken as base, as in Mr. Wood's index numbers of consumption for the United Kingdom.

TABLE 9.[1]

Index Numbers of Consumption in France, based on the *per capita* consumed quantities.

Average Consumption 1870–9 = 100.

Commodity.	1870–9.	1880–9.	1890–9.	1900–9.	1910–13.
Wheat-flour	100	103	105	101	103
Potatoes	100	106	128	128	120
Sugar	100	160	166	204	249
Wine	100	72	82	112	114
Spirits	100	137	155	129	137
Beer	100	110	120	137	160
Tea	100	150	217	315	366
Coffee	100	135	148	188	222
Cocoa	100	140	173	231	290
Tobacco	100	114	146	154	160
Cotton	100	127	140	237	273
Wool	100	156	239	245	260
Average of index numbers	100	126	152	173	204

From the period of 1870–9 to the period of 1910–13, the wheat consumption increased by 3 p.c.; potatoes increased by 20 p.c.; sugar by 149 p.c.; wine by 14 p.c.; spirits by 37 p.c.; beer by 60 p.c.; tea by 266 p.c., on account of the small initial amount; coffee by 122 p.c.; cocoa by 290 p.c.; tobacco by 60 p.c.; cotton by 173 p.c., and wool by 160 p.c. The considerable increase in tea and cocoa consumption is

[1] Calculated from *Stat. Annuaire* (see Appendix, Tables V and VI).

due to the small initial consumed amounts, and as in the case of cocoa in the United Kingdom, tea and cocoa raise the average of twelve commodities. But coffee, although consumed in larger quantities and being the substitute of tea, in the case of the United Kingdom, more than doubled ; similarly the sugar consumption. The cotton and wool consumption increased very conspicuously, probably the high percentage is due again to the small initial consumed amount. The tobacco and beer consumption show just the same percentage of increase. Forming groups of commodities as necessaries, semi-luxuries, and clothing, the average increase is as follows :

Table showing the Average Increase of Groups of Commodities.

	1870–9.	1910–13.	Average rise p.c.
Necessaries (wheat, potatoes) . .	100	111·5 [1]	11·5
Semi-luxuries (wine, spirits, tobacco)	100	142·7	42·7
Semi-luxuries (tea, coffee, cocoa) .	100	192·6	92·6
Clothing (cotton, wool)	100	166·5	66·5

The general average of consumption was 104 p.c. higher in the period 1910–13 than in the period 1870–9. The decennial rise of consumption was 26 p.c. in 1880–9, 52 p.c. in 1890–9, and 73 p.c. in 1900–9. Comparing France's growth of consumption with that of the United Kingdom, we notice that the increase in wheat consumption was 6 p.c. lower in France than in the United Kingdom, but the sugar consumption increased by 100 p.c. more in France than in the United Kingdom. The average consumption of the group of commodities, tea, coffee and cocoa, was 92 p.c. higher in France than in the United Kingdom, and that of beer, wine and spirits, 168 p.c. higher than in the United Kingdom.

1 Assuming a 40 per cent. rise for meat consumption during the same time, this group would show 121 per cent. increase.

Germany.

The growth of consumption of commodities in Germany is satisfactorily measurable only with regard to imported commodities, as raw cotton, coffee, tea, cocoa, groceries, rice, tropical fruits, and jute; or dutiable goods, as sugar, salt, beer, and spirits. The statistics of the consumption of wheat and meat are rather incomplete.

If we suppose that the consumption of wheat in "mahlsteuerpflichtigen" towns was the same as in the whole country, we get the following numbers (Table 10) from 1831 onwards.

TABLE 10.[1]

Consumption of Wheat and Rye in Germany from 1831–1913, per head of Population.

Years.	Wheat.	Rye.	Total.
	Kg.	Kg.	Kg.
1831	112·6	30·6	143·2
1838–40	110·1	35·7	145·8
1844–6	112·0	45·5	157·5
1850–2	114·6	45·1	159·7
1856–8	120·7	52·5	173·2
1864–6	111·9	51·9	163·8
1870–2	105·2	48·4	153·6
1879–84	121·0	51·6	172·6
1884–9	115·9	56·6	172·5
1889–94	112·6	63·4	176·0
1893–1913	147·4	90·6	238·0

Considering the consumption of the towns of Prussia as representative for the whole of Germany, the consumption of the aggregate wheat and rye amount rose 66 p.c. in eighty-two years. The average consumption of the years 1864–6 and 1870–2, the periods of the Prusso-Danish, Austro-Prussian and Franco-Prussian

[1] The years 1831–72 are taken from K. Apelt, *Die Konsumption*, p. 22, and they represent the consumption in "mahlsteuerpflichtigen" towns of Prussia; the other numbers represent the consumption for the whole of Germany: *Stat. Jahrbücher*, diff. years.

Wars, is lower compared with the previous years 1856–8.

For meat consumption we have no direct statistics for the whole of Germany. But the following table, illustrating the growth of meat consumption in Saxony [1] (Table 11), may be taken as indicating the trend and the proportion of its growth for the whole of Germany.

TABLE 11.

Index Numbers of Meat Consumption in Saxony.

Average Consumption in 1835–44 = 100.

Period or Year.	Beef.	Pork.
1835–44	100	100
1845–54	102·8	109·3
1855–64	122·2	140·7
1865–74	140·3	173·0
1875–84	161·1	211·6
1885–94	187·5	245·3
1895	190·3	277·3
1896	200·0	310·5
1897	215·5	301·2

It is obvious that the growth is very considerable; in about sixty years the beef consumption more than doubled, and that of pork trebled. The more recent growth of meat consumption in Germany was estimated by Huckert [2] as being 43 p.c. higher in 1892 than in the year 1872; that is a growth of 43 p.c. in twenty years. All meat, imported and slaughtered, is included. Assuming the same rate of growth, we might conclude that the meat consumption in the period 1910–13 was about 40 p.c. higher than in 1870–9; this figure seems to be too high compared with the index numbers of meat consumption in the United Kingdom.

[1] *Stat. Jahrbücher für Sachsen*, 1898. K. Apelt, *Die Konsumption*, p. 49.

[2] "Zur Geschichte und Statistik des Fleischkonsums in Deutschland." *Zeitschrift für Socialwissenschaft*, III. Jrg.

The consumption of some imported articles whose statistics have been more exactly noted [1] than those of home-grown commodities seems to have increased from the level consumed in the period 1836–40 to a considerable amount in the quinquennium 1906–10. So the consumption of raw cotton was 19·5 times greater in the period 1906–10 than in the period 1836–40; this is due probably partly to the fact that ready-made clothing was imported from the United Kingdom in the middle of the nineteenth century, and therefore the imports of raw cotton and its use throughout Germany were very low. The consumption of coffee was trebled, and that of currants more than three (3·6) times as great in 1906–10 as in 1836–40. Cocoa, as in the United Kingdom, grew considerably: its consumption reached in 1906–10, 57 times the initial amount in 1836–40; similarly the tropical fruits rose to 53 times, rice to 14 times, tea to 15 times, and jute to 18·5 times the initial amount.

The aggregate average increase of tea, coffee, cocoa, amounted to 41·6 p.c., a figure not very far from the 34 p.c. increase in the United Kingdom, in which case it relates only to sixty years, whereas for Germany it relates to seventy-five years. The growth of tropical fruits is to be explained by the economic prosperity of the wealthier classes.

Making index numbers of consumption with a similar base as for France and the United Kingdom, the growth of consumption is apparent for every article except tobacco (see Table 12).

So wheat consumption rose 35 p.c., rye consumption, 22 p.c., while the consumption of wheat in the United Kingdom during forty-three years increased only 11 p.c., in France 3 p.c. Cotton consumption increased 152 p.c., while in the United Kingdom it increased only 15 p.c., and in France 127 p.c.; the relative growth of French and German cotton consumption as compared with the British is probably due to

[1] Appendix, Table VIII.

France's and Germany's relatively low initial average amount consumed during the 'seventies, when the United Kingdom's consumption was approaching the optimum point.

Initial Cotton Consumption per head during the years 1870–1879.[1]

Period.	U.K. lb.	France. lb.	Germany. lb.	U.S.A. lb.
1870–9	36·9	5·1	5·9	14·4

TABLE 12.

Index Numbers of Consumption of Commodities in Germany.[2]

Average Consumption of 1871–80 = 100.

Article.	1871–80.	1881–90.	1891–1900.	1901–10.	1911–13.
Wheat	—	100 [3]	122	130	135 [4]
Rye	—	100	113	124	122
Rice	100	111	152	153	181
Coffee	100	105	111	130	112
Cocoa	100	160	440	950	1,540
Tea	100	140	200	220	240
Groceries [5]	100	118	140	154	145
Tropical fruits	100	139	262	444	679
Sugar	100	130	187	254	276
Beer	100 [6]	110	122	123	117
Spirits	100	110 [7]	129	137	118
Tobacco	100	83	89	90	91 [4]
Cotton, raw	100	132	184	224	252
Wool	100 [8]	145	189	165	—
Average index number	100	124 [9]	174	236	300
A.I.N. without cocoa and tropical fruits	100	118	145	151	163

[1] *Stat. Tables and Charts*, Cd. 4954, 1909.
[2] See Appendix, Table VII, the absolute quantities.
[3] Average consumption of 1880–9 = 100.
[4] Only two years, 1911 and 1912.
[5] Corresponding partly to currants and raisins in the U.K.
[6] Average consumption of 1872–80 = 100.
[7] Only the years 1880–1, 1887–8, 1888–9, 1889–90 considered; human and technical consumption.
[8] Base 1870–9 and consequently the subsequent periods.
[9] Only twelve commodities without wheat and rye.

The rice consumption increased 81 p.c. in Germany, while in the United Kingdom it increased only 24 p.c.; sugar rose 176 p.c., while in the U.K. it rose 50 p.c., and in France 149 p.c.; tea rose 140 p.c., in the U.K. 51 p.c., and in France 266 p.c. The high average rise in the consumption of tea in France is due to the relatively small initial consumed amount (·030 kg. in 1913). The same remark is valid for Germany too (·06 kg. in 1911–13). Coffee consumption in Germany during forty-two years increased 12 p.c., in France, 122 p.c., and in the U.K. it decreased 37 p.c.; cocoa consumption increased to the "colossal" percentage of 1,440 in Germany, while in France it attained only 190 p.c., and in the U.K. 431 p.c. Taking the average consumption of the three articles, tea, coffee, and cocoa, we get the result that their consumption, from the period 1871–80 to the period 1910–13, in Germany increased 530 p.c., in France 192·6 p.c., and in the U.K. 148 p.c.

The aggregate average consumption of beer and spirits in Germany increased 17·5 p.c., in France 37 p.c. (wine included), and in the U.K. the aggregate consumption of the three articles decreased just 33·3 p.c.

The wool consumption of the corresponding periods in Germany increased 65 p.c., while in France it increased 39 p.c., and in the U.K. 4 p.c. (1900–9), but 31 p.c. taking the period of 1910–13 into account. The consumption of currants and raisins increased 8 p.c. in the U.K., while groceries and tropical fruits in Germany increased 308 p.c.; the explanation is again that the Germans were poorly off in the above articles during the 'seventies and earlier. The tobacco consumption for Germany decreased 9 p.c. from the period 1871–80 to the period 1911–13.

Grouping the commodities and calculating the average rise in consumption, we get the following percentages indicating the progress in consumption.

Groups of Commodities consumed in Germany in 1911–13, as Percentages of the *per capita* Consumed Average Amount of the Years 1871–9.

Groups.	Average Rise.
Necessaries (wheat, rye, rice, groceries, meat) [1]	45 p.c.
Sugar	176 p.c.
Semi-luxuries (tea, coffee, cocoa, tropical fruits, beer, spirits, tobacco)	331 p.c.
Cotton and wool (1901–10)	94·5 p.c.

The table indicates clearly that the average rise of the groups was considerable, and compared with those in France, the relative growth of consumption in Germany seems to be twice as great as in France.

United States of America.

The statistics of the U.S.A. are incomplete concerning the consumption of meat.

From the Appendix, Tables X and XI, we see the growth of consumption of sugar from 1865, of coffee, tea, spirits, wines, and malt liquors from 1830 and 1840 respectively, and that of wheat from 1871.

Expressing the growth of consumption of commodities in 1914 as the increase p.c. of the initial amount of consumption in 1830, 1840, or 1865, the sugar consumption increased from 1865 to 1914, 395 p.c.; the consumption of coffee, tea, spirits, wine, and malt liquors increased from 1830 and 1840 respectively: coffee, 268 p.c.; tea, 102 p.c.; wine, 58 p.c.; beer, 1,193 p.c.; it decreased only for spirits, 46 p.c.

Examining the growth of consumption (Table 13) in the U.S.A. during forty-five years, it does not seem so conspicuous as one might perhaps expect it to be. The wheat consumption rose 23 p.c. during forty years (1871–1910), and only 15 p.c. from 1911–16, while the wheat consumption in Germany rose 24 p.c. during thirty years (1880–1910), in the U.K., 11 p.c., and in France, 3 p.c. during forty years. It is higher than in France and the United Kingdom, but it is lower than in Germany.

[1] Assumed a 40 p.c. rise.

The coffee consumption increased 36 p.c., but the tea consumption decreased by 26 p.c.; or the aggregate increase is only 5 p.c., while the aggregate average increase of tea and coffee is 76 p.c. in Germany and 194 in France; it decreased by 3 p.c. in the U.K.

The growth of tea and coffee consumption in the U.S.A. is behind that of France and Germany, but above that of the United Kingdom.

The sugar consumption increased 114 p.c.; it comes again behind the German (176) and French (149) consumption, but before that of the U.K. (50 p.c.).

The wool consumption during about forty years (1871–1908) increased 6 p.c., and 5 p.c. from 1911–16; the corresponding figure in the U.K. is 4 p.c., in France, 39 p.c., and in Germany, 65 p.c. The cotton consumption increased 100 p.c. for the period 1911-16.

TABLE 13.

Consumption Index Numbers of Commodities in the U.S.A.[1]

The Average Consumption per head of the Years 1871–80 = 100.

Article.	1871–80.	1881–90.	1891–1900.	1901–10.	1911–16.
Wheat	100	104	90	123	115
Indian corn	100	109	97	112	94
Coffee	100	118	130	151 [4]	136
Cotton	100 [2]	127	148	182 [4]	200
Rice [5]	100	151	137	370	479
Sugar	100	124	161	190	214 [3]
Tea	100	101	95	83	74
Wool	100	121	117	106 [5]	105
Wine	100	102	87	118	111
Spirits	100	96	99	102	100
Beer	100	179	221	269	283
Average of index numbers	100	112	117	163	174

[1] See Appendix, Table IX, for actual quantities.

[2] The periods are 1870–9, 1880–9, etc.

[3] Only 1911–14 (four years). [4] Only 1900–8 from Cd. 4954.

[5] Index number calculated according to the production statistics; therefore too high. Exports not taken into account.

The consumption of wine rose 11 p.c.; the consumption of spirits remained stationary, while that of beer rose 183 p.c.; or the aggregate average increase is 64·5 p.c.

The corresponding consumption increased in France 37 p.c.; in Germany 175 p.c., while the decrease of consumption in the U.K. of the articles of this group (wine, spirits, beer) amounted to 33·3 p.c.

To get a correct statement about the consumption of corn, it is necessary to supplement the index numbers of wheat consumption by the index numbers of consumption of Indian corn; the aggregate consumption of both during forty years (1871–80 to 1901–10) increased 175 p.c., and only 4 p.c. from 1911–16.

The cotton consumption rose 82 p.c., nearly half of the German figure, 152 p.c.; about two-thirds of the French, 127 p.c., and it is five and a half times as great as the British percentage of growth of consumption.

The rice consumption is very considerable in the table, for the index numbers were calculated on the basis of production statistics, which does not seem a correct method; the increase for the period 1911–16 was 379 p.c.; exports were not considered.

No index numbers of the consumption of meat are to be found in the table.

According to groups, the average rise for the period 1911–16 was for necessaries (wheat, rye, rice) 126 p.c. (too high on account of rice index numbers of consumption); for semi-luxuries (tea, coffee, wine, spirits, beer), 51 p.c.; for sugar, 114 p.c., and for cotton and wool consumption, 52·5 p.c.

The average level of consumption for the decades was: 100 for 1871–80; 112 for 1881–90; 117 for 1891–1900; 163 for 1901–10, and 174 for 1911–16.

Italy.

The statistics of consumption of commodities do not stretch into the period of 1870–9, so I used as base for consumption index numbers (Table 14) the average consumption per head of the years 1881–90, and calculated them for only nine commodities. The consumption of wheat in the period 1911–13 is 39 p.c. higher than in 1881–90; of maize, 11 p.c.; of wine, 49 p.c.; of beer, 184 p.c.; of sugar, 65 p.c.; and of coffee, 51 p.c.; that of tobacco decreased 4 p.c., and of spirits 25 p.c., but this decrease is compensated by the large increase of beer consumption. The average rise of consumption for groups of commodities in the latest period, 1911–13 was:

For necessaries (wheat, maize) . . . . 25 p.c.
For sugar . . . . 65 p.c.
For semi-luxuries (alcoholic beverages, coffee, tobacco, etc.) . . . . 70 p.c.

Professor Mortara's[1] index numbers were made on another base, that is by dividing the returns for any year by the means of the returns for the years 1901–5, inclusive, and multiplying by 100. By chance, the index number of coffee consumption is not very far from the index number given in Table 14; Pro-

TABLE 14.

Consumption Index Numbers of Commodities in Italy.[2]
Average Consumption per head in the Years 1881–90 = 100.

Article.	1881–1890.	1891–1900.	1901–1910.	1911–1913.
Wheat	100	97	125	139
Maize	100	87	104	111
Wine	100	107	140	149
Spirits	100	69	68	75
Beer	100	75	161	284
Sugar	100	84	122	165
Coffee	100	82	118	151
Tobacco	100	87	91	96
Average of index numbers.	100	86	116	146

[1] "Sintomi Statistici delle condizioni economiche d'Italia." *Giorn. degli Economiste e Rivista di Statistici*, 1914.

[2] See Appendix, Table XIII, for actual quantities.

fessor Mortara's are 144 for 1911 and 151 for 1912, while mine is 96 for 1911–13.

The statistics of consumption in Eastern Europe, including Austria-Hungary, the Balkans, and Russia, are neither complete nor trustworthy concerning the growth, nor available for many commodities. But one has to remember that they fluctuate more violently, and have not the stability of Western Europe. The people in Eastern Europe consume more if the commodity is in stock, more after a good harvest and less after a bad one, and, generally speaking, the quantities consumed of cereals are greater than in Western Europe.

The following table shows this difference in the consumed quantities of wheat and rye in Eastern and Western Europe [1] for recent periods, per head of population per annum.

Period.	Western Europe.		Eastern Europe.		Europe.	
	Wheat.	Rye.	Wheat.	Rye.	Wheat.	Rye.
	Kg.	Kg.	Kg.	Kg.	Kg.	Kg.
1891–5 . .	83	54	99	113	89	77
1896–1900 . .	86	53	92	117	88	80
1901–5 . .	87	57	116	118	99	82

It seems that wheat consumption rose considerably in the last decade, a sign of the rising standard of living, and that correspondingly rye consumption remained stationary.

The average wheat consumption per head in Austria-Hungary increased from 1871–80 to 1901–10 by 53 p.c.

The following table shows the growth of wheat consumption per head of population.

Index Numbers of Wheat Consumption in Austria-Hungary.

1871–9.	1881–90.	1891–1900.	1901–10.	1911–13.
100 (70 Kg.) .	158 .	. 146 .	. 153 .	. 168

[1] *Das Getreide im Weltverkehr.* III. Folge. 1909, Vienna.

That is the highest relative increase among all the countries examined. The other commodities [1] do not seem to have risen much; tea is consumed in insignificant quantities; the coffee consumption [1] remained stationary until 1891–5, and the same is the case for groceries; the rye consumption declined from the initial amount by about 20 p.c. in the period of 1911–13.

Comparative Growth of Consumption.

Comparative growth of the consumption in different countries may be taken as indicated by the level of average of index numbers of consumption in some periods, if the base is equal and if the number of commodities does not differ much. The table given below gives an approximate indication of the growth of consumption in five countries: United Kingdom, Germany, France, United States, and Italy.

TABLE 15.

The Comparative Growth of Consumption indicated by the level of the general average of the index numbers of consumption in decennial periods.

The average per head consumption in the period 1870–9 (or 1871–1879 Germany and U.S.A., and for Italy 1881–90) taken as base = 100.

Country.	1870–9.	1880–9.	1890–9.	1900–9.	1910–13.
United Kingdom [2]	100	104	115	124	138
France [3] . . .	100	126	152	173	204
Germany [4] . .	100	124	174	236	300
U.S.A. [5] . . .	100	112	117	163	174 [7]
Italy [6]	—	100	86	116	147

The greatest rise of the level of consumption is in Germany, France and the United States, then Italy

[1] *K. Apelt*, p. 33, pp. 110–113.
[2] Average of 14 commodities.
[3] Average of 12 commodities.
[4] Average of 14 commodities.
[5] Average of 11 commodities.
[6] Average of 8 commodities.
[7] 1911–16.

and the United Kingdom. Yet the number of commodities differ and the base differs, as in the case of Italy and the United Kingdom.

It is therefore necessary, in order to reach a sound judgment on the relative growth of consumption, that commodities should be equal in number and significant for the consumption of the country.

Table 16 gives some idea of the progress of consumption in five countries, in the period just preceding the war, that is 1910–13 or 1911–16 for the United States; the number of commodities is nine for four countries and eight for Italy, and they are so chosen as to represent the consumption of the country significantly. So coffee has been dropped for the United Kingdom, tea for France and Germany, and wine for Germany, as these articles are consumed in insignificant quantities.

The level of general consumption was in the United Kingdom 20 p.c. higher in the pre-war period than in the basal period; in France, 86 p.c.; in Germany, 61 p.c.; in the U.S.A., 49 p.c.; and in Italy, 47 p.c.

We see that Germany loses her rank in progress if the commodities are so chosen as to represent the comparative average progress. At the same time the United Kingdom's progress was the least pronounced, partly on account of diminished consumption of alcoholic beverages and coffee; but the chief reason why her average of index numbers is lowest among the countries is that the consumed initial amounts in the period 1870–9 were already considerable, and greater if compared with the initial consumed amounts of commodities in the other four countries, and therefore the progress could not be at the same rate as in the other countries. Or we could say also that the consumed amounts are nearer to the optimum point of consumption, and it is therefore that the progress was not so pronounced.

While making index numbers of consumption, we fix an average of a period as 100, and express the subsequent periods as percentages of the fixed period, but they indicate only the rate of increase or growth, and comparing the index numbers of different countries, we state only the difference in the rate of increase or in the velocity of growth with regard to the fixed period, but the actual figures may be different in different countries, and therefore the rate of increase differs too.

TABLE 16.

Comparative Index Numbers of Consumption of Commodities in the U.K., France, Germany, U.S.A., and Italy, in the Pre-war Period 1911–13 (1911–16 in U.S.A.).

The average consumption per head in the period 1871–9 (or 1871–80 and 1881–9 Italy) taken as base = 100.

Commodity.	U. Kingdom.	France.	Germany.	U.S.A.	Italy.
Wheat	111	103	135	115	139
Sugar	150	249	276	214	165
Rice	124	—	181	—	111 (maize)
Coffee	—	222	112	136	—
Tea	151	—	—	74	151
Wine	—	114	—	111	149
Spirits	57	137	118	100	75
Beer	97	160	117	283	284
Tobacco . . .	142	160	91	—	96
Cotton	115	273	252	200	—
Wool	131	260	165 [1]	105	—
General average .	120	186	161	149	147

The index numbers do not give any idea of the actual amount of commodities, if compared with the amounts of the other countries. So the index numbers of consumption may perhaps be very small indeed, for a country like the United Kingdom, and yet the amount consumed may be greater in the United Kingdom than in Germany. For instance: the index number of wheat consumption is smallest for France (3 p.c.), although the actual amount per head of popu-

[1] 1900–8.

lation is the greatest in France; the increase of wheat consumption from 1870–80 to 1901–10 amounted to 33 p.c. in Germany, 23 p.c. in U.S.A., and only 11 p.c. in the United Kingdom, and yet the actual amount is nearly in inverse proportion, greatest in U.S.A., then in the United Kingdom, then in Germany. Table 17 gives the actual amounts of wheat, consumed per head of population in each of the under-mentioned countries.

TABLE 17.[1]

Period.	U. Kingdom.	France.	U.S.A.	Germany.
	Lb.	Lb.	Lb.	Lb.
1880–4 . . .	364	548	382	134
1885–9 . . .	356	516	340	134
1890–4 . . .	367	534	295	159
1895–9 . . .	358	535	302	179
1900–4 . . .	358	499	363	199
1905–8 . . .	361	511	401	201

The amounts of wheat consumed in the United Kingdom may be put as 100, and the amounts of other countries expressed as percentages of the consumption in the United Kingdom, as was done by the Board of Trade.[1]

TABLE 18.

Showing the Wheat Consumption per head of Population in France, Germany, and U.S.A. as Percentages of Consumed Amount in U.K.

Period.	U. Kingdom.	France.	Germany.	U.S.A.
1880–4 . . .	100	151	37	105
1885–9 . . .	100	145	38	96
1890–4 . . .	100	146	43	80
1895–9 . . .	100	149	50	84
1900–4 . . .	100	139	56	101
1905–8 . . .	100	142	56	112

[1] Stat. Tables and Charts, Cd. 4954.

The following table represents another example :—

TABLE 19.[1]

Showing the Consumption per head of Cotton and Wool.

The Average Consumption of U.K. = 100.

Period.	U.K.	France.		Germany.		United States.	
	Cotton or Wool.	Cotton.	Wool.	Cotton.	Wool.	Cotton.	Wool.
1870–9 . .	100	14·5	94·0	15·5	36·5	39·5	53·0
1880–9 . .	100	15·5	114·5	19·9	54·0	45·0	65·5
1890–9 . .	100	21·5	114·0	27·0	58·5	52·0	52·5
1900–8 . .	100	28·0	123·0	34·5	56·0	65·5	52·5

The drawback of such a representation of consumption is the fact that the consumption of the fixed country is not at all stationary, but changes as the index numbers of consumption indicate. A combination of both methods would give the most satisfactory representation of progress in consumption, as it would indicate not only the relative growth from a fixed period and for a fixed country, but it would give a true picture of the comparative progress.

Looking at Table 19, the reason is clear why the index numbers of consumption could increase in France 127 p.c. and in Germany 124 p.c., while in the United Kingdom it increased only 5 p.c. and in the United States 82 p.c. The consumption of cotton in the United Kingdom could not increase so rapidly as that of the United States, France, or Germany, because the actual quantities consumed were much greater than in France or Germany or the United States. The same may be applied to the consumption of wool. In Germany, where the smallest initial amount of wool was consumed, the consumption increased with the greatest rapidity, 65 p.c.; the consumption of France increased 39 p.c.; while in U.S.A. there

[1] Stat. Tables and Charts, Cd. 4954. 1908. Given by Board of Trade.

seemed to have been a shortage of wool, as the consumption increase is only 5 p.c., compared with 17 p.c. in the 'nineties and 21 p.c. in the 'eighties.

The consumption of wool in the United Kingdom could not increase as fast as the consumption in other countries; it showed 4 p.c. higher consumption in 1900–9 than in 1870–9, but the consumption was 13 p.c. higher in the previous period of 1890–9.

We may conclude in a general manner that the increase of index numbers of consumption depends on the initial amount, or the growth of index numbers of consumption is in inverse proportion to the initial consumed amount.

IX

CONSUMPTION AND WAR-EQUILIBRIUM THEORY

THE war equilibrium theory asserts that the tendencies of the growth of the rate of natural increase in a population, and of consumption before and after a war are of antagonistic nature. I demonstrated the pre-war declining and the post-war ascending phase of the rate of natural increase previously, as far as possible. In the last chapter, I showed the general tendency of the growth of consumption, visible in the differentiation and quantitative increase of consumption of commodities; beside this general tendency of growth of consumption, there is a short pre-war ascending phase of consumption, and thirdly, a phenomenon indicating a pressure of consumption, just before war. In this chapter we are concerned with the last two phenomena.

Although the consumption of most commodities is in an ascending phase before a war, there may be commodities the pre-war consumption of which is stable and stationary, because it is nearer to an optimum of satisfaction, or is compensated by consumption of other commodities. The declining phase of these commodities, as well as of those with a general tendency to increase, appears clearly after the war. The war period is perplexed; the consumption of commodities may begin immediately to decline, or be stationary, or even, in the case of some semi-luxuries, may increase. But the ultimate effect of war is a general decline of consumption, thereby restoring the economic equilibrium in stabler form, and balancing the pre-war ascending phase. The commodities the consumption of which increases during the war period, begin to decline a little later on ; but the effect is again a lowering of consumption.

Although the assumption of a general ascending phase of consumption is valid if we consider the tendencies of longer pre-war periods, and of short pre-war periods (some years), it is not valid if we compare the average consumption of some commodities in the short pre-war period with the average consumption of an equal period preceding it. In this case the consumption of the pre-war period is in numerical decline, and this phenomenon is termed "pressure on consumption" (see Fig. 4).

Not taking into account the pressure on consumption, the general characteristics of the war equilibrium of modern communities are: a pre-war declining phase of the natural growth of population, and a pre-war ascending period of consumption, and, through balancing of forces, a post-war ascending phase of natural growth and a post-war or war declining period of consumption.

There is no necessity to discuss the post-war declining period of consumption, as the fact alone, that there is loss of human material and scarcity of productive labour, at least from the standpoint of consumption, explains that production must diminish during the war, if it is long enough, and certainly after, and that therefore consumption *per capita* cannot reach the level of pre-war consumption. If the consumption during the war increases or remains stationary, it is possible only on account of accumulated stocks, and loans; as long as the stocks last, and borrowing is possible, consumption may keep on the same level as in the pre-war period, but with the exhaustion of the general stocks, it must diminish. The diminution of the stocks and the lack of labour available for production influence the prices, which go up, but not in the same proportion with the wages of the workmen.

The declining period is therefore clear, and it is not necessary to dwell more upon it.

But the reason for the ascending period of consumption does not seem so clear ; yet it was noticed by some writers who tried to observe the pre-war conditions in a general manner. So L. L. Price [1] says about the South African War : " It has coincided with a period of economic prosperity, when manufacturers and traders have been busy and employment has been steady and abundant. It is possible that the series of reverses which occurred in one eventful week of last December might have been faced in a different spirit and have led to other consequences, had they happened at a season of depression, when labourers were out of work, when factories and shops were standing idle, and when employers and merchants were disheartened by losing trade. Such at any rate was not the case. The demand for armaments and stores, however, has undoubtedly been reflected in the special activity of particular trades ; and, when the war is over, a certain slackness should follow, corresponding to the unusual briskness, so far as it is not counterbalanced by a permanent increase of military expenditure."

South African War, 1899–1902.

Before examining the table, we should remember that consumption of each article is dependent on its supply, and as food-stuffs are governed by natural factors over which people have no control, so the consumption must show variations which are to be attributed, not to the tendency of consumption, but to supply difficulties or to harvests. It is probable therefore that the irregularity of consumption of

[1] " Economic Consequences of the South African War." *Econ. Journ*, vol. 10, pp. 323–39, 1900.

potatoes and wheat, for example, is to be ascribed to this variation of crops. Besides this, there are competitive articles, which may replace their fellow articles, as for instance, tea, coffee, and cocoa.

Having regard to these remarks, we may state that all the articles as food-stuffs, drinks, retained for home consumption in the United Kingdom show a rise in quantities more or less continuous from 1893 to 1900 or 1901, as did bacon and hams, beef (salted and fresh), cocoa, coffee, pork, tea, tobacco, wine; some articles reached the maximum height earlier, as beer, currants and raisins, wheat-meal and flour, which reached the maximum in 1899 and began to decline after this year (Table 20). Some of them, as butter, rice, mutton, and eggs, show a continuous growth through the war; their consumption is probably compensatory, and they show this rise on account of this action. Consumption of butter rises to 1907, then begins to be slowly substituted by margarine. The decline of consumption in rice begins in 1903 with 12·18 lb., and 12·15 in 1904; 1905 begins to approach the former quantities. Consumption of mutton rises to 10·63 in 1903, declines to 9·17 in 1904, and rises to 9·92 in 1905. Consumption of eggs rises to the maximum of 55·86 in 1903, falls to 55·59 in 1904, 52·04 in 1905, 51·84 in 1906, and to 50·53 in 1907.

Besides this, we should remember the remark of Sir R. Giffen,[1] that although the South African War has caused a great disturbance of local industries, greater in proportion to the industry of localities which are the seat of war than any similar disturbance upon record, yet this war altogether has not caused any great disturbance because it has really been small in proportion to the resources of the British Empire. Yet although comparatively small, I was able to trace all the features of an approaching state of war

[1] Sir R. Giffen, "Some Economic Aspects of War." *Econ. Journ.*, vol. 10, p. 191.

TABLE 20.

Quantities of Articles retained for Home Consumption per head of Total Population in United Kingdom.

Article.		1893.	1894.	1895.	18 6.	1897.	1898.	1899.	1900.	1901.	1902.
Bacon and ham.	lb.	11·73	13·29	14·63	15·90	17·95	19·90	20·16	19·62	19·87 [1]	17·15 [1]
Beef, salted and fresh	lb.	5·68	6·59	6·72	8·11	8·83	9·05	10·85	11·74	12·14	9·83
Butter . . .	lb.	6·59	7·27	7·92	8·46	8·85	8·77	9·22	9·11	9·85	10·51
Cocoa, raw . .	lb.	·54	·58	·63	·63	·70	·80	·84	·92	1·02	1·09
Coffee . . .	lb.	·69	·69	·70	·69	·69	·69	·72	·71	·76	·68
Wheat . . .	lb.	188·82	201·48	233·20	197·95	175·89	180·54	182·02	187·02	187·14	216·11
Maize	lb.	95·67	101·80	97·02	145·19	149·18	156·43	171·17	146·81	137·62	118·73
Wheat meal and flour	lb.	58·83	54·71	51·89	59·35	51·95	57·44	62·08	57·90	59·99	51·66
Currants and raisins	lb.	5·02	4·90	4·97	4·95	4·80	4·84	4·83	3·72	4·09	4·78
Eggs	No.	34·39	36·68	38·97	40·25	42·23	43·04	47·78	49·48	49·26	54·17
Mutton, fresh .	lb.	5·74	6·62	7·46	8·20	8·97	9·22	9·51	9·28	9·12	9·77
Pork	lb.	1·03	1·12	1·40	1·50	1·58	2·22	2·55	2·54	2·13	1·74
Potatoes . . .	lb.	8·14	7·68	10·73	6·26	10·92	18·69	14·04	24·13	18·54	14·63
Rice	lb.	8·54	7·26	8·00	6·49	8·62	7·55	8·81	10·20	11·43	17·14
Sugar, refined .	lb.	33·17	39·89	40·09	41·53	43·91	45·29	48·68	52·23	—	—
Tea	lb.	5·41	5·52	5·67	5·77	5·81	5·86	5·98	6·11	6·16	6·07
Tobacco . . .	lb.	1·63	1·66	1·67	1·73	1·75	1·83	1·89	1·96	1·89	1·93
Wine	galls.	·37	·36	·37	·40	·40	·41	·41	·39	·37	·36
Beer	galls.	29·59	29·47	29·65	30·89	31·42	31·91	32·70	31·75	30·77	30·29

[1] Fresh and refrigerated.

in the decline of the rate of natural increase, as well as the rise in consumption, which harmonizes with the theory treated in this essay.

The period of recovery of equilibrium is different for different articles; it depends on the length of the war, or it is a function of time.

The consumption index numbers in Table 21 show that the years 1897 and 1898 are to be considered as a pre-war ascending period; so consumption of wheat rose from 100 to 110, of cocoa from 259 to 293, of cotton from 101 to 125, of meat from 118 to 120, of sugar from 139 to 147, of tea from 135 to 136, of tobacco from 117 to 123, of wool from 110 to 127, of wine from 75 to 79, and of beer from 113 to 114. The consumption of coffee (69 and 69) and of currants and raisins (109 and 109) is stationary, but that of rice (83 and 73) and of spirits (86 and 67) is lower in 1898 than in 1897. That may be due to compensatory increase of consumption of other commodities, as, for instance, meat, and beer or wine.

The average consumption of wheat in the years 1897–8 is five points lower than in 1895–6; that of coffee, 2·5 p.c. lower; of currants, 4 p.c.; of sugar, 11·5 p.c.; of wool, 8 p.c.; of spirits, 9 p.c.; we may therefore state that the pressure on consumption is visible on wheat, coffee, currants and raisins, sugar, wool, and spirits, or on six commodities out of fourteen.

Cocoa and tea show a continuous pre-war and war period of increase, but the tea consumption declines immediately after the war (1903) by 1 p.c.; partly tobacco consumption is of the same type, but the continuous increase was interrupted in 1897 and 1901.

The declining period of consumption during the war and after the war is evident from the following commodities: cotton, currants and raisins, meat (1898 and 1903), rice (1898 and 1903), sugar, wool, wine, beer, or from the general unweighted average, which is 122 in 1898 and 121 in 1903, or from the weighted average (System 5), 122 and 116 respectively.

TABLE 21.

Index Numbers of Consumption of Certain Commodities, according to G. H. Wood.[1]

Average of 1870–9, inclusive, = 100.

Article.	1893.	1894.	1895.	1896.	1897.	1898.	1899.	1900.	1901.	1902.	1903.
Wheat and wheat-flour	108	109	112	104	100	110	110	104	105	110	114
Cocoa	200	214	233	229	259	293	307	341	378	404	359
Coffee	71	71	72	71	69	69	72	72	73	69	72
Cotton	81	104	103	104	101	125	85	98	102	96	92
Currants and raisins	114	112	113	113	109	109	109	84	93	109	103
Meat	104	109	112	118	118	120	123	121	122	115	118
Rice	83	76	73	70	83	73	85	59	67	100	71
Sugar	140	142	157	152	139	147	146	152	163	146	142
Tea	126	128	132	134	135	136	139	142	144	142	141
Tobacco	115	117	117	122	117	123	126	132	128	130	132
Wool	114	120	122	125	110	127	114	110	117	103	93
Wine	72	70	72	78	75	79	79	73	71	69	63
Spirits	83	83	85	86	86	67	92	95	92	89	84
Beer	106	106	106	111	113	114	117	114	111	109	107
Unweighted average	108·3	111·5	114·9	115·5	115	122	122	121	127	128	121
Weighted, System 5	108·2	113·1	116·3	117·2	114	122	119	118	121	117	116

Franco-Prussian War.

As there are two parties in every war, one aggressive, the other defensive, we cannot assume that economic factors have the same significance for both. It is more likely that the aggressive party is the more representative for the general theory of war equilibrium than the defensive. We may assume that the intentional aiming at war by the aggressors is due to nothing else than the unconscious influence of economic factors on the rulers, if the economic situation is ripe for war, or if economic equilibrium is approaching a state of " war equilibrium." But although the aggressor is likely to be more representative for the theory than the defender, there is yet no reason to believe that the economic forces affecting the aggressor do

[1] *R. Stat. Soc. Journ.*, 1899, p. 656.

not influence the defender too. As the economic forces, as they exist now, are interwoven in a state of economic interchange and exchange, it is likely that some features of war equilibrium will be apparent with the defender too.

The statistics of consumption in Prussia before 1870, per head of population, are rather defective, and only available for some articles. But the available statistics confirm the theory. As consumption was not registered carefully except in towns, so the statistics given below are taken from the statistics of towns. The consumption of towns is perhaps representative for the country in general, although not showing the actual correct numbers, yet indicating the proportionate growth.

Table 22 shows the fluctuations of rye and wheat consumption and of their totals.

TABLE 22.

Consumption of Rye and Wheat in the "Mahlsteuerpflichtigen" Towns of Prussia [1] per head of Population. In Kgs.

Years or Average of Years.	Rye.	Wheat.	Total.
1850– 2	114·6	45·1	159·7
1853– 5	115·0	44·3	159·3
1856– 8	120·7	52·5	173·2
1859–61	116·9	52·9	169·8
1862	115·2	45·9	161·1
1863	112·7	50·7	163·4
1864	113·0	53·9	166·9
1865	109·1	53·1	162·2
1866	113·5	48·7	162·2
1867	113·4	42·5	155·9
1868	108·9	40·9	149·8
1869	109·3	46·7	156·0
1870	115·8	52·7	168·5
1871	105·0	45·6	150·6
1872	104·9	47·0	151·9

[1] K. Apelt, *Die Konsumption der wichstigsten Kulturländer.* Berlin, 1899, p. 22.

The average total consumption of wheat and rye in 1856–8 or 1859–61 or 1862–7 is higher than the average consumption of the years 1868–70, which represents the pre-war ascending period of consumption, and that indicates the pressure on consumption.

Prussia had three wars during the period of 1816 to 1872, and she was always the aggressor. All these wars, the Prusso-Danish in 1864, the Prusso-Austrian in 1866, and the Franco-Prussian in 1870–1, show a distinct confirmation of the theory. The total consumption of wheat and rye in 1864 is 166·9 kgs., 4.7 kgs. above the quantity of 162·2 for the following year 1865, and 3.5 kgs. above the quantity consumed in 1863; so the war period coincides with an increase in consumption; the after-war period with a decline of consumption. The consumption of 1865 remained stationary at 162·2 kgs. in 1866, during the Austro-Prussian War, fell to 155·9 kgs. in 1867, and declined still further to 149·8 in 1868; then it rose to 156·0 in 1869, and to 168·5 in 1870, which represents the highest number; it fell to 150·6 kgs. in 1871, and slightly rose to 151·9 in 1872. As we see, the period of increased or stationary consumption coincides with the war period and declines after the war.

I have no other statistics for Prussia.

For France, the statistics of consumption of meat in Paris, the consumption of coffee, cocoa, spirits, tea, sugar, wine, pepper, and vanilla, agree with the theory; the consumption of wheat and potatoes is more irregular, probably due to bad harvests.

Table 23 shows the pre-war ascending period of

TABLE 23.

Period.	Sugar.	Wine.	Spirits.	Beer.	Cocoa.	Tea.
	Kg.	L.	L.	L.	Kg.	Kg.
1867 . .	3·1	68	2·47	18·4	·172	·008
1868 . .	6·1	71	2·55	19·2	·191	·008
1869 . .	7·3	72	2·63	19·7	·207	·008

consumption of commodities, consisting of two or three years.

Wheat and potato consumption is highest in 1867, probably due to a bountiful harvest; coffee consumption is rising in 1870, the war period.

Table 24 shows the declining period of consumption during and after the war.

TABLE 24.

Article.		1870.	1871.	1872.	1873.
Wheat . . .	Hectol	2·84	2·30	3·38	2·36
Potatoes . . .	Kg.	2·44	2·33	2·28	2·48
Tea	Kg.	·010	·007	·006	·007
Coffee	Kg.	1·977	1·109	·462	1·233
Cocoa	Kg.	·308	·221	·092	·203
Sugar	Kg.	5·8	7·8	5·1	6·9
Wine	L.	65·0	66·0	77·0	76·0
Beer	L.	17·8	19·1	20·5	21·1
Spirits. . . .	L.	2·32	2·81	2·09	2·59

The declining period is noticeable in wheat consumption during the war; in 1872 the wheat consumption rose, probably in consequence of a good harvest, but in 1873 it fell again to below the level of the war consumption. Potato consumption declined from 1870 to 1872, and it begins to recover in 1873; similarly tea, coffee and cocoa consumption. Consumption of sugar and alcoholic beverages declined violently during the first year of the war period, 1870, but then it rose slightly in 1871, again declined in 1872, and after this year it began to recover the previous amounts.

The pre-war ascending phase of consumption of meat in Paris (Table 25) extends three years, from 1867 to 1869; the war consumption of meat is stationary, and the decline is abrupt in 1872, more than 14 p.c. The statistics of wine consumption in Paris indicate a continuous ascending period as far as 1860;

the war consumption is unknown and therefore the year 1872 cannot be compared.

TABLE 25.

Consumption of Meat and Wine in Paris, per head of Population, from 1860–72.[1]

Year.	Meat. Beef and Pork. Kg.	Wine. L.
1860	79·6	129·0
1861	71·8	134·6
1862	72·5	148·8
1863	75·6	159·6
1864	80·4	170·0
1865	79·6	187·0
1866	77·7	193·0
1867	77·5	195·6
1868	79·3	198·7
1869	81·2	203·5
1870	81·2 } Average	No data
1871	81·2 } Average	No data
1872	72·8	217·0

Lastly, Table 26 indicates the fluctuations of vanilla and pepper consumption in France per head of population.

TABLE 26.[2]

Period.	Vanilla. Kg.	Pepper. Kg.
1867	·0008	·077
1868	·0009	·077
1869	·0006	·078
1871–2	·0004	·060
1873	·0004	·049

The course of pepper consumption is normal, according to the war-equilibrium theory, but that of vanilla is of the same type as that of coffee, that is, with a decline in 1869, a year earlier than other commodities.

Looking at the average consumption of quinquennial periods, before and after the war, we find (Table 27)

[1] M. Block, *Stat. de la France*, vol. 4, 1875, pp. 400, 405–13.
[2] K. Apelt, pp. 74–76, 146.

that in the war period and the immediate after-war period the average consumption in the years 1871–5 is the lowest on record during forty years.

TABLE 27.

Consumption of Coffee and Tea in France and Germany.[1]

Period.	Coffee.		Tea.		Sugar.		Tobacco.	
	France.	Germany.	France.	Germany.	France.	Germany.	France.	Germany.
1866–70	1·45	2·20	·1	·02	6·8	—	·83	1·3
1871–5	1·06	2·27	·1	·02	6·3	6·7	·78	1·8
1876–80	1·45	2·33	·1	·02	7·3	6·4	·86	1·7
1881–5	1·75	2·44	·01	·03	10·7	7·8	·93	1·4
1886–90	1·74	2·38	·02	·04	11·3	8·5	·94	1·5
1891–5	1·88	2·41	·02	·05	11·5	10·7	·94	1·5

We could assume about the consumption of coffee in France that the equilibrium of the average consumption was disturbed in the years 1871–5, but restored in 1876–80, and that in the following year the average consumption rose, through the action of the law of increasing wants. On the contrary, the average consumption of tea is so low that one place of decimals is unable to give any evidence of the rise and decline during the years of 1866–80, although, as we saw it, it exists. The decline of consumption of tea is a compensatory action of the increased consumption of coffee in France. In Germany the average consumption of five years does not show a change, as we showed in the case of France; it rises in the subsequent quinquennial periods, owing to the action of the law of increasing wants.

The consumption of sugar is similar to that of coffee in France; in Germany the data are not very trustworthy for comparisons. The average consumption of tobacco is in accordance with the other com-

[1] K. Apelt.

modities in France, but in Germany it is increasing in the quinquennial period of 1871–5, instead of decreasing as in France. The high number is probably due to the increased consumption during the war, and during the immediate period after the war in the winning country; as tobacco is very much used by soldiers, the custom persisted after the war, and the decline was delayed.

The consumption of wine in Paris, as well as in France, is in some respects similar to that of tobacco, and we may say of beer in Germany.

The average consumption of wine in France and of beer in Germany was as follows, per head of population in each of the quinquennial periods, in litres.

TABLE 28.

Period.	Beer. Germany.	Wine. France.
1871–5 [1]	89·6 litres	150·1 litres
1876–80	87·0 ,,	109·1 ,,
1881–5	87·2 ,,	115·2 ,,

The average consumption per head of wine in France is greatest during the period of 1871–5, that is, the war period and the immediate after-war period; it declines in the period 1876–80 from 150·1 to 109·1 litres, then rises again. The consumption of beer in Germany is also greatest during 1872–5, then slowly declines. It is probable that these numbers for Germany are not representative for Prussia, which conducted the war, and I have not got other data. These statistics show that there are more and less sensitive commodities in consumption, and according to the elasticity of demand they show a quicker or slower recovery.

We could distinguish, according to the sensitiveness, commodities which decline immediately during war, and either recover slowly, as rye and wheat, and also meat, or recover quickly, as tea and pepper.

[1] The exact periods are for Germany, 1872–5, 1876–80/81, 1881/82–1885/86.

The period of decline may last for a very short time or for a longer period, and therefore the recovery of equilibrium may also come after a longer or shorter time. We have the recovery of consumption in France for coffee, sugar, and tobacco, after about five years (quinquennial period of 1876–80); the recovery of tea consumption comes after a very short period, so that the quinquennial average is unaltered.

The period of increase, on the other hand, may last longer or be very high, so that the quinquennial average consumption does not indicate a fall in the period of 1871–5, but it comes a period later, as, for instance, in the consumption of tobacco in 1876–80.

Russo-Japanese War, 1904–5.

Russia is an agricultural community, and her statistics given in Table 29, concerning the consumption of wheat, rye, barley, and oats, indicate a clear pre-war ascending and a post-war declining period of consumption, if we average the annual consumed quantities of the period. That is necessary, because as in all agricultural communities, the quantities fluctuate violently, and the consumption of necessaries is dependent on the harvests. It should be noted that rye and wheat are the stable food articles of the Russian peasant.

TABLE 29.[1]

Showing the Average Consumption of Cereals in Russia, per head of Population (60 Gov.).

Period.	Wheat.	Rye.	Barley.	Oats.	Period.
	Kg.	Kg.	Kg.	Kg.	
1902–3 .	64·89	147·07	31·81	72·93	Pre-war
1904–5 .	60·25	137·66	26·88	79·77	War
1906–7 .	39·13	119·15	23·79	55·29	Post-war

[1] K. K. Stat. Zentral Komission. *Das Getreide im Weltverkehr*. 3 Folge. 1909. Vienna.

X

CONSUMPTION BEFORE THE WORLD WAR, 1914

THE war-equilibrium theory assumes that a war period is a more or less fixed turning point of balancing forces, acting in opposite directions. We are able to examine only the pre-war economic phenomena of consumption; the decline of consumption during the war is a common truth, although not stated in exact amounts.

Germany.

Examining now the figures of consumption in Germany, we find the ascending phase in the following commodities: Wheat, rye, potatoes, spirits, tobacco, sugar, salt (for eating), groceries, rice, tea, jute, tropical fruits, and herrings, from 1909 or 1910 to 1913.

Table 30 shows the actual numbers. All the sub-

TABLE 30.

Article.		1910.	1911.	1912.	1913.
Rye	Kg.	—	139·3	140·1	145·2
Wheat	Kg.	—	87·6	87·6	93·6
Potatoes	Kg.	—	565·8	438·8	656·1
Spirits	L.	—	5·2	5·3	5·4
Tobacco	Kg.	1·4	1·5	1·5	1·7
Sugar	Kg.	—	19·0	16·9	12·2
Salt	Kg.	—	—	7·6	7·9
Groceries	Kg.	·15	·16	·16	·16
Rice	Kg.	—	2·71	2·43	3·56
Tea	Kg.	·05	·06	·06	·06
Tropical fruits	Kg.	3·94	4·09	4·52	4·44
Herrings	Kg.	—	2·71	2·71	2·89

sequent figures refer to consumption per head in all countries.

Beer, cotton, coffee, cocoa, and tropical fruits do not agree completely, probably on account of difficulties in supply (Table 31).

TABLE 31.

Showing the Consumption of some Commodities in Germany.

Year.	Beer.	Cotton.	Coffee.	Cocoa.	Tropical Fruits.
	L.	Kg.	Kg.	Kg.	Kg.
1910 . . .	99	5·87	2·60	·64	3·94
1911 . . .	99	6·70	2·79	·75	4·09
1912 . . .	106	7·56	2·53	·81	4·52
1913 . . .	101	7·33	2·44	·77	4·44

Of these commodities, four, beer, cotton, cocoa, and tropical fruits, are increasing to 1912, and begin to decline a year before the war. Coffee is in a progressive declining state of consumption, so that this explains the steady falling off in consumption.

I may repeat here that the consumption of coffee and vanilla in France began to decline also just a year before the beginning of war; I infer, therefore, that the phenomenon is not accidental.

As these commodities are more or less luxuries or semi-luxuries, so probably the pressure on consumption acts first on them, and that is the cause of the diminution of consumption of beer, tropical fruits, and cocoa, vanilla and coffee. The high figure of consumption of cotton in 1912 or the lower figure of 1913 may be due to some irregularities of supply.

I represent in Table 32 the pressure on consumption by three-yearly averages, during the periods 1911–13 and 1908–10.

Only sugar, rice, cocoa, and tropical fruits do not show any pressure on consumption. The reason is either that they are consumed in comparatively small quantities, as cocoa, or that they are consumed by

TABLE 32.

Article.		1908–10.	1911–13.
Rye	Kg.	145·2	141·5
Wheat	Kg.	89·2	82·8
Potatoes	Kg.	627·2	552·3
Spirits	L.	6·1	5·3
Beer	L.	105·0	102·0
Tobacco	Kg.	1·6	1·6
Salt	Kg.	7·8	7·8
Herrings	Kg.	3·90	2·77
Groceries	Kg.	·18	·16
Coffee	Kg.	2·98	2·59
Tea	Kg.	·063	·06
Jute	Kg.	2·29	2·15

the well-to-do classes, which do not feel the pressure, e.g., in the case of tropical fruits, or that they are used in manufacturing processes, as sugar, and therefore the disentanglement of personal consumption from the technical is not easy, and that may be the source of the steadiness of progress in consumption.

Germany's social and economic phenomena agree best with the theory of war equilibrium ; so the declining phase of the rate of natural increase was nearly an ideal confirmation of the theory. The phenomena of consumption, considered for short or long periods, agree with the theory too. We may infer that Germany's economic and social situation was quite ripe for a war, and her rulers, without consciously knowing, were driven to war by the economic phenomena. And if they started the war for other reasons, they obeyed also the pressure of economic phenomena.

United Kingdom.

The situation in the United Kingdom shows some irregularities with regard to the theory of war equilibrium. So taking the last three years before the war, 1913, 1912, 1911, we do not notice an agreement with the theory, but taking the two last years, 1913, 1912, the agreement, an ascending phase of consumption, is evident. The ascending phase of three years is noticeable in the consumption of rice, tobacco, and wool; of two years in the consumption of currants and raisins, meat, sugar, and beer. The consumption of wine and coffee, which declines after 1898, is stationary from 1911–13, which for such commodities may be counted as equivalent to an ascending phase for other articles.

TABLE 33.[1]

Showing the Consumption of Commodities in U.K.

Article.		1911.	1912.	1913.
Currants and raisins	lb.	4·89	4·66	4·79
Meat	lb.	126·12	122·92	123·65
Rice	lb.	13·02	14·81	15·01
Sugar	lb.	80·22	79·13	82·54
Tea	lb.	6·47	6·46	6·64
Tobacco	lb.	2·01	2·05	2·08
Wool	lb.	13·80	14·03	14·53
Wine	galls.	·25	·25	·25
Spirits	galls.	·68	·67	·69
Beer	galls.	27·22	26·74	27·31
Coffee	lb.	·62	·61	·61

Coffee, cocoa, and cotton show the same phenomenon as in Germany; that is, they decline just a year prior to the beginning of the war.

TABLE 34.

Showing the Consumption of Cocoa and Cotton in U.K.

Article.		1911.	1912.	1913.
Cocoa	lb.	1·23	1·73	1·70
Cotton	lb.	41·9	54·36	41·23

[1] The figures for some commodities (meat, wheat, etc) in the last years were given me by Professor A. Bowley.

The consumption of cocoa belongs to the same category of economic phenomena as the consumption of beer, cocoa, and tropical fruits in Germany before the World War, or the consumption of vanilla and coffee in France before the Franco-Prussian War. The maximum point of cotton consumption in the United Kingdom in 1912 coincides with the maximum point in Germany in the same year.

The consumption of wheat, if the figures are correct, is not in agreement with the theory, as the ascending phase of wheat consumption is not prolonged into the year 1913 but finishes in 1912; the consumption amount was for 1911, 6·02 bushels; for 1912, 6·28 bushels; and for 1913, 6·17 bushels.

The pressure on consumption of commodities is shown in Table 35. Meat, rice, sugar, coffee, wine, and spirits are the commodities which show the pressure. For coffee, wine, and spirits, being in a declining state of consumption, we may assume that the pressure accelerated decline.

TABLE 35.

Showing the Pressure on Consumption of Commodities per head.

Average of Years.	Meat.	Rice.	Sugar.	Coffee.	Wine.	Spirits.
	Lb.	Lb.	Lb.	Lb.	Galls.	Galls.
1908–10 .	126·17	16·69	84·29	·66	·27	·74
1911–13 .	124·99	14·97	80·63 [1]	·61	·25	·68

Wheat, cocoa, cotton, tobacco, wool, and beer are in a progressive state of consumption, considering the averages of the subsequent periods; so wheat has an average consumption of 6·04 and 6·18 lb.; cocoa, 1·14 and 1·55 lb.; cotton, 40·2 and 45·8 lb.; tobacco, 19·6 and 20·5 lb.; wool, 11·78 and 14·12 lb.; beer, 26·44 and 27·09 galls. But, shifting the periods to

[1] Taking as amount of sugar consumed in 1911, 90·07 lb., we get an average of 83·72.

six years, we get the figures of average consumption of wheat in the United Kingdom for 1908-13 as 6·11 bushels, and for 1902-7 as 6·20 bushels, which clearly indicates the existing pressure on wheat consumption, as the average consumption of 6·20 bushels is well within the limits of average consumption, and there is no reason to believe that the consumption of wheat, although near to the optimum, has reached it, and that it could not go beyond the 6·20 limit.

France.

The consumption per head in France is more similar to that of the United Kingdom than to that of Germany. The ascending phase of consumption covers, for most articles, two years, as was the case in the United Kingdom.

TABLE 36.

Showing the Ascending Phase of Consumption in France before the World War.

Year.	Wheat.	Sugar.	Spirits.	Beer.	Coffee.	Cocoa.	Silk.
	Kg.	Kg.	L.	L.	Kg.	Kg.	Kg.
1911	—	—	—	—	2·805	·609	·1
1912	3·22	16·8	3·86	32·0	2·810	·679	·2
1913	3·38	18·1 [1]	3·93	32·4	2·910	·700	·2

The consumption increase for two years, 1912-13, is visible in the following commodities: wheat, spirits, beer; the consumption of coffee and cocoa is in an ascending phase from 1911; silk and sugar consumption is stationary; cotton, as in England or Germany, begins to decrease in 1913.

Besides cotton there are other articles showing a fall of consumption, the beginning of a declining period, in 1913, shown in Table 37.

[1] *Ann. Stat.*, vol. 34.

TABLE 37.

Showing the Decrease in Consumption of Some Commodities in France in 1913.

Year.	Cotton.	Potatoes.	Wine.	Tea.
	Kg.	Kg.	L.	Kg.
1911 . . .	6·3	3·26	133	·033
1912 . . .	7·0	3·69	168	·032
1913 . . .	6·8	3·29	126	·030

We may conceive the decrease of consumption of some commodities a year prior to the beginning of war as a sign of pressure on consumption, which is visible if looking at the averages of periods preceding the war.

So pressure on wheat consumption is visible, if we compare the average consumption of the periods 1902-7 and 1908-13, as we have done for the United Kingdom. The average wheat consumption of the years 1902-5 was 3·50 kgs., and of 1908-13, 3·12 kgs.

TABLE 38.

Showing the Pressure on Consumption in France.

Period.	Potatoes.	Wine.	Wheat.
	Kg.	L.	Kg.
1908–10 .	3·53	(1906–9) 124	(1902–7) 3·50
1911–13 . .	3·41	(1910–13) 103·5	(1908–13) 3·12

Coffee, cocoa, cotton, beer, spirits, and sugar are in a progressive state of consumption ; tea indicates a slight pressure by decrease of consumption after 1912.

Russia.

The statistics of the consumption of corn and potatoes [1] show a pronounced pre-war ascending period

[1] *Annuaire Stat. de la Russie,* 1904–14.

of corn consumption, and a stationary pre-war period of potato consumption. Table 39 represents the consumption statistics, assuming that the net produce of these commodities available for consumption are the quantities consumed per head of population in Russia, including Poland (sixty Governments).

TABLE 39.

Year.	All Corn.	Potatoes.	Wheat.[1]
	Poods.	Poods.	Kg.
1911	16·18	9·6	56·6
1912	20·20	9·6	88·0
1913	25·22	9·6	112·6
1914	18·88	9·1	93·2

There is an indication of a decline of consumption during the war year 1914: about 12 p.c. for corn, 5 p.c. for potatoes, and 18 p.c. for wheat.

The consumption of rye[1] fluctuates irregularly, the amounts being per head 89·5 kgs. in 1911, 128·5 in 1912, and 120·4 in 1913. The relatively high quantity in 1912 is due to a good harvest.

Italy.

I could not get the consumption statistics of the year 1914, which belongs to the pre-war ascending period in Italy. Table 40 shows the inclusive consumption in 1913, per head of population.

TABLE 40.

Year.	Wheat.	Maize.	Wine.	Spirits.	Beer.	Sugar.	Coffee.	Tobacco.
	Kg.	Kg.	L.	L.	L.	Kg.	Kg.	Kg.
1911 .	173	80	119	·60	2·27	4·66	·75	·53
1912 .	164	82	121	·65	2·06	4·80	·77	·55
1913 .	176	78	139	·66	2·16	4·81	·81	·54

[1] From Internat. Agricult. Inst., Rome, 1917.

Wheat consumption indicates an ascending phase in the years 1912-13, and also beer; wine, spirits, sugar, and coffee consumption show an ascending phase of three years, 1911-13. Tobacco and maize consumption slightly decreased in 1913, if compared with the preceding year, but the tobacco consumption of 1913 represents just the average of three years. There is no indication of pressure on consumption.

Hungary.

Hungary's wheat consumption is irregular; the annual *per capita* fluctuations show a decrease from 1911 to 1913 (149·2, 147·3, and 137·3 kgs.), but taking the average of two consecutive years, 1910–11 and 1912–13, the consumption indicates a decrease, 148·85 and 142·3 kgs., which could be accounted as a slight pressure, but taking the average consumption of four years, the period 1910–13 is in ascending phase compared with the period 1906–9.

Austria-Hungary.

Austria-Hungary as a whole exhibits similar features. Considering the average wheat consumption per head in the periods 1906–9 and 1910–13, we find the latter in ascending phase (117·7 kgs. per head of wheat), while the average wheat consumption in 1906–9 was only 106·6 kgs.

The rye consumption approaches more the state required by the theory, although the annual fluctuations are irregular; the figures were: 72·2 kgs. in 1908, 71·8 in 1909, 70·7 in 1910, 67·8 in 1911, 78·3 in 1912, and 70·9 in 1913. The average consumption in 1908–10 was 71·6, and in 1911–13, 71·0 kgs., and this difference may indicate a pressure on consumption.

United States of America.

The United States entered the war in 1917, and the pre-war ascending period should be taken corresponding to the date of entering into the war, that is from 1914 to 1916.

In Table 41 the consumption of coffee, tea, salt, spirits, wine, and malt liquors is represented, per head of population.

TABLE 41.[1]

Year.	Coffee.	Tea.	Salt.	Spirits.	Wine.	Malt Liquors.
	Lb.	Lb.	Lb.	Proof galls.	Galls.	Galls.
1914	10·06	·90	99·2	1·43	·52	20·54
1915	10·52	·91	98·1	1·25	·32	18·24
1916	10·97	1·07	103·9	1·35	·46	17·59

There is a distinct ascending period of consumption (probably spurious) of coffee for 1914–16, of tea, salt, spirits, and wine for 1915–16, and there is a decrease in the consumption of malt liquors in 1916 if compared with 1915 or 1914. So the pressure on consumption had already started.

The pressure on consumption is visible in the following articles if we compare the average consumption of 1914–16 with 1911–13.

TABLE 42.

Period.	Tea.	Spirits.	Wine.	Malt Liquors.
	Lb.	Galls.	Galls.	Galls.
1911–13 . .	1·01	1·46	·60	20·41
1914–16 . .	·96	1·34	·46	18·76

All the commodities are more or less semi-luxuries.

[1] *Stat. Abst. U.S.A.*, 1916, No. 39.

XI

THE DISPROPORTION IN THE PRODUCTION OF PRIMARY AND SECONDARY GOODS

A. *The General Phenomena.*

THE pre-war economic phenomena of the natural growth of population, as referred to previously, indicate an unstable state of economic equilibrium and the approach of a state of "war equilibrium."

This tendency to an unstable state of general economic equilibrium is still more emphasized by some peculiarities of production in agriculture and industry, as well as in commerce. They could be shortly characterized as a disproportion between the production of primary and secondary goods; this proportion relates to the general tendency of the rate of growth in production in some productive branches above the rate of growth in others, which is not at all in accordance with the real needs and wants of the community.

The tendency to disproportionate production is continuously pushed forward, and it effects an enormous increase in the production of some goods, but at the same time there is a diminution in others, for the community cannot embark upon the production of some goods beyond a certain limit without a corresponding diminution in production in other branches. A proportionate division of the labour cannot be effected when the production in one branch is increasing at such a rate as to diminish it in another.

A stable state of equilibrium in production requires certain proportions between the amount of land, the amount of labour, and the amount of fixed and circulating capital, and it requires a proportionate distribution of these agents among the different branches of production. The law of co-efficients of production of Walfras and Ponto holds good if applied to the distribution of the general agents in productive branches.

Now this proportionate distribution of the agents in the different branches of production does not seem to be realized in modern communities. Some authors already noticed this, as for instance for agriculture.[1] " L'agriculture est aujourd'hui soumise à des influences économiques diverses, qui en se modifiant sans cesse, la place dans des conditions en quelque sorte instable, et il semble qu'on ne puisse arriver à un certain équilibre avant le terme, encore lointain, de la prodigieuse évolution qui marque la fin de ce siècle." It is not necessary to dwell upon the periodical crises [2] in industrial communities, which indicate an unstable equilibrium in industry and commerce.

It is not the intention of this essay to investigate these economic phenomena inside of a branch of production, but more to indicate the general disproportion between the branches themselves. It may be assumed as an axiom, that the general economic equilibrium is stable if the different branches of production progress at the same rate as consumption and the growth of population, and if they do not lag behind these rates. Another axiom is that the rate of increase in the different branches should correspond to the total utility of the commodities, but not only to the degrees of utility. It may be that the degrees of utility of some secondary goods are greater for a particular class in a community, or for the whole community itself, than that of the primary ones ; but the total utility of the primary goods, viewed from the standpoint of the whole community, is greater, and the

[1] Say and Chailley, *Dict. d'Econ. Pol.*, p. 40.
[2] See D. H. Robertson, *A Study of Industrial Fluctuation*. London, 1915.

production is more stable if it corresponds to the total utility of commodities than to the degrees of utility.[1]

The economic equilibrium is therefore stable if the agricultural production progresses as rapidly or at the same rate as the manufacturing, in accordance with the total utility of the commodities, and if it keeps pace with the progress of the population.

This is not the case in modern communities. The agricultural production does not keep pace with the industrial production, nor with the growth of population, whose demands are increasing according to the law of increasing wants.

Agricultural production decreases in industrial communities, sometimes absolutely, as in the United Kingdom, or relatively in *per capita* production, and in each case it does not keep the same rate as the growing consumption and population.

Turning to the factors of production, we mentioned already that the equilibrium in production requires a certain amount of land, a proportionate amount of labour, and a proportionate amount of fixed and circulating capital, and that it corresponds to the total utility of commodities. The first quantity is limited in a given community, and it may be changed, and it is changed nowadays, by war. The exchange of territories through peaceful understanding is negligible. So the meaning of war is to steady the unstable and disproportionate production of primary and secondary goods by supplementing new territories, which balance the loss of agricultural production in the industrial communities themselves.

The decrease in agricultural production is due chiefly to the employment of less labour in cultivation, and that is due to the fact that the agricultural population forms a decreasing part of the total population almost everywhere.[2]

[1] Jevons, *Theory of Political Economy*, pp. 45–49.

[2] E. Merritt, "The Agricultural Element in the Population." Amer. Stat. Assoc., vol. 15, 1916, pp. 50, 51.

Why is the agricultural element a decreasing part of the total population? Is it that the efficiency of the agricultural labourers and the better methods of producing and distributing agricultural products decrease the need for workers, where formerly more were required? Now it is not proved that the decrease of the agricultural element is effected only by the efficiency of methods and the consequent decreasing need for labourers. There seems, however, to be a little truth in it, particularly if we look at the following numbers. According to H. C. Taylor [1] the number of acres of leading crops in the United States per male worker increased from 23·3 in 1881 to 31 in 1900; the number of acres of these crops per working animal was 13·5 at both of these dates. But the average number of horses to one worker increased from 1·7 in 1880 to 2·3 in 1900.

From these figures it appears that in twenty years, by the aid of machinery and the substitution of horse power for hand labour, the effectiveness of human labour on farms increased to the extent of 33 p.c., the agricultural element decreased at the same time about 20 p.c.

The percentage of the population engaged in agriculture declined during these two decades at the same rate, which did not endanger the production of staple food crops, and the production *per capita* was at the same rate for the total population.

Now, looking more closely at the facts, we find that the persons engaged in agricultural pursuits in the U.S. formed in 1880 44·3 p.c. of the total population, and in 1900, 35·7 p.c., or there was a decline of 20 p.c.; now the average yield of wheat per acre in the decade 1881–90 was 12, and in 1900–10, 14, or an increase of 14·3 p.c. So it does not seem that the elimination of the agricultural labourer from farming increased the yield very much, and there is reason to believe that the application of more hand labour,

[1] *Agricultural Economics*, pp. 31, 32. New York, 1905.

with supervision and scientific insight, would surely increase the yield per acre. The substitution of machinery for hand labour leads to an efficient exploitation of the soil, but only in extensive cultivation, the intensive cultivation wants brain and hands, which cannot be replaced by machinery. It is therefore our conviction that as long as the agricultural element forms a decreasing proportion of the total population the culture of soil and the raising of agricultural products cannot keep pace with the rate of production of other commodities, but must proportionately decrease.

A look at the following table gives an idea of the urbanization and industrialization of Western Europe and America.

TABLE 43.

Proportion of Urban to Total Population,[1] as Percentages of the Total Population.

Census Year.	England and Wales.	U. Kingdom.	France.	Germany.	Austria.	U.S.A.
1861 .	54·6	47·3	28·9	—	—	21·8
1871 .	61·8	54·5	31·1	36·1	—	27·1
1881 .	67·9	60·7	34·8	41·4	29·6	29·9
1891 .	72·0	65·6	37·3	47·0	32·4	36·8
1901 .	77·0	71·3	40·9	54·3	38·1	41·7
1911 .	78·1	—	—	60·1	—	—

Through urbanization of the total population, the production of primary goods in the world slackens continuously, but the agriculture of the industrial communities declines most, and therefore the agricultural depression from 1875 onwards.[2]

Is the foreign competition a cause of the agricultural

[1] Cd. 4954. *A Century of Population Growth*, 1790–1900. Dep. of Com. and Lab.

[2] F. Aus. Ogg, *Economic Development of Modern Europe*. New York, 1917, pp. 158–211.

depression in industrial countries? It is obvious that in some respects it is, but foreign competition was caused by the fact that foreign agricultural lands had to pay somehow for the manufactured goods which they got from the industrial communities.

So the foreign agricultural countries gave in exchange what they had, that is food and raw material, and the industrial communities had to take what they could, and the easiest and best way of exchange was that of giving manufactured goods for food and their commercial services.

"Food was, so to speak, the currency in which foreign nations paid for English manufactured goods, and the cheapness was an undoubted blessing to the wage-earning community. Thrown on their own resources, agriculturists fought the unequal contest with courage and tenacity. But as time went on, the stress told more and more heavily. The manufacturing population seemed to seek food markets everywhere except at home."[1]

The facilities of rapid distribution and the enormous development of transport by sea and land helped the industrial communities to get food cheaply and on good terms. While exchanging manufactured products for food and raw materials (which in this sense belong to the primary economic goods), as long as the manufactures are relatively scarce, the exchange is favourable to the communities producing them, but as their supply grows, the demand for them, although not decreasing, the exchange turns against them and their prices fall, while the prices of the agricultural products rise.

Agricultural decline is the effect of the industrialization of modern communities. It effects a shifting of the labour to industrial production. This shifting is effected by giving to the agricultural workmen better employment and higher wages, and they leave their homes only for these better prospective wages. Indus-

[1] R. E. Prothero, *English Farming*, 1917, p. 379.

trialization is dependent on the free capital wanting employment, and the incessant accumulation of capital does not seem to have any limits.

The accumulated capital is employed nowadays more profitably in the industrial processes, and as the accumulation of capital is going on, its employment is continuously increasing in those processes. The effect of that is the depopulation of the rural districts and the urbanization of modern communities. It is quite true that the transport facilities make this depopulation of the rural districts easier, but the depopulation is not caused by the over-population of the rural districts, as Vandervelde asserts.[1] There is no proof of that; the agricultural labourers leave their homes mostly in the hope of getting better employment somewhere else. The over-population is only artificial, and it may be caused by the existence of great land estates, in which case the over-population exists because the greatest part of the yield is taken by the landowners in the shape of rent.

The difference of wages in agricultural and industrial production is the primary cause of the attraction of the rural population, and this difference is the effect of the abundance of employed capital in industrial production. As long as a great difference of wages exists between agricultural and industrial workmen, the rural exodus is bound to last. But as the application of capital and labour increase at the same rate as in industrial processes, the shifting of workmen will cease, and the economic equilibrium will become more stable.

It will be more stable if the redistribution of the land comes, because it is not the want of soil, as M. Kovalevsky[2] argues, that drives the Russian peasants to emigration, but the great land estates and the landowner class, which prevent the intensive cultivation of the soil. Great estates are pushing the pro-

[1] *L'Exode Rural et le Retour aux Champs*, p. 40. Paris, 1903.
[2] *Le Régime Econ. de la Russie*, pp. 248–86. Bibl. Soc. Int. Paris, 1898.

duction of primary goods to extensive cultivation, and although they may involve some economies in general expenses and partly of labour, their effect is to diminish the number of producers and to reduce the quantity of products. In some highly civilized countries the yield of crops from the great estates may be larger than from the small ones in some backward countries, but that does not prove that this yield could not be raised if the capital and labour were employed in intensive cultivation on small farms.

Whatever is the state of cultivation now in the industrial communities, compared with that in the backward ones, the general effect of the great estates is the extensive cultivation of the soil.

So the disproportionate employment of capital in industrial processes, and the great estates, help each other and effect the extensive cultivation of soil, driving the agricultural population to decrease continuously in comparison with the population in other branches.

The agricultural production in industrial communities must ultimately decrease, whatever may be the improvements in the agricultural methods; it neither keeps pace with the increase of population in the communities, nor with the growth of consumption. The efficiency of the agricultural methods is not such as to balance the loss of manual workers, nor the gain of the natural growth of population, nor to cover the increasing consumption in the progressive communities.

The disproportionate production of primary and secondary goods in industrial communities disturbs the economic equilibrium not only in these countries, but by the immense development of industrial activity in the whole world. So the world production of primary goods does not keep the same rate as the world production of the secondary ones, but it lags behind. This will effect a general slackening of commerce in food-stuffs, indicating the irrelative scarcity, and consequently a disproportionate rise in the price of food-stuffs and raw materials. Both these phenomena are helped by the extensive cultivation of the soil, now existing, and they all effect a tendency to geographical expansion in the industrial communities. Now, geographical expansion is a means to readjust the economic equilibrium and to make it stable. This kind of readjustment is usually carried out by war, and it is therefore the function of war to stabilize the economic equilibrium by supplementing an area of industrial activity by an area of production of primary goods (food-stuffs and raw materials).

But war may effect a redistribution of values, as now in Russia, in the sense of the above consideration; where an expansion becomes impossible, the redistribution of land and capital takes place, and a movement to intensive cultivation is bound to come. Besides, war stabilizes the economic production, through lowering the standard of living; the demand for secondary goods slackens and the supply slackens too, while the demand for primary goods cannot slacken at the same rate as the former, so the supply does not diminish at the same rate, but, on the contrary, it increases. This phenomenon of increasing the supply of agricultural products in the industrial countries during war, we shall consider statistically too.

As long as there are supplementary areas easy to subdue, there is no fear of a great world conflagration, but as the supplementary areas get scarce, as at the beginning of the twentieth century, a world struggle was bound to come, and it came in 1914. It was indicated by a disproportionate rate of growth in the world production of primary and secondary goods in the last decades, by a disproportionate rate of increase in the growth of population and production of primary goods in the industrial communities in the last decades, by the limit of extensive cultivation, which was reached in these decades, by a slight rise in the intensive culture in the world production of primary goods, and lastly by having reached the limits of geographical expansion in the last century.

B. *The Disproportionate Rate of the Growth in Production of Primary and Secondary Goods in the World.*

The disproportionate growth in the production of primary and secondary goods in industrial communities may be without any visible effect on the general economic equilibrium in the world, if the disproportion is not sufficiently large, and if the industrial communities are small compared with the total number of the world population. But as the population of the industrial communities increases continuously, and as the industrialization continues without interruption, and as there are new countries added to the industrial communities, the effect on the general production of primary and secondary goods is bound to be visible.

The general disproportionate growth of production cannot go on in several of the most populous countries without endangering the general economic equilibrium in the world, and the rates of the growth in production of primary and secondary goods prove that the secondary goods increased at double the rate of the primary ones during the last three decades.

Examining the growth of the estimated increase of population, gold, pig-iron, and wheat production in the world, we see the actual disproportion (Table 44) existing in the production of goods, because pig-iron and gold may be taken as representing secondary and wheat primary goods.

The average population in the decades 1891–1900 and 1901–10 was 8·7 and 17·5 p.c. higher than in the period 1881–90, while the average production of wheat rose 10 p.c. and 43 p.c., the production of gold 95 and 222 p.c., that of pig-iron 40 and 139 p.c. in the corresponding decades above that in the years 1881–90. So it seems that wheat production was nearly 25 p.c. above the level of the growth of population in 1901–10,

TABLE 44.[1]

Showing the Growth of Population, and of Wheat, Gold, and Pig-iron Production, as Percentages of the Average Population or Production in 1881–90 in the World.

Period.	Population.	Wheat.			Gold.	Pig-iron.
		Area.	Harvest.	Yield.		
1881–90	100	100	100	100 p. acre	100	100
1891–1900	108·7	110	114	103 ,,	195	140
1901–10	117·5	126	143	113 ,,	325	239

but having regard to the rise of consumption actually taken place in all European countries, this surplus percentage is not so great. Besides, it should be noted that the rate of increase of European stock, of which wheat is the chief food article, is relatively larger than that of the whole world, and therefore this difference between the rates of increase in population and wheat production is getting still smaller. It is therefore justifiable to conclude that the actual wheat production covers the actual demand, but not in proportion to the action of the law of increasing wants ; an optimum of satisfaction is likely to be approached or reached only in one or two countries.

We get the following increase in the amounts available for *per capita* consumption in different successive periods.

TABLE 45.[2]

Showing World's *per capita* Wheat Production.

Period.	Quarters.
1873–80	·199
1881–90	·197
1891–1900	·210
1901–10	·246
1911–12	·276

[1] Population growth and gold and pig-iron production, calculated from J. Kitchin's *Trade Cycles Chart*, 3rd ed. Wheat area, harvest and yield, from J. F. Unstead, *Statistical Study of Wheat Cultivation and Trade*, 1881–1910. Wheat production on the basis of Mr. Kitchin's figures, is in 1881–90, 100 ; 1891–1900, 115 ; and in 1901–10, 149 ; therefore yields per acre : 100 104·5, and 118.

[2] J. Kitchin, *Trade Cycles Chart*, 3rd ed,

Taking the average amount in the period 1873–80 as 100, the successive periods show the following increase or decrease respectively: in 1881–90, 99; in 1891–1900, 105·5; in 1901–10, 124; and in 1911–12, 137. So there was a relative rise in the amounts available for consumption in the period preceding the World War, this confirming the theory that consumption is in ascending phase in the period just preceding war. The greatest amount of this surplus of wheat produced was and is consumed by the European stock or industrial communities.

The following figures show the difference between the average amount available for the world and the approximate actual amounts consumed in the modern communities during the period 1880–1910. The average quantities of wheat available for consumption during 1880–1910 per head[1] were in lbs:

Period.	World.	Germany.	United Kingdom.	United States.	Italy.	France.
1880–1910	5·76	168	327	330	290	522

On the average, the population in these five countries consumed about fifty-six times more of wheat than the amount available for the consumption of the world.

The effect of the actually decreasing production of agricultural products, or of their lagging behind the production of secondary goods in industrial communities during longer periods, must be an increasingly unstable economic equilibrium of the whole world, as well as of the industrial communities themselves.

Shorter Periods.

This tendency to a slower rate of increase in the production of primary goods in comparison with that of secondary goods, is to be seen in the world production of the three chief articles of food of Western and Eastern Europe, America, and Asia, that is wheat,

[1] From Cd. 4544, 1909. The periods are exactly 1880–1903 for the U.K., U.S.A., France, and Germany.

rye, and rice; and also of the three most important industrial commodities, that is of copper, pig-iron, and gold, in the most recent period.

TABLE 46.

Index Numbers of the World Production of Wheat, Rye, Rice, Copper, Pig-iron, and Gold.

The Production Amount of the World in 1901 = 100.[1]

Period.	Wheat.	Rye.	Rice.	Copper.	Pig-iron.	Gold.
1902–1904	109·8	118·7	112·9	113	111	123
1905–1907	114·3	104·6	104·9	135	142	152
1908–1910	118·7	117·2	125·2	159	143	171
1911–1913	142·5	127·2	144·5	185	176	184

Taking the amount produced in the world for metals in 1901 or for crops in 1901–2 as 100, the increase in the average world production of wheat, rye, and rice was 42·5, 27·2, and 44·5 p.c. respectively, in the period 1911-13, while the increase in the world production of copper, pig-iron, and gold was 85, 76, and 84 p.c. Or the increase in the three primary commodities, taking an average, was less than one-half of that of the production of the three secondary commodities.

The following table shows the growth of production of some six other commodities: pig-lead, tin, spelter, cotton, sugar, and tobacco.

TABLE 47.

Index Numbers of the World Production of Pig-lead, Tin, Spelter, Cotton, Sugar, and Tobacco.

Production in 1901 = 100.

Period.	Pig-lead.	Tin.	Spelter.	Cotton.	Sugar.	Tobacco.
1902–4	107	105	114	117·8	102·5	101·5
1905–7	117	118	138	123·6	110·6	95·3
1908–10	128	131	152	124·7	118·0	119·4
1911–13	138	142	189	—	—	—

[1] Index numbers of production of wheat, rye, and rice, from *Ann. Int. de Atat. Agricole*, 1910. Inst. Int. d'Agric., Rome. Those of metals are calculated from H. R. Merton & Co., *Comp. Stat. of Lead, Copper, etc.* London, 1914. Gold production from J. Kitchin.

Tobacco is a semi-luxury, sugar is partly a necessary of life, partly used for manufacturing purposes; cotton is a raw material; but all the three commodities may be taken as significant by the methods of production as belonging more to the primary goods, while pig-lead, tin, and spelter belong to the secondary goods, although not of the same importance as pig-iron, copper, and gold.

The average production of pig-lead, tin, and spelter increased from the level in 1901 in the period 1908–10 by 28, 31, and 52 p.c., while the average production of cotton, sugar, and tobacco increased by 24·7, 18·0, and 19·4 p.c. respectively. Or the increase in the average production of the three agricultural (semi-primary) goods, was a little more than one-half of that of the three metallic goods.

The following table (48) shows the average increase of three years in the world production of barley, oats, maize, coal, and steel.

TABLE 48.

Index Numbers of World Production of Barley, Oats, Maize, Coal, and Steel.

The Production in 1901–2 or 1901 = 100.

Period.	Barley.	Oats.	Maize.	Coal.	Steel.
1902–1904 .	111·3	119·0	137·6	110	114
1905–1907 .	115·0	123·6	156·7	130	153
1908–1910 .	127·1	139·5	157·1	139	166
1911–1913 .	141·5	155·1	143·9	174 [1]	204 [1]

The average increase in the production of these three primary commodities (barley, oats, maize) was 34·8 p.c. lower than that of gold, copper, and pig-iron, about 9 p.c. lower than that of pig-lead, spelter, and tin for the period 1911–13, and about half of that of coal and steel (43·8 p.c.).

[1] 1911–12.

Altogether the increase in the production of the primary economic goods seems to be one-half of that of the secondary products, during the last pre-war decades (see Fig. 3).

C. *The Disproportion in the Growth of Population and the Production of Primary Commodities.*

In the preceding sub-chapter we have seen that the population of the world has increased in the decade 1901–10, 17·5 p.c. from the level of 1881–90, while the world production of wheat increased 43 p.c., so that in general the wheat supply of the world may be taken to be secure. But at the same time the consumption and the standard of living has rapidly progressed, particularly in the industrial communities, so that the surplus has been mostly consumed by the industrial communities. Another feature of the rising of the standard of living in the industrial communities is the increased consumption of meat.

Notwithstanding this fact, that consumption in modern communities is steadily increasing either in the direction of cereal or meat diet, their production tends to decrease, and to lag behind not only the increased consumption, but the rate of increase of population.

Table 49 shows this tendency, measured by the average growth of population and the average production of wheat, cattle, sheep, and pigs in the last three decades, in the four most important modern communities. The average population in the United Kingdom in 1900–9 increased 20 p.c., cattle 12 p.c., sheep 4 p.c., while the wheat production decreased 28 p.c., if the average population and production in 1880–9 is 100.

The population of the United States increased 66 p.c., wheat 54 p.c., cattle 49·5 p.c., and sheep only 21 p.c.

In France the population increased 3·2 p.c., wheat production 6 p.c., cattle 8 p.c., but sheep decreased

13 p.c., so the average increase of cattle and sheep is a negative quantity. So France's situation is favourable regarding wheat production, but taking into account the rise of consumption, this advantage

TABLE 49.

Index Numbers showing the Disproportionate Growth of Population and of Production of Primary Commodities.

The Average of the Population, Wheat Harvest, and of Numbers of Cattle and Sheep in the Decade 1880–9 = 100.[1]

	1880–1889.	1890–1899.	1900–1909.
United Kingdom :			
Population	100	109	120
Wheat	100	79	72
Cattle	100	106·5	112·5
Sheep	100	107	104
United States :			
Population	100	123	166
Wheat	100	131	154
Cattle	100	110·5	149·5
Sheep	100	90	121
Germany : [2]			
Sheep	100	77	63
Population	100	111	129
Wheat	100	132	143
Pigs	100	138	182
Cattle	100	109	113
France :			
Population	100	101·3	103·2
Wheat	100	101	106
Cattle	100	106	108
Sheep	100	100	87

[1] The percentages of the population based on the figures given by Statistical Abstracts for Foreign Countries (various years) and Cd. 4954. Cattle and sheep on figures given by P. G. Cragie, "Comparative International Statistics of Agriculture," *Bull. de l'Inst. de Stat.*, Tom. 11, 1899, and Tom. 15, 1906, and completed by the available figures given in Statistical Abstracts for Foreign Countries.

[2] There are no available statistics to compute the average number of cattle, sheep, or pigs, for the decades. The percentages of animals obtained from the averages of two successive census years, e.g., 1880 and 1890, 1890–1900, etc. By the same method, rye production gives the following index numbers: 100 for 1880–9, 129 for 1890–9, 169 for 1900–9.

is annihilated, and France still has to import a part of her wheat. The average imported amount was in 1880–9, 39 millions, in 1890–9, 36 millions, and in 1900–9, 10 millions of bushels.

Germany's population increased 29 p.c. in 1900–9, wheat 43 p.c., due probably to the tendency of the people to consume more wheat than rye, which was the chief food article in the previous years. The other percentages are not very reliable; cattle increased 13 p.c., pigs 82 p.c., sheep decreased 27 p.c. The average increase of the three meat-supplying animals was in 1900–9 only 19 p.c., 10 p.c. behind the rate of increase of population. Rye production increased 69 p.c., but this figure is not reliable; it was obtained by averaging the amounts produced in 1900 and 1910.

The average imports of wheat were as follows:

Period.	United Kingdom.	Germany.	France.	Italy.	Austria-Hungary.
	Million bushels.				
1880–9 . .	144	18	39	23	—
1890–9 . .	177	41	36	22	—
1900–9 . .	209	70	10	38	3

Turning to the other wheat-consuming countries, the wheat production of Italy, Austria-Hungary (Hungary is a grain-exporting country), and the Balkans was under the general level of world production (Table 50). The European general average of wheat production on the decade 1900–10 was 11 p.c. below the world's level, although including the Russian high percentage, which was 46 p.c. above the general world average (Table 50).

TABLE 50.[1]

Showing the Growth of Wheat Production.

The Average Production in the Decade 1881-90 in Individual Countries and in the World = 100.

	1881–1890.	1891–1900.	1901–1910.
World	100	110	143
North America	100	131	163
Europe	100	108	132
Russia	100	122	189
Austria-Hungary	100	115	132
Italy	100	104	138
Balkan Peninsula	100	97	101

Only the Argentine shows a considerable rise of wheat production, during the last decades, and that is only on account of the application of extensive cultivation, which is to be observed from the following table (51).

TABLE 51.

Showing the Increase of Wheat Production and Wheat Area in the Argentine during Three Decades.

The Average of Wheat Area and of Wheat Harvest = 100.

Period.	Wheat Area.	Wheat Amount.
1881–1890	100	100
1891–1900	285	270
1901–1910	600	541

[1] The figures based on J. F. Unstead, "Statistical Study of Wheat Cultivation and Trade." *The Geographical Journal*, 1913.

So the wheat amount produced was 59 p.c. lower than the wheat area sown, or the yield per acre diminished.

Another method to measure the disproportion in the growth of population and of the primary commodities is to take single years at intervals of ten years, and to express the subsequent changes in percentages (+ increase, − decrease). Mr. W. S. Thompson [1] used this method in his study of Malthusianism. Yet the yearly fluctuation in crops and in the number of animals may be very sharp, and these percentages do not express the phenomena so correctly as the percentages obtained from the averages of the whole periods. Yet as there are no complete statistical data they are very useful, and I shall give some of Mr. Thompson's figures in Table 52, partly corrected for the United Kingdom, the U.S., and France, by three-yearly averages (for instance, 1889–1890–1891, or 1909–1910–1911) for cattle and other animals (see Table 52).

The increase of the cereals is behind the actual increase of population in Germany and the United Kingdom; it just covers the increase of population in the U.S., and there is a surplus of increase in cereal production in Russia and Hungary, and partly in France, in 1910.

The percentages of increase of cereals for Austria and Italy do not represent the actual facts, at least from the standpoint of food-stuffs, as these are grain-importing countries. The high percentage of Austria in 1910 is probably a slip one.

[1] Population. 1915, New York. *Columbia Studies*, vol. 63, No. 3, pp. 65–71, and Appendix B.

TABLE 52.

Growth of Population and Primary Commodities. Increase or Decrease as Percentages of the Previous Year.

	1880.	1890.	1900.	1910.
GERMANY.				
Actual Increase of population . .	12·5	9·2	13·8	15 8
Natural increase	12·1	12·4	14·9	13·3
Increase of cereals	—	15·6	40·0	11·4
Increase of animals (cattle, sheep, pigs)	3·1	6·5	7·9	8·8
UNITED KINGDOM.				
Actual increase of population . .	10·8	8·2	9·9	9·1
Natural increase	12·9	10·9	10·7	10·5
Increase of cereals	—	—	− 8·7	1·5
Increase of animals (cattle, sheep, pigs)	− 7·2	22·2	− 2·2	0·7
RUSSIA.				
Actual increase of population . .	8·0 (1867)	29·3 (1885)	15·5 (1897)	23·4
Natural increase	—	12·8	17·0	17·0
Increase of cereals	− 0·1	26·5	17·2	31·3
Increase of animals (cattle, sheep, pigs)	6·0	11·2	18·6	− 14·9
U.S.A.				
Actual increase of population . .	30·1	25·5	20·7	21·1
Natural increase	24·2	18·5	16·8	13·3
Increase of cereals	64·7	29·2	5·9	21·4
Increase of animals (cattle, sheep, pigs)	50·0	24·2	8·7	− 1·6
FRANCE.				
Actual increase of population . .	4·3	1·8	1·6	1·6
Natural increase	2·5	0·4	1·1	0·4
Increase of cereals	19·3	7·1	5·7	5·7
Increase of animals (cattle, sheep, pigs)	− 1·5	7·8	3·1	− 2·3
AUSTRIA.				
Actual increase of population . .	9·5	7·9	9·4	9·2
Natural increase	7·9	8·8	11·9	10·8
Increase of cereals	− 3·3	14·7	− 6·6	35·9
Increase of animals (cattle, sheep, pigs)	1·0	6·1	7·4	11·6
HUNGARY.				
Actual increase of population . .	1·5	10·9	10·2	8·3
Natural increase	11·0	9·3	11·7	11·2
Increase of cereals	—	25·6	16·0	11·6
Increase of animals (cattle, sheep, pigs)	− 13·6	13·4	10·9	− 7·2
ITALY.				
Actual increase of population . .	6·2	7·3	6·3	6·8
Natural increase	7·7 (1876-81)	10·7	10·7	11·2
Increase of cereals	− 7·7	− 4·1	− 2·6	12·9
Increase of animals (cattle, sheep, pigs)	11·3	13·7	19·3	17·7

Taking the increase of cereals and animals together, the average increase of the primary commodities is actually lagging behind in all these countries, except Italy and Austria, due to the faulty high percentages. It is the case in the United Kingdom, Germany, Russia, U.S.A., and Hungary. In France the gain by cereals covers the loss from decrease of animals. In Italy the people must have had a miserable production in the previous years, because although the increase in cereals and animals is high, yet it does not cover the demand in the country.

The most prominent feature of these figures is the fact that the increase in animals is almost everywhere lagging behind the increase of population. In Austria it is a little ahead of the increase of population, and in Italy too, due to the previous low production.

XII

THE SLACKENING OF COMMERCE IN FOOD-STUFFS, AND THE DISPROPORTIONATE RISE OF PRICE

A. *The Greatest Cereal Producers.*

BESIDES the immediate effect of industrialism on the agricultural production in the industrial communities themselves, there is a more remote influence, but none the less inevitable, on the agriculture of the whole world. The increasing rate in the production of secondary goods must absorb the greater part of human labour and energy, and supposing the time is sufficiently long, it effects a decreasing rate of production and therefore a slackening of commerce in food-stuffs.

Now, the whole of humanity, including the white races, on the average is still maintained and fed by vegetable food, and the white races by cereals (wheat, rye, maize). It is therefore the production of cereals that gives an indication of the state of food-stuffs. Table 53 shows the greatest cereal producers in the world during the decade 1901–10, with the amount of world production.

Wheat.—Ten countries produced 69 p.c. of the whole supply of the world. The greatest producers were: Russia (European and Asiatic), United States, France, and India. Minor producers, but wheat-exporting countries, were Hungary, the Argentine and Canada. There are countries, as the Australian Commonwealth and Rumania, which are wheat-exporting, but they are comparatively small producers. According to the average amount of exported wheat, the following countries showed a surplus of production during the most recent pre-war period, 1909/10–1913/14: (1) Russia, 44·8; (2) U.S., 29·6; (3) Canada, 25·9; (4) Argentine, 22·6; (5) Rumania, 14·6; (6) Australia, 14·4; (7) India, 13·5; and (8) Hungary, 13·0 millions of quintals.

So we see that the smaller countries (Australia, Rumania, Argentine, Canada) are covering the wheat balance of the wheat countries. The wheat amount of the United States destined for export approaches that of Canada. Only Russia exports a considerable amount, but if industrialism had enough time to spread, this surplus would very soon disappear.

TABLE 53.

The Greatest Cereal Producing Countries during the Decade 1901–10.[1]

WHEAT. 000,000 Quintals.		RYE. 000,000 Quintals.		BARLEY. 000,000 Quintals.	
Russia (Eur. & Asiatic)	191	Russia	213	Russia	84
U.S.A.	181	Germany	99	U.S.A.	33
France	89	Austria	24	Germany	32
India	80	France	13	Japan	19
Italy	46	Hungary	12	Austria	15
Hungary	44	U.S.A.	8	U.K.	15
Argentine	37	Spain	7	Spain	15
Germany	36			Hungary	13
Spain	33			Canada	9
Canada	30				
Total world production	838	Total world production	398	Total world production	268

[1] Ann. Intern. Agric. Inst., 1910, Rome.

Oats. 000,000 Quintals.	
Russia	135
U.S.A.	132
Germany	78
France	46
Canada	38
U.K.	31
Austria	20
Hungary	12
Total world production	535

Maize. 000,000 Quintals.	
U.S.A.	637
Hungary	39
Argentine	34
Italy	24
Rumania	21
Russia	19
Spain	6
France	6
Serbia	5
Bulgaria	5
Total world production	793

Rye.—The greatest rye producers during the decade 1901–10 were: Russia, Germany, Austria, France, Hungary, United States, and Spain; or seven countries produced 94 p.c. of the whole world supply. Among these countries only Russia is the truly exporting country. Germany imports; Austria and France consume their own supply, and the exports of the other three are of no great importance or weight.

Barley.—Nine countries produced 88 p.c. of the whole world supply. These were: Russia, United States, Germany, Japan, United Kingdom, Spain, Austria, Hungary, and Canada. The United States exported a comparatively small amount.

Oats.—Oats are more used for animal feeding. Eight countries produced 92 p.c. of the whole world supply. They were: Russia, the United States, Germany, France, Canada, the United Kingdom, and Austria-Hungary. The truly exporting ones were: Russia, Canada, and the United States (a small amount). Germany, France, and the United Kingdom consume their own supply. Hungary's surplus just balances the requirements of Germany and Austria.

Maize.—Maize is used as human food in the United States and is of importance for the national diet. The United States are the greatest producers of maize, and alone produce 80 p.c. of the whole world supply.

Nine countries, Hungary, Argentine, Italy, Russia, France, Spain, Austria, and Japan, produce 18 p.c., and all the other countries only 2 p.c. The more prominent exporting countries were: United States, Russia, Argentine, and Hungary.

The broad facts regarding the supply of cereals, are that the largest countries consume their own supply. The only exceptions are Russia and partly the United States, which seems to approach the ordinary state of modern communities and to cease to be a food-exporting country. Therefore, the smaller producers cover the balance and the requirements of the larger countries, and they are supplementary areas in this respect. If a large industrial community has already got a large supplementary area under its influence, as the United Kingdom or France, the problem of supplementing the area of the industrial community does not seem to be acute. Or if it is still possible for a country to be self-supporting, as the United States, the area of industrial activity is still comparatively stable; but in other cases, such as Austria and Germany, the question of supplementing the area of industrial activity by an area of production is of vital economic importance to stabilize the economic equilibrium of a community.

It does not seem to me, therefore, that there is an abundance of food-stuffs, particularly if we remember that consumption tends everywhere to increase, and that the wheat- or cereal-producing countries tend, in the course of time with the rising standard of living, to consume all the food and cereals they produce.

"Au fur et à mesure, que le bien-être d'une nation exportrice de froment se developpe, elle en absorbe une plus grande quantité et elle diminue la part relative de son exportation," says Y. Guyot.[1] He further observes that "Loin qu'il y ait surproduction des matières alimentaires dans le monde, il y a insuffisance

[1] Les Ressources et les Besoins dans le Monde. *Journ. de la Soc. de Stat. de Paris*, 58ième année, 1917, p. 251.

de production ; de plus, aucun pays, pas même les États Unis, malgré l'étendu de leur territoire et le variété de leur climat et de leur sol, ne peut se suffire à lui-même. Ils ont importé en 1916 pour plus de 260 millions de dollars d'objets d'alimentation brut, et pour 339 millions de dollars d'objets d'alimentation fabriqués, en tout ou en parties" (p. 245).

B. *The Slackening of Commerce in Food-stuffs.*

A better index of the general state of the food situation than either the one year referred to by Guyot, or the general consideration of the greatest food producers and exporters, is the commerce in food-stuffs. We shall consider the average values of food-stuffs, imported and exported, and their relation to the total value of imports and exports during the two decades preceding the World War, in the principal countries.

Table 54 gives the average of the imported and exported food values as percentages of the total value of imports and exports during two decades, 1890–1900 and 1901–10. It shows a general decline of imported and exported food value in the period of 1901–10, compared with the total value of imports or exports. That indicates either that the food was cheaper, causing the relative decline of the value of food-stuffs in comparison with the total value, which is not the case, or that on the contrary the prices of food-stuffs in general and on the average were rising in the last decade. This would explain the proportionate diminution of the volume of trade in food-stuffs, compared with the other manufactured or semi-manufactured commodities, and that indicates a proportionate reduced supply of food-stuffs, compared with the other commodities, which is the first proof of the disproportionate production between primary and secondary commodities.

Examining the details, we find another general tendency, that the values of food exports have fallen more than the values of imports; or expressing the same tendency in another way, that the value of imported food-stuffs tends to increase, while that of exported tends to decrease.

TABLE 54.

The Average Imported and Exported Food Value, as Percentages of the Total Value of Imports and Exports during Two Decades.

Period.	Living Animals.		Food Articles.	
	Import.	Export.	Import.	Export.
	RUSSIA.			
1890–1900 . . .	·59	2·26	18·68	54·41
1901–1910 . . .	·73	2·19	20·89	59·91
	AUSTRIA-HUNGARY.			
1890–1900 . . .	—	—	19·59	18·43
1901–1910 . . .	—	—	13·43 [1]	13·48
	FRANCE.			
1891–1900 . . .	—	—	27·92	19·77
1901–1910 . . .	—	—	17·67	15·24
	ITALY.			
1891–1900 . . .	—	—	22·49	29·22
1901–1910 . . .	—	—	18·35	26·09
	GERMANY.			
1891–1900 . . .	—	—	34·38	12·96
1901–1910 . . .	—	—	30·93	9·53
	UNITED STATES.[2]			
1901–1905 . . .	—	—	25·16	36·30
1906–1910 . . .	—	—	22·85	27·19
	UNITED KINGDOM.			
			Food, Drink, and Tobacco.	
1901–1905 . . .	—	—	46·0	5·7
1906–1910 . . .	—	—	43·6	5·8

[1] Classification changed.
[2] U.S. Food-stuffs. Cols. I and II.

Expressing the values of the first period, 1890–1900 as 100, and those of the following as percentages of the first one, we see the following relations.

TABLE 55.

Period.	Living Animals.		Food Articles.	
	Import.	Export.	Import.	Export.
Russia.				
1890–1900 . . .	100	100	100	100
1901–1910 . . .	124	97	111	110
Austria-Hungary.				
1890–1900 . . .	—	—	100	100
1901–1910 . . .	—	—	69	73
France.				
1890–1900 . . .	—	—	100	100
1901–1910 . . .	—	—	64	77
Italy.				
1890–1900 . . .	—	—	100	100
1901–1910 . . .	—	—	82	89
Germany.				
1890–1900 . . .	—	—	100	100
1901–1910 . . .	—	—	90	73
United States.				
1901–1905 . . .	—	—	100	100
1906–1910 . . .	—	—	91	75
United Kingdom.				
1901–1905 . . .	—	—	100	100
1906–1910 . . .	—	—	95	101

Russia, which is one of the greatest food producers, shows this tendency quite clearly. The value of imported living animals is increasing, while that of exported is decreasing; the average value of imported food in the two decades is increasing faster than that of exported food; we see therefore that Russia is approaching the state of an importing country.

The United States exhibit the same phenomenon: the average value of the imported food-stuffs in the quinquennium 1906–10 decreased (9 p.c.), but that of the exported decreased more still (25 p.c.); Germany's imports of food-stuffs decreased 10 p.c. in the decade 1901–10, while that of her exports decreased 27 p.c.; the United Kingdom's imported food-stuffs, drink and tobacco decreased in the quinquennial period 1906–10 by 5, from the period of 1901–5, while her exported goods increased 1 p.c.; the reason is because the shipping service is paid by food, a part of which can be re-exported.

Austria-Hungary's imports decreased 31 p.c., and her exports 27 p.c.; it seems as if Austria-Hungary were becoming more self-supporting, which is not the case. The reason is probably that the statistical classification was changed in 1906, and the difference in percentage indicates more a stationary condition.

The same stationary state seems to have existed in Italy, with 18 p.c. decrease in imports and 11 p.c. in exports. Only France is an exceptional country; the value of imported food-stuffs decreased 36 p.c. from 1890–1900 to 1901–10, while that of exports decreased 23 p.c., which indicates an abundance of food. The cause is that France is not an industrial country, and is not on the way to become so, and the artificial limitation of population and the governing policy helped the development of agriculture.[1]

C. *The Disproportionate Rise of Prices.*

So long as the growth of industrial production serves to free the people from dependence on the accidental action of natural forces, and tends to stabilize the conditions of human life, it is most beneficial; as long as it serves to increase the variety and the quality of consumption and to raise the standard of living,

[1] Ogg, pp. 158–211.

it may be beneficial. But as the industrial production serves only to induce people to create all possible products, and to oblige other people to exchange them for the necessaries of life, it may become harmful. And it is harmful if industrialization is going on without any corresponding increase in the agricultural production.

The sequence of this process of the exchange of products, and if besides there are no good agricultural lands to be added to the cultivation, is a disproportionate advance in the prices of agricultural products and of food-stuffs.

Prices [1] move up and down, but not only with the amount of gold produced, although the gold production is one of the most important factors, determining the purchasing power of money.

In methods of business, the number of gold-using countries, the quantity of gold available for currency, and the volume of transactions to be performed in gold-using countries, establish the value of gold, and thereby they influence the prices of commodities. Fluctuations in the prices of individual commodities or of whole groups of commodities may be caused in various countries by tariffs, speculation, and by temporary inflation of credit or other accidental factors.

But such a general tendency to rise in the prices of agricultural productions in all countries, as it will be shown, cannot be explained except by the general state of production and of economic equilibrium in general. The disproportionate diminution of agricultural production must have an effect on the prices of the products, disproportionately raising them. To quote Ch. Gide,[2] " Let us suppose (*a supposition which coincides with the present conditions*) that industry, thanks to the marvellous increase of productive power, throws an enormous quantity of manufactured goods

[1] W. T. Layton, *The Study of Prices*. London, 1914.
[2] *Principles of Political Economy*. 2nd Eng. ed. 1904.

on the market. The result is a general glut. Why? Because agricultural production has not kept pace with manufacturing; it has increased only slightly, and consequently the value of agricultural goods has, compared with the value of manufactured goods, increased." This unequal advance in price is to be attributed to the disproportionate production of primary and secondary goods.

Mr. D. Durand[1] expresses himself similarly: "The general advance of prices has been due primarily to the increased production of gold. The general tendency of wages and salaries to lag behind commodity prices, when the supply of money is augmented, is the source of the much higher cost of living. But no small part of it is due to the fact that the agricultural products have risen faster in price than the other products."

On the Continent there is a general rise of prices from 1895 onwards. In the United States the prices of farm products were in recent years not merely higher than during the 'nineties, but they were the highest, reckoned in gold, ever known, and that was due to the filling up of the United States.

Now, the general disproportionate rise in prices of agricultural products indicates the approach of the time when the balancing action of war is an action of necessity, because it finds a relief in supplementing the industrial activity by geographical expansion.

The following tables show the rise of prices in different groups of commodities in different countries during three periods, 1900–4, 1905–9, and 1910–12 or 1910–11. The average of the index numbers during the period 1900–4 is put as 100, and the following periods are expressed as percentages of that period.[2]

[1] American Statistical Association. 1916. Vol. 15.

[2] Index numbers recalculated from: Cost of Living of the Working Classes. Report of an inquiry by the Board of Trade into working class rents and retail-prices. 1912. Cd. 6955. 1913.

TABLE 56.

Showing the Disproportionate Rise in Wholesale Prices in the United Kingdom from the Period 1900–4.

The Average of the Index Numbers during the Period 1900–1910 = 100

Article.	1900–1904.	1905–1909.	1910–1912.
Coal and metals	100	96	97
Textiles	100	113	126
Corn	100	107	113
Meat, fish, and dairy produce	100	102	111
Whole of Group 3 [1]	100	104	113
Miscellaneous	100	101	113
All forty-seven articles	100	104	113

The raw materials (textiles) show the greatest advance, 25·5 per cent.; the whole of Group 3, food, drink, and tobacco, advanced proportionately to the general advance of prices of all forty-seven articles. Corn in general is at the same level as the food-stuffs and all forty-seven articles; the sub-group, meat, fish and dairy produce, is 2 p.c. below the general level, due mostly to the cheapening of fish.

Germany.—The prices of rye, wheat, and potatoes were in the period 1910–12, 38 p.c. above the level of prices in the quinquennial period 1900–4; they were 7 p.c. higher than those of oxen, pigs, calves, and sheep; 14 p.c. above the prices of cotton and wool; 39 p.c. above the group of metal, and 32 p.c. above the group of coal and petroleum in the same period (Table 57).

Russia.—The prices in the Russian Empire show the same tendency. The highest advance in price was 27 p.c. in 1910–11, in the group of oleaginous products, including linseed, hempseed, sunflower seed, and the oils; then come the animal products with 24 p.c., the textiles with 18 p.c., and the cereals with

[1] Including food, drink, and tobacco.

TABLE 57.

Index Numbers of the Wholesale Prices in Germany, based on the Figures of the Imperial Statistical Office, showing the Disproportionate Advance of Prices in Different Groups of Commodities.

The Average of the Index Numbers in the Quinquennium 1900–4 = 100.

Article.	1900–1904.	1905–1909.	1910–1912.
Rye, wheat, and potatoes .	100	118	138
Oxen, pigs, calves, and sheep	100	118	131
Wool and cotton	100	112	124
Copper and pig-iron . . .	100	99	99
Coal and petroleum . . .	100	98	106

16 p.c. Russia is an agricultural country, and there is no explanation necessary about the relatively slow advance of cereal prices; it seems more that there existed a relative scarcity of animals. The least advance was in the group of colonial (4 p.c.) and mineral products.

The general average rise was 17 p.c. in the period 1910–11, compared with the quinquennium 1900–4. The prices of cereals in the period 1910–11 have gone down if compared with those in 1905–9, but this period includes partly the Russo-Japanese War and the Russian revolution, the effect of which was that the prices of these products went up considerably in two or three years, and this explains the relatively large average of the period. The tendency of the prices in other groups (except cereal and mineral products) is a steady upward movement.

U.S.A.—The prices of farm products, of lumber and building materials, and of food show the greatest advance in the period 1910–11, compared with those in the quinquennium 1900–4. The general average rise was 15 p.c. in the same period, while farm products show a rise of 35 p.c.; lumber and building materials, 28 p.c.; food, 22 p.c.; miscellaneous, 19

TABLE 58.

Showing the Index Numbers of the Wholesale Prices in Russia, and the Disproportionate Rise in Different Groups.

The Average of the Index Numbers in the Quinquennium 1900–4 = 100.

Groups.	1900–1904.	1905–1909.	1910–1911.
Cereal products	100	126	116
Animals	100	119	124
Oleaginous products . . .	100	104	127
Textiles	100	106	118
Mineral products	100	119	114
Dyes and chemicals . . .	100	112	115
Colonial products	100	103	104
General average	100	103	117

p.c.; clothing, 16 p.c. On the contrary the group fuel and lighting shows a decrease of 4 p.c., and metals and implements advanced only 7 p.c., drugs and chemicals 4 p.c., and house furnishings 1 p.c. (see Table 59).

TABLE 59.

Showing the Index Numbers of the Wholesale Prices in U.S.A., and the Disproportionate Growth in Different Groups.

The Average of Index Numbers in the Quinquennium 1900–4 = 100.

Groups.	1900–1904.	1905–1909.	1910–1911.
Farm products	100	111	135
Food	100	110	122
Cloth, clothing	100	113	116
Fuel, lighting	100	100	94
Metals, implements. . . .	100	112	107
Lumber and building materials	100	115	128
Drugs and chemicals . . .	100	98	104
House furnishing goods . .	100	102	101
Miscellaneous	100	109	119
All commodities	100	108	115

Taking the average prices of 1890–9 as 100, we get the following average index numbers for 1912–13.[1]

Groups of Commodities.	Index Numbers.
Farm products, raw or very slightly manufactured	158
Manufactured food from domestic farm products.	142
Other foods (mineral, fish, or imported) . .	101
Clothes and clothing	120
Fuel and lighting	139
Metal and metal products	113
Lumber and building materials	149
Drugs and chemicals	111
House furnishing goods	90
Miscellaneous	118
All commodities.	137

These prices were, as has already been mentioned, not only higher than during the 'nineties, but the highest ever known in the United States.

Austria.—There are no general index numbers of prices for the whole of Austria, but the retail prices in Vienna may be taken as indicating the general course for the whole country. Table 60 shows the index numbers of the retail prices of food, fuel, and of sixteen articles in Vienna.

TABLE 60.

Showing the Index Numbers of Retail Prices in Vienna, and the Disproportionate Growth in Different Groups.

The Average of Index Numbers in the Quinquennium of 1900–4 = 100.

Groups of Commodities.	1900–1904.	1905–1909.	1910–1912.
Flour, bread, and potatoes .	100	120	137
Beef, veal, pork, and bacon .	100	115	137
General index numbers, including petroleum and coal (sixteen articles)	100	111	125
General index numbers, excluding petroleum and coal. .	100	113	127

[1] Dana Durand. **Amer. Stat. Assoc.**, 1916, p. 134.

So the advance in prices of vegetable and animal food was the same (37 p.c.), while the rise in prices for the whole group, including sixteen articles, was 12 p.c. less (25 p.c.), and for fourteen articles, excluding fuel, only 10 p.c. less.

Hungary.—The average cost of food rose 29 p.c. between the quinquennium 1900–4 and the years 1910–11, while the increase in the cost of food, fuel, and lighting was only 26 p.c., as is shown in the following table.

TABLE 61.

Showing the Index Numbers of Retail Prices of Food, Drink, and Lighting Materials in Hungary, and the Disproportionate Rise in Different Groups.

The Average of Index Numbers in the Quinquennium 1900–4 = 100.

Period.	Food, Drink, Fuel, and Lighting Materials.	Food only.
1900–4	100	100
1905–9	119	120
1910–11	126	129

Japan.—The average rise in prices of food, drink and tobacco was 26 p.c. higher in the period 1910–11 than in the quinquennium 1900–4; the price of clothing and textiles was 25 p.c. higher; and that of minerals, fuel, timber, and manufactured articles was 17 p.c. higher: the general average rise being 23 p.c.

TABLE 62.

Showing Index Numbers of the Wholesale Prices in Japan, and the Disproportionate Rise in Different Groups.

The Average of Index Numbers in the Quinquennium 1900–4 = 100.

Groups of Commodities.	1900–1904.	1905–1909.	1910–1911.
Food, drink, and tobacco	100	125	126
Clothing and textiles	100	120	125
Minerals, fuel, timber, and manufactured articles	100	112	119
General average	100	119	123

Canada.—The course of the wholesale prices in Canada exhibits the same disproportionate rise in the prices of agricultural articles, if compared with other groups. The rise in price for grains and fodder was 29 p.c.; for animals and meat, 39 p.c.; while for textiles it was only 13 p.c.; for metals, 1 p.c.; for fuel and lighting, 2 p.c.; and for drugs and chemicals, 8 p.c., from the level of the quinquennium 1900–4 to the years 1910–12. The general average rise was 17 p.c. So the rise in the prices of agricultural products was more than double, yet Canada is an agricultural exporting country.

TABLE 63.

Showing the Index Numbers of Wholesale Prices in Canada, and the Disproportionate Rise in Price for Different Groups.

The Average of Index Numbers in the Quinquennium 1900–4 = 100.

Groups of Commodities.	1900–1904.	1905–1909.	1910–1912.
Grains and fodder	100	124	139
Animals and meat	100	117	139
Textiles	100	112	113
Metals and implements	100	106	101
Fuel and lighting	100	101	102
Drugs and chemicals	100	102	108
General index numbers	100	110	117

XIII

THE LIMITS OF EXTENSIVE CULTIVATION AND OF GEOGRAPHICAL EXPANSION

A. *The Wheat Yield per Acre.*

THE phenomena considered in the two preceding chapters, the disproportionate rate of increase in the production of primary and secondary goods and the slackening of commerce in food-stuffs, point to the fact that the production of agricultural commodities did not proceed at a rate which could be called intensive cultivation.

Examining the wheat yield per acre in the European countries, we see that the greatest advance in the yield in the last three decades happened in Holland and in Germany (25 in 1891–1900 and 32 bushels in 1901–10), and this seems to indicate a great step forward to intensive culture. But some other countries in Europe already reached the same yield, as the United Kingdom, 32; Belgium, 35; Switzerland, 33; and Denmark, 35, in 1901–10. They advanced more because their previous standard was high, with the possible exception of Denmark.[1]

But the general European average wheat yield per acre did not advance much during the three decades 1881–90, 1891–1900, and 1901–10. Only in the last decade it was raised by 1 bushel per acre. The average wheat yield per acre in 1901–10 was 14 bushels, while in the previous decade it was 13 bushels.

The greatest wheat producers had the following

[1] J. F. Unstead, "Stat. Study of Wheat Cultivation and Trade, 1881–1910." *The Geographical Journal*, 1913, Appendix.

increase in yield per acre in the last decade 1901–10: Russia, 2; United States, 1; France, 2; India, 1 (probably); Italy, 2; Hungary (with Austria), 1; Argentine, 0; Germany, 4; Spain, 3 (probably); and Canada, 1 bushel. The increase in the wheat yield per acre in the decade 1901–10 from the level of the previous decade was 2 bushels in France, the United Kingdom, Austria-Hungary, Italy, Belgium, Switzerland, and Russia.

Now it is quite true that there is a great difference between the amounts of Russia and the other countries. But the methods of Russian agriculture are purely extensive, while the methods of industrial countries are said to be intensive, yet the relative advance is the same; perhaps it is reasonable to expect a greater increase in yield from industrial countries than from the agricultural communities. The average yield of the second wheat producers, the United States, is still less, only 1, while the chief prospective South American source of wheat supply shows no increase at all. Canada, one of the chief prospective sources of wheat supply, increased her yield by 1; Africa by 2; Australasia by 3 bushels, but her yield decreased in the previous decade 1891–1900, so there was really a rise of only 1 bushel per acre.

To sum up: the greatest two wheat producers and the chief prospective sources of the world wheat supply show an increase of 1 bushel per acre during the decade 1901–10 from the level of 1891–1900, and that is the average of the whole world. This proves that the wheat production, and perhaps that of cereals in general, is more or less stationary, or that the increase in amounts is obtained chiefly by the extensive cultivation of the soil.

B. *The Limits of Extensive Cultivation.*

Extensive cultivation has its limits. The products of primary economic importance compete with each other, and the increase in the production of one brings a decrease in the production of another. Animals and cereals have this sort of relation to each other: the increase in production of cereals by means of extensive cultivation brings a decrease of pasture for animals, and therefore a diminution of their number. The productive area in each country is limited by geological and geographic features, which can hardly be changed substantially. The productive land is divided into arable, meadows and pastures, vineyards, gardens and orchards, land for other sorts of culture, forests and marshes, heaths and uncultivated soil. Among these divisions, arable land, meadows and pastures, and forests, are the chief components of the productive land, and they occupy the greatest percentage of the whole productive area. Arable land serves for cereal growing; meadows and pastures for animal growing, and forest land for getting fuel and timber, and for a general regulation of the rainfall. The proportion among these three chief divisions in European countries seems to be fairly fixed; on the average the arable land forms about 50 p.c. (47·7 exactly), meadows and pastures, 21 p.c. (20·6), and forest land 22 (21·6) p.c. Or their relation may be roughly fixed as 2½, 1, and 1. We have seen in the preceding lines that animal (cattle) growing is in decline, and lagging behind the growth of population or production of cereals. Supposing now, as there is a tendency to a meat diet, that the people of European countries decide to raise the number of animals: it could be done either by the reduction of arable or forest land, as the percentages of the other divisions of the productive land are either small, or they could not be used for animal growing, as marshes, heaths, and uncultivated land. But a diminution in the area of arable land would proportionately diminish the cereal crops, and that again partly the human and animal food. A diminution of the area of forest land would endanger the course of rainfalls, and therefore the production of cereals.

Arable land forms the following percentages of the total productive area: 37·7 in Austria, 50·4 in Germany, 55·6 in Belgium, 53·8 in Bulgaria, 47·8 in France, 26·8 in the United Kingdom, 45·6 in Hungary, 51·9 in Italy, and 60·2 in Rumania; or the average of the nine European countries is 47·7.

Meadows and pasture land form the following percentages of the total productive area: 25·4 in Austria, 16·9 in Germany, 15·2 in Belgium, 5·1 in Bulgaria, 20·2 in France, 43·4 in the United Kingdom, 22·9 in Hungary, 21·2 in Italy, and 15·1 in Rumania; or the general average of nine countries is 20·6 p.c.

Forest land forms the following percentages of the total productive area: 34·7 in Austria, 27·4 in Germany, 20·6 in Belgium, 39·8 in Bulgaria, 18·8 in France, 4·6 in the United Kingdom, 28·8 in Hungary, 17·3 in Italy, and 22·9 in Rumania; or the general average is 21·6 (Table 64).

Arable land was 31·4 p.c. of the total productive area in Canada, 62·6 in British India, and only 8·3 in the Argentine. Meadows and pastures formed 17·8 p.c. in Canada, and 72·0 p.c. of the total productive area in the Argentine.

Forests were 26·5 p.c. in Canada, 17·5 p.c. in British India, and 19·4 p.c. of the total productive area in the Argentine.

We could therefore expect an increase of arable land in the Argentine by a diminution of meadows and pastures without any danger to the raising of animals.

The distribution of the productive area among different usages in Canada does not leave a big margin for a great change; it seems that the percentage of forest area can be diminished, and that the marshes, heaths, and uncultivated soil give a possibility for an increase in either animal or cereal growing. There is also a possibility of diminution of forest area in Austria, Bulgaria, and Hungary, but it is a question whether this land is suitable for arable land or for other purposes. The division of marshes, heaths, and uncultivated land is exceptionally high in the United Kingdom, Canada, and British India. It is probably a miscalculation for the United Kingdom. There does not seem to be much land available from this division which would be suitable for productive purposes, without a great investment of labour and capital.

If we examine further the use of arable land (Table 65) for different sorts of cultivation, we shall notice that the cereal crops occupy on the average 60 p.c. in twelve countries, and that the cereal-exporting countries are exporting only because their percentage of arable land used for cereal crops is exceptionally high. In Hungary it is 72·7 p.c.; in Rumania, 83·9 p.c.; in Bulgaria, 65·4 p.c.; in Canada, 58 p.c.; in British India, 54·8 p.c., and in the Argentine, 52·9 p.c. of the total area of arable land.

So Canada is approaching the average percentage, while British India and the Argentine are under the average. The remaining 40 p.c. of the average total

TABLE 64.

Productive Land according to Usage as Percentages of Total Area.

Country.	Arable Land.	Meadows and Pasture.	Vine-yards.	Gardens and Orch-ards.	Other Cul-tures.	Forest Land.	Marshes, Heaths, and Uncult. Soil.
Austria . . .	37·7	25·4	·8	1·2	·1	34·7	4·1
Germany . .	50·4	16·9	·3	·9	—	27·4	4·1
Belgium . .	55·6	15·2	—	1·8	·2	20·6	6·5
Bulgaria . .	53·8	5·1	1·1	·3	—	39·8	—
France . . .	47·6	20·2	3·4	·1	2·2	18·8	7·7
U.K. . . .	26·8	43·4	—	·4	·1	4·6	24·7
Hungary . .	45·6	22·9	1·1	1·4	·2	28·8	—
Italy . . .	51·9	21·2	3·3	2·4		17·3	3·9
Rumania . .	60·2	15·1	·9	1·0	—	22·9	—
Canada . . .	31·4	17·8	—	·6	—	26·5	23·8
British India .	62·6	—	—	·9	1·0	17·5	24·7
Argentine . .	8·3	72·0	—	—	·3	19·4	—

TABLE 65.

Arable Land according to Crop Cultures as Percentages of Total Arable Area.

Country.	Cereals.	Grass Land and Forage.	Other Cultures.
Austria	62·8	14·3	23·0
Germany	56·8	14·8	28·4
Belgium	55·9	17·0	27·1
Bulgaria	65·4	12·6	21·9
France	57·6	21·5	20·9
U.K.	44·4	43·7	11·9
Hungary	72·7	10·8	16·5
Italy	53·3	18·3	28·4
Rumania	83·9	0·9	15·1
Canada	56·0	34·3	7·7
British India	54·8	1·6	43·6
Argentine	52·9	37·8	9·3

arable land is nearly equally divided among grass land and forage (18·9) and other cultures (21·1 p.c.). So we get a general proportion of cereal crops, grass land, and other cultures as 3, 2, and 2.

Supposing there were a diminution of other crops or grass land, in order to increase the cereal crops, that would either diminish the already decreasing meat supply (and wool supply), or it would cause a diminution in the variety of foods, or a shortage in commercial crops. Grass land could be diminished in Great Britain and Canada, but in the case of Great Britain it would lower the already decreasing meat supply, and in the case of Canada it would require more population. A diminution of other crops in India would lower the supply of rice in the whole world, and rice is a food of importance for the Indians themselves.

As the margin of the productive land which could be used for other than arable purposes is small, and cannot be shifted without a proportionate lowering of the production of other agricultural goods, so also the margin of arable land which could be used for other purposes than to raise cereal crops is very small, and cannot be increased without a decrease of other goods, in extensive cultivation.

Therefore the distribution of the productive and arable land among different cultures is such as not to permit an increase of one kind of culture without diminishing the others, with very few exceptions. The proportions of the two chief food articles, the cultivation of cereals and the raising of animals, do not seem to allow much alteration in the arable area, without endangering the already diminished supply of animals. So extensive cultivation is reaching its limits.

C. *The Geographical Limits.*

In the above lines no reference was made to the situation of the United States, but the following lines of E. Dana Durand [1] on the geographical limits of agricultural production will help to clear the point: "At the beginning of the nineteenth century, a large part of the fertile temperate regions of the earth was still virtually unoccupied. Discovery and improvement in transportation brought enormous rich areas suddenly into the service of the European stock. Hundreds of millions of acres of excellent land in the United States, in Canada, in the Argentine, and elsewhere were brought into cultivation by European settlers and their descendants. This new land was for the most part quite as productive as the best of Europe itself. Geographical expansion of agricultural production for a long time involved no descent to inferior lands with consequent diminishing returns to labour" (p. 130). Considering the remaining undeveloped territories, we find the largest areas in the United States, Canada, and Siberia.

[1] "Some Problems of Population Growth." Amer, Stat. Assoc., vol. 13 1916, pp. 129–148.

"First of all, the United States. Only one-fourth of the total area of this country is under cultivation, and less than half is in farms at all. Nevertheless, the unused or slightly used lands are either permanently deficient in some of the qualities essential to the best agricultural results, or they require great investment of capital to make them satisfactory agents of production. In fact such geographical extension of agriculture as has taken place in this country in the last decade or two has for the most part been under distinctly unfavourable conditions. From 1901–10, 64,000,000 acres were added to the improved farm land of the United States, plus an increase of 15 p.c. of this total; 54,000,000, or fully five-sixths, were west of the ninety-fifth meridian, that is, west of the first tier of states on the farther side of the Mississippi River. The great bulk of this new uncultivated land was in fact west of the hundredth meridian. That meridian marks substantially the limit of normal humidity. West of it, irrigation or dry farming is in most cases necessary to make land productive. Irrigation, save in a few favoured localities, requires very heavy investment of capital; the results of more recent projects have not been altogether encouraging. Dry farming gives far less yield per acre per year, and usually less production per man than farming under conditions of normal rainfall. The increase of our agricultural production through geographical extension during recent years has been accomplished only at increasing unit cost. Much is expected of the enormous area of Canada. Great areas in the West and in the North of that country can unquestionably be brought under cultivation. But in much of this territory the rainfall is not sufficient to assure the regular production of good crops and in most of it the cold is a serious handicap, both to production and to the comfortable living. The life of the farmer in a region where for months the days are exceedingly short and the cold intense, can hardly be considered a thing of joy. Even more unfavourable are the conditions in the vast unsettled area of Siberia.

"Turning to the Southern hemisphere, we find great proportions of Argentina, of South Africa, and of Australia are cursed with drought. In fact, it is evident that were there anywhere in the temperate regions large areas of good land still available for settlement, the people of the United States would scarcely be extending their agriculture into regions so ineligible as those where lie the greater part of recent additions to our own cultivated area."

From whatever side we examine, whether from the view of the distribution of the use of productive land or of the arable land, we see that the margin or percentage of the available land, which could be used for increasing the general production of primary goods is relatively small, and that a proportionate increase of one kind of products cannot be done without endangering or diminishing the production of other component or connected or subsidiary branches of production.

For example, there is perhaps a relatively large percentage of arable land which could be used for increasing the cereal crops, but that is impossible without a compensatory diminution of the raising of animals.

The margin of available land free to use does not seem therefore to be great, if the land is cultivated extensively, and this extensive cultivation of land is approaching its limits, as is clear from the consideration of the geographical limits.

Mr. W. Thompson [1] comes to the same conclusion, although starting from another basis: "The conditions which made possible the unprecedented expansion of the European peoples in the last fifty years are passing away. The agricultural development which came as a result of rapid transportation, the invention of labour-saving farm machinery, and the

[1] *Population*, p. 130.

abundance of new and fertile land cannot be duplicated. The system of transportation can be greatly improved, but no revolution such as came with the development of the steam engine seems likely to take place. The efficiency of agricultural implements will probably be greatly increased, but they have already reached the limit of practicability for extensive farming, not because the implements might not be improved upon, but because the days of extensive farming are rapidly passing as the new countries become more thickly settled. Fertile land is no longer to be had for the asking in the unlimited states and will soon be taken up in other places where Europeans can thrive."

Although the conclusion that the day of extensive farming is passing or has passed is correct, yet it does not seem to me that there is anything to be regretted. The point is that extensive farming has to be either substituted by intensive cultivation, or as intensive cultivation is an effect of the disproportionate production of primary and secondary goods, the disproportion may be removed either by a proportionate increase in the production of primary goods or by a proportionate decrease in the production of secondary goods. In each case the actions of the economic forces tend to balance each other and to make the economic equilibrium more stable. In the latter case, war partly checks the transformation of extensive cultivation into intensive, but it balances the proportions by raising the production of primary goods and by lowering the production of secondary goods. We have already observed the latter similar phenomenon while considering the post-war effects in consumption; the rise in the production of primary goods we have to treat later on.

D. *The Meaning of Supplementary Area.*

Can the rate of increase in the production of secondary goods go on without a proportionate rise in the production of primary goods? Or to put the question in another form, can the exchange of manufactured articles be on a firm basis when the production of food and raw materials is lagging behind?

The exchange could probably be continued for a long time, and the above disproportion would only influence the rate of exchange, that is the price, which would go down disproportionately. Besides this influence on exchange, the disproportionate production inevitably leads to a state where the economic equilibrium of the communities themselves and of the whole world becomes unstable. For though the manufactured articles may be exchanged for manufactured commodities between industrial communities, this cannot be done in the case of exchange between an industrial and an agricultural community, when the exchange must be only on the basis of raw materials and food for manufactured articles. But as the primary goods are not increasing at the same rate as the secondary goods, the exchange is getting more difficult, and the industrial communities are giving away their products, not because of their generosity, but because they have to do it in order to bring some profits. Besides this, many services, as shipping commerce, are paid by the agricultural communities by goods, or booked in as debts, and that increases the capital which wants investment, and finds it in industrial processes, or commerce. So in any case the production of primary goods is not growing at the same rate as the production of secondary goods, and the economic equilibrium of the industrial communities becomes more unstable. We have seen in a previous chapter that the stabilization of consumption is carried out by lowering it, and that the ascending pre-war phase of consumption is balanced by a descending phase. That is the peculiarity of economic equilibrium, if we look from the standpoint of the individual. We have considered the stabilization of the rate of natural growth, which increases after war; but the post-war increase is partly balanced by a pre-war descending phase, and partly by actual losses through war.

Now the stabilization in the production of secondary goods may be carried out by supplementing the industrial area by areas of production of primary goods, and the balancing action of such supplementary areas is sure to render the economic equilibrium of production in industrial communities more stable, if they are under the complete political as well as the economic domination of the industrial areas. This may be done most effectively by conquest and war.

Therefore if we look at the exchange of products, or commerce, from the point of view of the colonies themselves, and determine the share in colonial trade which falls to the industrial mother country, we find that it constitutes a very considerable part of the total trade of the colony, bound to be done with the industrial country. Thus,[1] 30 p.c. of the trade of Indo-China, 83·7 p.c. of the trade of Algeria, and 57·9 p.c. of that of Tunis is with France. Great Britain had 52 p.c. of the trade of British Guiana, 62 p.c. in Natal, 44 p.c. in Canada (33 p.c. of imports, 55 p.c. of exports), 69·5 p.c. in Australia, and 53 p.c. in India. To Germany belonged 70 p.c. of the trade of South-West Africa. The proportion of French trade to the total in Indo-China has risen from 16 p.c. in 1890 to 30 p.c. in 1899.

These percentages were probably not changed, and they clearly indicate this function of the supplementary areas of industrial communities. Besides this, the colonies actually relieve the mother country from the pressure of population by giving opportunity for emigration.

But the primary function of the supplementary areas is to stabilize the economic equilibrium in the production of secondary and primary goods, by supple-

[1] P. S. Reinsch, *Colonial Government*, p. 63. New York, 1902.

menting the area of production of secondary goods by areas of production of primary goods.

Supposing the production of primary commodities kept the rate of increase of the population in industrial communities, this fact still would not mean stability of equilibrium, because the growth of consumption at the same time may have disturbed it. So in Germany the population increased during the nineteenth century 135 p.c., while wheat and rye production increased 136·7 p.c. Now, this illustrates that the economic equilibrium during the whole century was in a stable position. But considering the shorter periods, the disturbed state of economic equilibrium may arise not only from the disproportionate growth of population and production, but from the disproportionate increase of consumption.

The great problem of the industrial communities is not only the problem of finding markets for their surplus manufactures, but at the same time to find food to feed their population, and raw materials to feed their industries. The standard of living is not stationary, but rising, and the demand for food is increasing while the supply is decreasing. And as the population grows and industrialization progresses, other countries must one by one be added to the ranks of those dependent on the outside world. And so, " when enough nations have come to rely on the outside world for means of subsistence, there will be no outside world." [2]

" A nation that is primarily devoted to manufactures and that can maintain its standard of living only by exporting them, largely in exchange for food and materials, naturally seeks to secure itself exclusive sources of supply, or, in the common phrase, exclusive markets for its products."

" It is all but inevitable that this industrial and commercial struggle should result in war." [3]

[1] J. Rybark, *Die Steigerung der Productivität der deutschen Landwirtschaft.* Mitt. der Landwirt. Inst. der Kgl., Univ. Breslau, vols. 3–4, pp. 459–514.

[2] Dana Durand, pp. 139–140. [3] Dana Durand, pp. 139–40.

XIV

THE WAR EFFECTS ON THE PRODUCTION OF PRIMARY GOODS

THE production of primary commodities is more dependent on the as yet but partly known course of natural phenomena; on account of their complexity they cannot be so easily handled as the mechanical, electrical and chemical forces employed in industrial processes. A scientific production of primary commodities and a complete knowledge of all the biological, meteorological, and other phenomena is far more difficult than an invention and utilization of new mechanical and electrical engines.

It is therefore necessary to simplify the economic phenomena, and for this reason the average yield of the crops and the crops in general are a less convenient measure of economic considerations than the area utilized for this purpose. The average yield of crops may be due to the improvement of the agricultural methods of cultivation, but the yearly fluctuations indicate more the influence of the natural forces, the course of which is not subdued to the human will.

Therefore the area sown indicates more clearly the trend of economic phenomena, for thus a lot of unknown influence of natural factors can be eliminated.

This method shall be used for arguing in favour of the war-equilibrium theory in the following lines. In preceding chapters, I said that the stabilization of the economic equilibrium of an industrial area requires a supplementary area of production of primary commodities, and that this is due to the disproportionate growth in the production of primary and secondary economic goods.

During war, the struggle for supplementary areas is still undecided, and the industrial or semi-industrial countries which are fighting have to supplement the production of the primary goods in their own territories. Now this could be carried out either by an intensive or extensive cultivation of the soil (as far as the cereals are concerned). Intensive cultivation is impossible on account of the lack of human labour, which is employed in making war, and on the contrary the cultivation becomes worse, or the yield per acre diminishes during war. So extensive cultivation is used to supplement the primary production, and that means an increase in the area sown with cereals and wheat.

This increase may be caused by interruption of communications during the war and be only temporary, but probably a part of it will be of lasting effect in several countries.

The increase may be due partly to the loss caused by invasion of the territories of a belligerent party, and the effect is again of a temporary character.

And lastly, this increase may be due to the lack of human labour, which effects a loss in intensive cultivation, and this loss is balanced by the use of a larger area; the yield per acre is less during the war, because the work done is of inferior quality, and the methods of cultivation are less expert. So the yield per hectare diminished in France during the Franco-Prussian War; it was 15·34 quintals in 1869–70; it fell to 10·78 in 1871, and then rose again.[1]

In the winning country, the effect of getting supplementary areas (won by war) is that the area used for the production of primary commodities in the country decreases, because it is supplemented by a

[1] M. Block, vol. 2.

new area. In the losing country the area for production of primary goods increases, for the supplementing cannot be carried out in new areas.

South African War.

This view is confirmed by the index numbers showing the fluctuations of the areas sown with wheat and other cereals. If the area in the year 1900 = 100, and the subsequent years are expressed as percentages of this year, we see the following fluctuations in the area of cereals in the United Kingdom.

TABLE 66.[1]

Showing the Index Numbers of the Cereal Area in U.K.

Article.	1901.	1902.	1903.	1904.	1905.
Wheat	100	101·5	92·8	80·6	105·2
Barley	100	97·3	94·5	93·7	87·5
Oats	100	101·0	103·5	105·0	100·5

So the wheat area increased during the war; it was 100 in 1901, and 101·5 in 1902, but after the conclusion of peace it fell to 92·8 in 1903, and to 80·6 in 1904. The barley area fell in 1902, probably due to the time of sowing (the war was concluded in May), to 97·3, to 94·5 in 1903, to 93·7 in 1904, and to 87·5 in 1905. The oats area increased during 1903 and 1904, but the following years suggest a stationary state (100·5 in 1905, 100·6 in 1906, 102·5 in 1907, 101·8 in 1908, and 98·1 in 1909).

Russo-Japanese War, 1904–5.

The fluctuations of the cereal area in Russia and Japan confirm the view of supplementary areas. Table 67 shows the fluctuations of the cereal area in Russia and Japan, with the same base (1901 = 100).

[1] Int. Agric. Inst., Rome. *Ann. Int. de Stat. Agricol.*, 1910.

TABLE 67.[1]

Country.	Article.	1901.	1902.	1903.	1904.	1905.	1906.	1907.	1908.
Russia, Europe	Wheat	100	102·3	105·4	109·6	114·8	118·2	110·8	110·3
,, Asia .	,,	100	93·3	105·6	102·4	111·6	106·8	124·6	140·2
Average		100	97·8	105·5	106·0	113·2	112·5	122·7	125·2
,, Europe	Rye	100	100·2	99·7	98·4	101·4	100·1	96·0	97·2
,, ,,	Barley	100	101·7	107·8	112·3	113·0	112·2	115·9	124·4
,, ,,	Oats	100	98·4	99·4	101·1	101·8	102·6	100·8	100·4
Japan . .	Wheat	100	99·4	96·4	94·1	93·1	90·9	91·1	92·3
,, . .	Barley	100	99·4	100·0	101·0	102·6	103·1	101·8	100·3

Russia's wheat area increased from 1901 to 1903 5·5 p.c., while during the war 1904–5 it increased 13·2 p.c. ; in the post-war years, 1906, 1907, and 1908, the increase was slow for the first year, but considerable in 1907 (10 p.c. above the previous year). The fluctuations in European Russia's wheat area are more significant in some respects than those of Russia as a whole, including the Asiatic provinces. Her wheat area increased during the three pre-war years by 5·4 p.c., while during the war period it increased nearly 10 p.c. above the level of the pre-war year 1903, and in the first post-war year it increased 6 p.c.

The rye area suggests a more stationary state ; it fluctuated slightly in the pre-war years (100 in 1901, 100·2 in 1902, and 99·7 in 1903) ; it fell slightly (to 98·4) in the first war year 1904, but rose to 101·4 in the second war year 1905 ; in the post-war period it fell beneath the level of the previous years. That is probably due to the fact that rye, as a food article, is on the way to be replaced by wheat, and the slight fall is due to this competition of commodities. The barley area in Russia increased during the three pre-war years, 1901–3, by 7·8 p.c. ; in the second war year it increased 13 p.c. from the level in 1901 ; it fell in the first post-war year, but rose in the second and third more than 10 p.c. above the level of the war area.

[1] *Ann. Int. de Stat. Agricole,* 1910.

An increase is noticeable in the oats area during the war period (98·4 in 1902, and 99·4 in 1903); it rose in the first post-war year to 102·6, and afterwards it is more stationary.

Russia was the losing party, so her area of cereals, according to the theory, should increase in the post-war period; but Japan being the winning party, her area should decrease, or at least remain stationary.

Now Japan's wheat area exhibits clearly a diminution in the post-war period; it fluctuated as follows: 100 in 1900, 99·4 in 1901, 96·4 in 1902 (pre-war period); 94·1 in 1904, 93 in 1905 (war period); 90·9 in 1906, 91·1 in 1907, 92·3 in 1908.

So the after-war decrease is clearly pronounced; it decreased already during the war and pre-war periods, probably due to the industrialization of the country. The barley area was stationary during the pre-war years (100, 99·4, 100); it increased slightly during the war (101 and 102·6); it is nearly equal in the first post-war year 1906 to that in 1905, and then it declines (101·8 and 100·3 in 1903).

So taking into account all possible counteracting causes, the fluctuations of the area of cereals in Russia and Japan may be said to be in accordance with the above theory.

The World War, 1914.

The wheat area before the beginning and during the World War indicates the same phenomena.

The most marked increase in the wheat area was in the United Kingdom, the most advanced of the industrial countries. The average wheat area in 1909–13 was 764,000 hectares; it increased in 1914 to 771,000 hectares, in 1915 to 944,000 hectares, and it decreased in 1916 to 830,000 hectares, due probably to the lack of labour. But, according to Sir Henry Rew,[1] the increase of the wheat acreage in 1917 was

[1] Sir H. Rew, "The Prospects of the World's Food Supplies after the War." *Journ. R. Stat. Soc.*, Jan., 1918.

198,000 acres, compared with that in 1914. The arable land increased 238,000 acres, and the oats acreage 836,000 acres, while the barley acreage decreased 76,000 acres in 1917, compared with the year 1914. Potato acreage increased 156,000 acres; cattle increased 158,000 in number; sheep and pigs show a decrease in number of 193,000 and 954,000.

The decrease of the barley area is due partly to the fact that the oats area increased enormously; the numbers of sheep and cattle may be due to the compensatory action of the general increase in acreage, and to the high demands of the army.

Although there was a general increase in the arable land in the United Kingdom during the World War, the yield per acre decreased for almost all crops, so the action of the increase in area is partly annihilated, and the general effect must be a proportionate decrease in consumption.

Sir Henry Rew also states that the yield per acre in England and Wales decreased in 1915-17, compared with the years 1905-14: for wheat, 2·6; for barley, 2·9; for oats, 1·4; for beans, 5·3; for peas, 3·2 bushels; only the seed-hay yield per acre increased slightly (0·1 tons). The same phenomenon of decrease of yield per acre is to be observed in the yield of wheat, barley, and seed-hay in Scotland; beans show a slight increase of 0·2 bushels, and oats of 1·4 bushels.

According to Sir H. Rew, these figures tend to support the assumption "which is *a priori* probable, that the fertility of the soil is being reduced under the stress of war conditions." It seems to me more likely that the diminution of the yield per acre is due to the lack of human labour and brain, and to the more careless methods of cultivation and dearth of fertilizers, and that it is not connected with the fertility of the soil itself.

The wheat area [1] of France decreased, because of the invaded territories; the average wheat area in

[1] *Notes of Int. Stat. Inst.* Rome, 1917.

1909–13 was 6,540,000 hectares; in 1914, 6,060,000 hectares; in 1915, 5,967,000 hectares. The same is true of Austria because of the invasion of Galicia and Bukovina during the first years of the war. The area in 1909–13 was 1,219,000 hectares; in 1914, 670,000 hectares. Hungary, on the contrary, shows an increase in area from 3,674,000 hectares in 1909–13 (or 3,433,000 in 1913) to 3,790,000 in 1914. The wheat area of Germany increased also during the first year of war, from 1,930,000 hectares in 1909–13 to 1,996,000 hectares in 1914; for other years no data are available.

A considerable increase in the wheat area took place in the first war year (1914) in Rumania. It rose from 1,623,000 hectares in 1913 to 2,112,000 hectares in 1914. Russia increased her wheat area in 1914 and 1915, although her territories were partly invaded. It was 24,772,000 hectares in 1909–13, 25,118,000 hectares in 1913, 25,392,000 hectares in 1914, and 24,487,000 hectares in 1915. In 1915 she lost her Polish provinces and therefore the area decreased to 20,542,000 hectares in 1916. The increase of wheat area in Asiatic Russia was remarkable; the average area was 3,853,000 hectares in 1909–13; 5,002,000 in 1913; 5,511,000 in 1914; and 5,881,000 hectares in 1915. Canada's was 4,262,000 in 1910–13, 4,518,000 in 1913; 4,166,000 in 1914; and 5,255,000 in 1915. The peculiarity of the fluctuations of Canada's wheat area is a slight decrease in 1914 and then an upward movement in 1915, but in 1916 it decreased, due to the lack of labour.

The increase in the world's wheat area from 1913 to 1914 was only 1,428,000 hectares, while in the following year (1914–15) it was 5,925,000 hectares, although the wheat area of Germany and Austria-Hungary is not correctly stated.[1] This increase is due mostly to the action taken by the countries to produce their own wheat supply, or to counterbalance the previous imports. In other terms it is due to the lack of supple-

[1] *Notes of Inter. Agricult. Inst.* 1917. (See Appendix.)

mentary areas, and that brings a tendency to self-support, and thereby stabilizes the economic equilibrium which was disturbed owing to the lack of supplementary areas.

It may be argued, and it is partly true, that this general increase is due to the supposition that part of the supply will be destroyed or annihilated or made useless by the war action of the belligerents, and therefore to the increased demand, and that this is the source of the increased area sown with wheat. This reasoning is partly correct, yet it cannot be denied that the increased wheat area in the industrial communities is due to the wish of these countries to be self-supporting, and this tendency, although it is not possible to separate it from other factors, is surely effective in raising the wheat area.

We could say that the increase in the wheat area in industrial countries is due to the vertical competition of the productive branches, and therefore to the tendency to stabilize the economic equilibrium, and that the increase of the wheat area in agricultural countries, if not directly concerned in the war, is due to partly horizontal and partly vertical competition of the same products.

XV

GENERAL SUMMARY

THE aim of this essay was to find out a possible statistical connexion between the state of economic phenomena in a community and an approaching war.

It was supposed that the readjustment of political power through war is connected with a readjustment of economic forces also. Therefore it seemed to be possible to apply the idea of the balancing of forces to the pre-war and post-war economic phenomena. The idea of balancing of forces implies a state of equilibrium, and in this case a pre-war unstable state of equilibrium.

This state of unstable equilibrium, shown in the pre-war economic phenomena in a modern community and connected with an approaching state of war, was called war equilibrium.

It was further supposed that the relations between the pre-war economic phenomena and the war are not exactly of causal nature, but that they are more loosely dependent on each other, that is of functional nature.

It was further stated that the instability of the pre-war economic equilibrium had a resemblance to the partial chemical equilibrium, indicating a possibility to profound changes, through war, and the after-war economic situation had its resemblance to a complete chemical or a stable statistical equilibrium.

Therefore the meaning of war is a stabilization of economic phenomena.

In this connexion it was shown how the idea of equilibrium was used in economics by various authors, and in connexion with various economic phenomena.

The relation between the economic phenomena and war during the past development of the human race was shortly treated; it was shown during the hunting, pastoral, and agricultural stages in Greek and Roman history, and during the Middle Ages. Then it was shown how the origin of modern wars was explained, and why the law of diminishing returns could not be accepted as the source of modern wars, but that their cause is in the state of general economic equilibrium, that is the state of the distributive, consumptive, productive and vital economic situation.

The distributive forces in modern communities effect a continuous accumulation of capital, and this pushes the whole productive forces to a disproportionate production of primary and secondary economic goods in these communities. Besides, the accumulated capital drives the agricultural communities to industrialization, and therefore the disproportion between the production of primary and secondary goods becomes more and more pronounced.

While the productive forces of modern communities are directed to an intensive production of secondary goods, the growth of consumption is extending to primary and secondary goods at the same time.

Besides this, the growth of the population is of importance. Now, in order that a population may grow continuously, and that its consumption and its standard of living may rise continuously, it is necessary that the production of all the goods should increase at the same rate in the industrial communities, or at least in the world's production. But that is not the case; the production of secondary goods does not go at the rate of increase of the growth of population and consumption, nor at the rate of increase in the production of primary goods. The production of primary goods lags behind the rate of increase in the production of secondary goods, and it just covers the rate of the growth of consumption, but it depresses the rate of natural growth.

The effect of this is an instability of the economic equilibrium in modern industrial communities, requiring from time to time a *stabilization*, by means of war.

As the population grows and as the consumption rises, the population cannot satisfy all its wants, on account of the difficulties in production, but a struggle has to arise in which a decision is carried out in favour of diminishing the size of families, and that means a diminution of the rate of natural increase. As the rate of natural increase diminishes, the standard of living and the consumption per head rises. Now if there is a steady and continuous decline in the rate of the natural growth of population, and a steady rise of consumption, war is probably approaching.

This is indicated particularly if a pressure on the pre-war consumption is shown ; this pressure on consumption is indicated chiefly by a diminished average of amounts consumed in the period just preceding the war, if compared with the period before.

Before the actual outbreak of war, we see in the modern communities the following pre-war phenomena :

(1) A declining phase of the rate of natural growth.

(2) An ascending phase of consumption, with a pressure on consumption in the period just preceding the war.

As the balancing of forces begins to operate through war, we notice during and chiefly after war the following phenomena :

(1) An ascending phase of the rate of natural growth.

(2) A declining phase of consumption.

All these phenomena have been statistically investigated in Chapters VI and IX, and their connexion with the general economic situation and their interrelation in Chapters V and VII. A survey of the comparative growth of consumption in the chief modern communities was given in Chapter VIII ;

that was done by means of comparative index numbers of consumption, constructed on a similar base.

But these pre-war phenomena of the natural growth of population and of rise in consumption are not the only ones representative for a war situation.

The phenomena of production in the industrial communities and in the world are significant for a war situation too. The disturbed state of the world's economic equilibrium has its source in the general and cumulative disproportionate production of primary and secondary goods, or in other terms in the production of necessaries of life (agricultural and partly raw materials) and of industrial products. The actual disproportion in the rate of increase in the production of primary and secondary goods was statistically demonstrated for the whole world, and for the chief primary and secondary articles during the last three years and the last pre-war decade (Chapter X).

It was found, generally speaking, that the rate of the production of secondary goods is twice as great as that of primary ones.

It was shown further how the disproportion in the growth of population and the production of primary goods is progressing in the chief modern communities. As the effects of this disproportionate production are cumulative, a slackening of commerce in food-stuffs is inevitable, and that was stated to be the case if we compare the relative average value of food-stuffs, imported or exported, with the total value of imports and exports during the last two decades preceding the World War.

A further effect of the disproportionate production of primary and secondary goods is a disproportionate rise in the prices of food-stuffs, compared with that of industrial products, and this was illustrated for the recent decade preceding the World War by means of comparative index numbers of prices.

Intensive production of secondary goods leads to extensive cultivation and production of primary goods in the world and in the agricultural communities. There seems to exist a certain amount of intensive production of primary goods in the industrial communities, but the relative progress in the industrial and agricultural communities does not vary very much, as is shown by the progress in the wheat yield during the last three decades. Examining the conditions of extensive cultivation in the chief modern communities, we found that the distribution of the productive area and of arable land into different uses is such that it leaves a very small margin for shifting and extending one kind of culture without endangering the other cultures, subsidiary or component branches. So an increase in cereal production could be effected in all the modern communities, but it would inevitably lead to a decline in animal raising, and as consumption in modern communities is progressing towards a meat diet, a diminution of pasture and grass land would bring a decline in animal raising and therefore a lowering of the standard of living in these communities. The conditions of extensive cultivation in the chief agricultural communities are such that they approach the limit of being just self-supporting, as in the United States; or that there is a rise in cereals, but a decline in animal raising, as in Russia; or that an increase in crops is effected by an extension of area, but with a diminution of yield, as in the Argentine; or that they are under very unfavourable climatic conditions, as Canada and Siberia; or that they are small producers, as Australia and New Zealand.

Taking all these facts into account, our conclusion is that the limit of extensive cultivation in modern communities is reached. That seems to be proved by examining the wheat yield per acre in the world and in particular countries. The wheat yield in the world's production advanced in the last pre-war decade, compared with the previous one (1901–9 and 1891–1900) by 1 bushel, and this rise in the wheat yield is one step to intensive culture.

As regards extensive cultivation and war equilibrium, the meaning of war for industrial communities is to supplement their area of production of secondary goods by an area of production of primary goods. So war is effecting a prolongation of extensive cultivation and a delay to intensive cultivation.

As the supplementing of an area of production of secondary goods by an area of production of primary goods is partly checked or made impossible by a war, we see that during war the industrial communities try to supplement their production from their own soil, and that means an increase in the cereal area. This was statistically demonstrated for some wars (Russo-Japanese, South African, World War).

As the industrialization of modern communities advances, the supplementary areas become scarcer, and it is more difficult to subdue them without touching the interests of other industrial communities, and therefore a world-wide conflagration is approaching, and it came in 1914.

The effects of this war will last longer and they will be of greater intensity. A lowered standard of living will last for a longer time and on a greater scale; an after-war rise of the rate of natural growth will be steadier, particularly for the winning communities; and a stabilization of economic equilibrium will be effected, which may last for a half or a whole century.

XVI

BIBLIOGRAPHY

Aftalion, A. . . Les Crises Périodiques des Surproductions. Vol. 2. Paris, 1913.

Annual Stat. Abstract to the Members of the British Iron Trade Association. London, 1903.

Annuario Statistico Italiano. 1878–1913. Roma.

Apelt, Kurt . . Die Konsumption der Wichtigsten Kulturländer in den Letzten Jahrzehnten. Berlin, 1899.

Atkinson, E., and Reinold, A. W. Canot's Elementary Treatise on Physics. 18th edition, 1910.

Baines, J. A. . . The Recent Growth of Population in Western Europe. *Journ. R. Stat. Soc.*, 1909, pp. 685–713.

Bateman, A., and Fountain, H. The Import and Export Statistics of Various Countries. *Bull. de l'Inst. Int. de Stat.*, Tome 15, 2ième livre, pp. 219–239. London, 1906.

Bateman, A. E. . Comparability of Trade Statistics of Various Countries. *Bull. de l'Inst. Int. de Stat.*, Tome 12, pp. 313–322. Kristiania, 1900.

Bernard, Fr. . . Capital (Econ. Rurale). *Nouveau Dict. d'Econ. Pol.*, pp. 320–322. Paris, 1891.

" " . . Agriculture. *Nouveau Dict. d'Econ.*, *Pol.* vol. 1, pp. 38–44. Paris, 1891.

Block, M. . . Statistique de la France. 2nd edition. Paris, 1875.

" " . . L'Europe Pol. et Sociale. Paris, 1892.

Board of Trade . Statistical Tables and Charts relating to British and Foreign Trade and Industry (1854–1908), Cd. 4954. 1909.

" " " . Cost of Living of the Working Classes. Cd. 6955. 1913.

" " " . Stat. Abst. for the Principal and other Foreign Countries. 39 Numbers. 1860–1912.

Board of Trade . Stat. Abstract for the United Kingdom. 61 Numbers. 1840–1913.

" " " . Stat. Abstract for Colonies. 49 Numbers. 1850–1912.

Bowley, A. L. . Elements of Statistics. 3rd edition. London, 1917.

" " . The Nature and Purpose of the Measurement of Social Phenomena. London, 1915.

" " . National Progress in Wealth and Trade since 1882. London, 1904.

Brentano, L. . . The Doctrine of Malthus and the Increase of Population during the Last Decades. *The Economic Journal*, vol. 20, pp. 371–393. London, 1910.

Cannan, E. . . Wealth. 2nd edition. London, 1916.

" " . . A Study in Malthusianism. *The Economic Journal*, vol. 26, pp. 218–222. London, 1916.

Carver, Th. N. . Sociology and Social Progress. Boston, Mass., 1905.

Cauderlier, G.. . Les Lois de la Population et leur Application à la Belgique. Bruxelles, 1899.

Comité Central de Statistique du Ministère de l'Intérieur de Russie. 1863–1913, Recueil Jubilaire. 1913.

Comité Central de Statistique. Annuaire Stat. de Russie, 1904–1914. Petrograd.

Conrad, J., Elster, L., Lexis, W., Loening, Edg. Handwörterbuch der Staatswissenschaften. 3rd ed. 1909.

Cragie, P. G. . . Comparative International Statistics of Agriculture. *Bull. de l'Inst. Int. de Stat.*, Tome 11, pp. 417–423. 1899.

" " . . International Comparisons of Cattle and Sheep on the Surface Areas and with Reference to the Population of Certain Countries Thirty Years Ago and at the Present Time. *Bull. de l'Inst. Int. de Stat.*, Tome 12, pp. 325–333. Kristiania, 1900.

Crookes, W.. . . The Wheat Problem. London, 1917.

Dana Durand, E.. Some Problems of Population Growth. *Quarterly Publication of the American Statistical Association*, vol. 15, pp. 129–148. Boston, 1916.

Department of Commerce and Labour. Bureau of the Census. A Century of Population Growth, 1790–1900. Washington, 1909.

Department of Commerce. Bureau of Foreign and Domestic Service. Stat. Abst. of the United States. Numbers 1–39. No. 39. Washington, 1916.

Eversley, Lord . The Decline in Number of Agricultural Labourers in Great Britain. *Journ. R. Stat. Soc.* 1907.

Furlan, V. . . Wirtschaftsgleichgewicht. *Handwört. der Staatswiss.*, vol. 8, pp. 825–831. Jena, 1910.

Gerlach, O. . . Fleischkonsum und Fleischpreise. *Handwört. der Staatswiss.*, vol. 4, pp. 353–368. Jena, 1909.

Gide, Ch. . . . Principles of Political Economy, translated by C. W. A. Veditz. 2nd edition. London, Norwood, Mass., 1904.

Giffen, R. . . . Essays in Finance. 2nd vol., 5th edition. 1890.

" " . . . Some Economic Aspects of the War. *The Economic Journal,* vol. 10, pp. 194–207. London, 1900.

Guyot, Yves . . Les Ressources et les Besoins dans le Monde. *Journ. de la Soc. de Stat. de Paris.* 58 Numbers. Nos. 8, 9.

Hibbard . . . Paris, 1917.

Hibbard, B. H. . The Decline in Rural Population. *Quart. Publ. of the Amer. Stat. Assoc.*, vol. 13, pp. 85–95. 1912–13.

Hirst, F. W. . . The Political Economy of War. London, 1916.

Hobson, C. K. . The Export of Capital. London, 1914.

Hodges, H. R. . Economic Conditions, 1815 and 1914. London, 1916.

Hooker, R. H. . The Meat Supply of the United Kingdom. *Journ. R. Stat. Soc.*, 1909, pp. 309–376.

" " . Is the Birth-rate Still Falling? *Transactions of the Manchester Stat. Soc* Session 1897–8. Manchester.

Huckert . . . Zur Geschichte und Statistik des Fleischkonsums in Deutschland. *Zeitschrift für Sozialwissenschaft,* 3. Berlin, 1900.

Institut International d'Agriculture. *Annuaire Internationale de Stat. Agricole,* 1910, 1913–14, and 1915–16. Rome, 1912–1915–1917.

International Institute of Agriculture. Bureau of Statistics. *Stat. Notes on the Cereals.* No. 4, Oct. 1916. No. 6, Dec. 1917, Rome.

Ironmonger, The . Metal Market Year-Book. London, 1917.

Jennings, H. S. . Behaviour of the Lower Organisms. Col. Univ. Biol. Series 10. New York, 1906.

Jevons, W. S. . The Theory of Political Economy. 4th edition. 1911.

Juraschek, Fr. . Übersichten der Weltwirtschaft. 6 Jahrg. 1878.

Kais. Stat. Amt. . Stat. Jahrbuch für das deutsche Reich. No. 39. 1880–1914. Berlin.

Kgl. Stat. Bureau in Berlin. Preussische Statistik. Vol. 30. Berlin, 1875.

K.K. Stat. Zentralkommission. Das Getreide im Weltverkehre. Vienna, 1905.

Kitchin, J. . . . Trade Cycles Chart. 3rd edition. 1917.

Kovalevsky, M. M. Le Régime Econ. de la Russie. Paris, 1898.

Layton, W. T. . An Introduction to the Study of Prices. London, 1914.

Levasseur, E. . La Population Française. Vol. 3. 1889–1892. Paris.

Lexis, W. . . . Die Allegemeinen Verhältnisse des Konsumption. *Handw. der Staatswiss*, vol. 6, pp. 117–123. Jena, 1910.

List, Fr. . . . The National System of Political Economy. London, 1904.

Mallet, B. . . . Vital Statistics affected by the War. *Journ. of the R. Stat. Soc.*, Jan. 1918.

Marshall, A. . . Principles of Economics. 6th edition. London, 1910.

Mayo-Smith, R. . Science of Statistics. (1) Statistics and Sociology, 1895. (2) Statistics and Economics, 1899. New York.

Mendeleef, D. . The Principles of Chemistry. Vol. 2. 1905.

Merritt, E. . . The Agricultural Element in the Population. *Quart. Publ. of the Amer. Stat. Assoc.*, vol. 15, pp. 50–57. Boston, 1916.

Merton, H. R. and Co. Comparative Statistics of Lead, Copper, Tin, and Spelter. London, 1903–14.

Metalgesellschaft und Metallurgische Gesellschaft. 12th Ann. Issue. Comparative Statistics of Lead, Spelter, Tin. Frankfort-on-the-Main, 1905.

Mill, J. S. . . Principles of Political Economy. Vol. 2. 1871.

Morley, H. F., and Muir, M. M. P. Watt's Dictionary of Chemistry. Vol. 4. 1888.

Mortara, G. . . Sintomi Statistici delle Condizioni Economiche d'Italia. *Giornale degli Econ. e Rivista di Statistici*, vol. 48, 1st sem., pp. 81–108. Roma, 1914.

Newsholme, A. . The Elements of Vital Statistics. London, 1889.

Newsholme, A., and Stevenson, T. H. C. The Decline of Human Fertility in the United Kingdom and other Countries as shown by Corrected Birth-rates. *Journ. R. Stat. Soc.*, 1906, pp. 34–87.

Nitti, Fr. S. . . Population and the Social System. London, 1894.

North, S. N. . . National Association of Wool Manufacturers. Boston, 1892.

Of, Ch. . . . The Mineral Industry during 1911. Vol. 20. New York, 1912.

Ogg, F. Au. . . Economic Development of Modern Europe. New York, 1917.

Palgrave, R. H. I. Dictionary of Political Economy. Vol. 3. 1908.

Patten, J. S. N. . The Consumption of Wealth. Publ. of Univ. of Pennsylvania. Philadelphia, 1889.

,, ,, . Dynamic Economics. Publ. of Univ. of Pennsylvania. Philadelphia, 1891.

Peacock, N. . . The Russian Year-Book, 1910–1916. London.

Pierson, N. G. . Principles of Economics. Vols. 1 and 2.

Porter, G. R., Hirst, F. W. The Progress of the Nation. London, 1912.

Price, L. L. . . Some Economic Consequences of the South African War. *The Econ. Journ.*, vol. 10, pp. 323–339. London, 1900.

Production and Consumption of Meat and Milk. Reports from the Committee appointed to Inquire into the Statistics, etc. *Journ. R. Stat. Soc.*, 1903 and 1904 (2nd and 3rd rep.).

Prothero, R. E. . English Farming, Past and Present. London, 1917.

Registrar-General 78th Annual Report (1915). London.

Reinsch, P. S. . Colonial Government. The Citizen's Library. 1902.

Rew, R. H. . . Observations on the Production and Consumption of Meat and Dairy Products. *Journ. R. Stat. Soc.*, 1904, pp. 413–427.

,, ,, . . The Prospects of the World's Food Supplies after the War. *Journ. R. Stat. Soc.*, Jan., 1918.

Rybark, J. . . Die Steigerung der Productivität der Deutschen Landwirtschaft. *Un. Vratislensis.* Vol. 3. 1905.

Say, L., and Chailley, J. Nouveau Dict. d'Economie Pol. Vol. 2. 1892.

Seligman, E. R. A. The Economic Interpretation of History. Col. Un. Press. New York, 1902.

Shepperson, A. B. Cotton Facts. New York, 1904.

Sombart, W. . . Der Moderne Kapitalismus. 2nd edition. München, Leipzig, 1916.

Statistique Générale de la France. Min. du Travail et de la Prévoyance Sociale. Ann. Stat. 1913 and 1914–15. Paris.

Statistique Internationale du Mouvement de la Population. Vol. 2. 1901–12. Min. du Travail et de la Prévoyance Sociale. Stat. Générale de la France.

Statistik in Deutschland. Vol. 2. 1911.

Statistisches Jahrbuch für das Deutsche Reich. 1870–1914.

Tait, P. G., and Thompson, W. Treatise on Natural Philosophy. 1877.

Taussig, F. W. . Principles of Economics. 2nd edition. Vol. 2. New York, 1915.

Thompson, W. S.. Population, A Study in Malthusianism. *Columbia Sudies in History,* etc. Vol. 153. 1915.

Tugan-Baranovsky, M. Les Crises Industrielles en Angleterre. Paris, 1913.

Unstead, J. F. . Statistical Study of Wheat Cultivation and Trade. *The Geographical Journal,* 1913. Vol. 42. Aug., Sept.

Vandervelde, E. . L'Exode Rurale et le Retour aux Champs. Paris, 1903.

Van Dyke Robinson, E. War and Economics. Carver's *Sociology and Social Progress*, pp. 134–174. 1905.

Watkins, J. L. . King Cotton; an Historical and Statistical Review, 1790–1908. New York, 1908.

Weber, A. F. . . The Growth of Cities. *Studies in History, Economics, and Public Law of Columbia University.* Vol. 11. 1899.

Willcox, W. F. . The Nature and Significance of the Changes in the Birth- and Death-rates in Recent Years, pp. 1–15. *Quart. Publ. of the American Stat. Assoc.* Vol. 15. Boston, 1916.

Wolfe, A. B. . . Economic Conditions and the Birth-rate after War. *Journ. of Pol. Econ.,* vol. 25, pp. 521–541. 1917.

Wood, G. H. . . Some Statistics Relating to Working Class Progress since 1860. *Journ. R. Stat. Soc.,* 1899, pp. 639–666.

Yule, Udny G. . On the Changes in the Marriage- and Birth-rates in England and Wales during the Past Half Century. *Journ. R. Stat. Soc.,* pp. 83–132. London, 1906.

Zeitschrift des Kgl. Preuss. Bureau. Jahrg. 1863.

APPENDIX

TABLE I

THE RATES OF NATURAL INCREASE IN SOME COUNTRIES PER 1,000 INHABITANTS.[1]

Year.	United Kingdom.	England and Wales.	France.	Germany.	Italy.	Austria.	Hungary.	Belgium.	Japan.	Rumania.
1896	12·1	12·5	2·5	15·5	10·8	11·6	11·5	11·6	8·6	—
1897	11·4	12·2	2·8	14·7	12·9	11·7	11·8	11·9	10·6	—
1898	10·1	11·8	·9	15·6	10·6	11·2	9·7	11·0	10·9	10·2
1899	10·3	10·9	·8	14·4	12·0	11·6	12·1	10·0	10·5	14·3
1900	9·8	10·7	–·6	13·6	9·2	11·8	12·4	9·7	11·3	14·6
1901	10·9	11·6	1·9	15·1	10·5	12·7	12·4	12·3	12·8	13·1
1902	11·5	12·2	2·1	15·6	11·2	12·4	11·8	11·1	12·0	11·3
1903	12·2	13·0	1·8	13·9	9·3	11·4	10·7	10·5	12·0	15·4
1904	11·1	11·7	1·5	14·5	11·7	11·9	12·4	10·3	9·4	15·7
1905	11·5	12·0	1·0	13·2	10·6	8·8	7·9	9·7	8·7	15·6
1906	11·3	11·7	·6	14·9	11·1	12·5	11·4	9·3	9·3	16·0
1907	10·8	11·4	1·5	14·2	10·6	11·4	11·0	9·5	12·2	15·0
1908	11·3	11·9	1·2	14·0	10·8	11·2	11·7	8·4	12·8	13·0
1909	10·7	11·1	·4	13·8	11·6	10·5	12·1	7·9	12·3	13·9
1910	11·0	11·6	1·8	13·6	13·3	11·3	12·1	8·5	12·8	14·6
1911	9·6	9·8	1·1	11·3	10·1	9·5	9·9	8·5	13·7	17·3
1912	10·2	10·5	1·5	12·7	14·2	10·8	13·0	7·8	13·4	20·5
1913	—	10·2	1·3	12·5	13·5	—	—	—	13·6	—
1914	—	9·7	–1·6	—	13·2	—	—	—	—	—
1915	—	6·8	—	—	—	—	—	—	—	—
1916	—	7·6	—	—	—	—	—	—	—	—

[1] Stat. Abst. for Foreign Countries, different years; *Stat. Int. du Mouvement de la Population*, and the original Abstracts and Census of the respective countries.

TABLE II

THE RATE OF NATURAL INCREASE IN RUSSIA PER 1,000 INHABITANTS.[1]

1871	12·6	1881	14·6	1891	14·2	1901	15·8
1872	8·6	1882	10·9	1892	15·1	1902	17·6
1873	15·5	1883	12·9	1893	13·9	1903	18·1
1874	16·0	1884	12·9	1894	14·7	1904	18·6
1875	16·7	1885	16·3	1895	14·4	1905	13·7
1876	15·7	1886	15·3	1896	16·9	1906	17·0
1877	15·1	1887	15·3	1897	18·1	1907	18·5
1878	9·1	1888	17·6	1898	15·5	1908	16·3
1879	15·2	1889	14·3	1899	18·0	1909	15·1
1880	13·4	1890	12·5	1900	18·3		

[1] 1863–1913. *Recueil Jubilaire du Comité Central de Statistique du Ministères de l'Intérieur.* 1913.

TABLE III

NATURAL INCREASE OF POPULATION IN SERBIA AND BULGARIA PER 1,000 INHABITANTS.

Years.	Serbia.	Bulgaria.	Years.	Serbia.	Bulgaria.	Years.	Serbia.	Bulgaria.
1862	11·9	—	**1880**	8·2	—	1898	12·2	16·3
1863	7·9	—	1881	21·0	17·3	1899	15·0	15·9
1864	13·8	—	1882	21·3	17·6	**1900**	18·9	19·7
1865	21·2	—	1883	24·2	18·7	1901	17·0	14·4
1866	21·4	—	1884	22·6	21·3	1902	15·8	15·0
1867	19·1	—	1885	19·7	20·9	1903	17·4	18·3
1868	13·0	—	1886	12·4	13·4	1904	18·4	21·2
1869	15·5	—	1887	21·4	20·2	1905	12·5	21·7
1870	11·6	—	1888	21·3	19·5	1906	17·5	21·7
1871	10·8	—	1889	18·6	18·2	1907	17·6	21·3
1872	7·0	—	**1890**	15·0	14·0	1908	13·1	16·4
1873	9·8	—	1891	18·5	12·4	1909	19·4	14·0
1874	5·3	—	1892	18·9	4·4	**1910**	16·6	—
1875	14·5	—	1893	12·8	7·4	1911	14·5	18·8
1876	−6·7	—	1894	14·4	10·6	1912	17·0	—
1877	−0·6	—	1895	17·1	17·1	1913	—	—
1878	4·7	—	1896	14·2	16·9	1914	—	—
1879	8·1	—	1897	16·1	16·3	1915	—	—

TABLE IV

NATURAL INCREASE OF POPULATION IN PRUSSIA AND FRANCE PER 1,000 INHABITANTS.[1]

Years.	Prussia.	France.	Years.	Prussia.	France.
1851	13·8	4·8	1866	5·2	3·2
1852	16·9	4·2	1867	12·7	3·7
1853	8·2	4·8	1868	9·5	1·6
1854	8·6	−1·9	1869	11·8	2·2
1855	4·0	−1·0	**1870**	11·1	−2·9
1856	8·6	3·2	1871	5·0	−12·2
1857	10·4	2·2	1872	10·4	4·7
1858	12·0	2·6	1873	11·6	2·7
1859	14·2	1·1	1874	14·3	4·8
1860	14·9	1·8	1875	14·1	2·9
1861	12·3	3·7	1876	15·2	3·6
1862	13·4	3·8	1877	14·3	3·9
1863	13·4	4·4	1878	13·0	2·7
1864	13·4	3·9	1879	14·3	2·6
1865	12·1	2·2	**1880**	12·3	1·7

[1] *Stat. Internat. du Mouvement de la Population jusqu'en* 1905, p. 391.

TABLE V

CONSUMPTION OF WHEAT IN FRANCE PER HEAD OF POPULATIONS.[1]

Years.	Hecto-litres.	Years.	Hecto-litres.	Years.	Hecto-litres.	Years.	Hecto-litres.
1827	1·78	1849	2·47	1871	2·30	1893	2·89
1828	1·87	**1850**	2·35	1872	3·38	1894	3·62
1829	2·04	1851	2·27	1873	2·36	1895	3·28
1830	1·69	1852	2·34	1874	3·88	1896	3·17
1831	1·76	1853	1·87	1875	2·69	1897	2·43
1832	2·48	1854	2·83	1876	2·60	1898	3·98
1833	2·00	1855	2·12	1877	2·69	1899	3·32
1834	2·02	1856	2·59	1878	3·04	**1900**	2·99
1835	2·15	1857	3·14	1879	2·91	1901	2·82
1836	2·01	1858	2·90	**1880**	3·37	1902	3·06
1837	2·01	1859	2·21	1881	3·03	1903	3·39
1838	1·87	**1860**	2·67	1882	3·70	1904	2·81
1839	1·92	1861	2·34	1883	3·11	1905	3·25
1840	2·43	1862	2·80	1884	3·39	1906	3·02
1841	2·07	1863	3·14	1885	3·12	1907	3·50
1842	2·06	1864	2·90	1886	3·06	1908	2·86
1843	2·17	1865	2·40	1887	3·62	1909	3·21
1844	2·42	1866	2·08	1888	2·98	**1910**	2·51
1845	2·05	1867	2·40	1889	3·23	1911	3·53
1846	1·85	1868	3·32	**1890**	3·42	1912	3·22
1847	3·03	1869	2·84	1891	2·73	1913	3·38
1848	2·46	**1870**	—	1892	3·53		

[1] *Annuaire Stat.*, vol. 33, 1913.

TABLE VI
CONSUMPTION OF SOME COMMODITIES IN FRANCE.

Years.	Potatoes.	Sugar.	Wine.	Alcohol.	Beer.	Tea.	Coffee.	Cocoa.
	Quintals.	Kg.	L.	L.	L.	Kg.	Kg.	Kg.
1830	—	—	44	1·12	9·2	—	—	—
1831	1·00	2·3	65	1·09	9·3	·003	·253	·020
1832	1·16	2·1	78	1·13	8·8	·005	·319	·016
1833	1·72	2·1	118	1·17	9·3	·003	·285	·027
1834	1·75	2·6	112	1·13	10·3	·004	·329	·028
1835	1·64	2·9	76	1·10	10·2	·004	·311	·031
1836	1·84	2·8	89	1·14	11·1	·004	·333	·033
1837	1·71	3·3	109	1·22	11·6	·003	·372	·042
1838	2·07	3·0	68	1·39	12·0	·003	·358	·037
1839	1·90	2·9	74	1·50	12·7	·002	·357	·038
1840	2·28	3·1	77	1·55	9·5	·004	·422	·042
1841	2·61	2·9	94	1·49	12·2	·005	·378	·048
1842	2·06	3·3	96	1·61	13·3	·006	·438	·045
1843	2·27	3·1	57	1·64	12·2	·004	·419	·048
1844	2·56	3·4	80	1·78	13·0	·004	·446	·052
1845	1·68	3·3	81	1·81	13·4	·004	·451	·051
1846	1·68	3·6	88	1·70	14·1	·005	·476	·049
1847	2·13	3·7	149	1·72	11·6	·004	·473	·060
1848	1·86	2·7	141	1·58	10·2	·003	·418	·043
1849	1·86	3·4	95	1·57	10·6	·009	·510	·058
1850	1·58	3·2	121	1·47	11·4	·003	·431	·056
1851	1·47	3·2	104	1·74	12·4	·004	·520	·058
1852	1·33	3·7	73	1·81	12·6	·006	·600	·071
1853	1·28	4·0	56	1·80	14·0	·004	·553	·083
1854	1·45	4·2	27	1·68	13·7	·005	·598	·098
1855	2·00	4·4	105	2·00	16·2	·005	·741	·120
1856	1·69	4·5	56	2·13	17·8	·005	·641	·109
1857	2·12	4·7	96	2·29	19·5	·006	·770	·087
1858	2·27	5·6	144	2·34	18·7	·007	·776	·105
1859	1·93	5·3	75	2·28	18·3	·008	·829	·104
1860	1·82	5·5	103	2·27	18·0	·007	·938	·121
1861	1·86	6·4	75	2·23	18·2	·006	1·003	·129
1862	2·34	6·5	94	2·30	18·9	·008	1·005	·127
1863	2·34	6·7	131	2·33	18·7	·007	1·051	·139
1864	2·22	5·5	128	2·33	19·1	·008	1·067	·142
1865	2·40	6·2	174	2·34	20·2	·008	1·143	·150
1866	1·92	7·1	159	2·53	21·2	·010	1·176	·165
1867	2·07	7·1	96	2·47	18·4	·008	1·235	·172
1868	2·79	6·1	130	2·55	19·2	·008	1·364	·191
1869	2·44	7·3	175	2·63	19·7	·008	1·310	·207
1870	2·44	5·8	135	2·32	17·8	·010	1·977	·308
1871	2·33	7·8	148	2·81	19·1	·007	1·109	·221

TABLE VI—*continued.*

Years.	Potatoes.	Sugar.	Wine.	Alcohol.	Beer.	Tea.	Coffee.	Cocoa.
	Quintals.	Kg.	L.	L.	L.	Kg.	Kg.	Kg.
1872	2·28	5·1	131	2·09	20·5	·006	·462	·092
1873	2·48	6·9	89	2·59	21·1	·007	1·233	·203
1874	3·00	6·3	166	2·69	20·7	·008	1·059	·205
1875	2·50	7·2	219	2·82	20·7	·009	1·307	·238
1876	2·30	7·2	106	2·71	21·3	·009	1·451	·270
1877	2·40	6·9	146	2·79	21·7	·010	1·289	·256
1878	2·21	7·2	128	2·98	21·2	·009	1·452	·265
1879	2·03	7·5	69	3·22	20·5	·011	1·520	·266
1880	2·75	8·6	92	3·64	22·9	·011	1·540	·289
1881	2·66	10·0	105	3·31	24·0	·012	1·719	·328
1882	2·40	10·8	95	3·85	23·0	·012	1·692	·311
1883	2·67	10·6	112	3·96	23·8	·013	1·802	·343
1884	2·80	10·9	106	3·98	23·2	·004	1·786	·323
1885	2·93	11·2	90	3·86	21·8	·012	1·793	·325
1886	2·93	11·5	87	3·53	21·6	·014	1·865	·327
1887	3·04	11·7	89	3·84	22·0	·014	1·669	·332
1888	2·68	11·3	105	3·87	21·2	·013	1·775	·322
1889	2·76	10·7	82	4·00	22·3	·014	1·700	·336
1890	2·85	11·9	94	4·35	22·5	·016	1·769	·369
1891	2·86	11·8	106	4·37	22·0	·016	1·829	·375
1892	3·49	12·3	97	4·56	23·7	·017	1·874	·379
1893	3·06	11·0	143	4·32	23·6	·018	1·798	·371
1894	3·31	11·8	110	4·04	22·3	·018	1·817	·386
1895	3·33	12·1	83	4·07	23·2	·019	1·881	·395
1896	3·34	10·7	133	4·19	23·5	·020	1·952	·410
1897	2·90	10·4	98	4·28	24·0	·020	2·005	·418
1898	3·03	11·0	100	4·70	24·7	·021	2·050	·449
1899	3·16	11·3	140	4·59	26·8	·023	2·102	·455
1900	3·13	11·7	180	4·66	27·7	·028	2·119	·451
1901	3·14	10·9	153	3·52	26·9	·021	2·216	·471
1902	2·83	11·8	108	3·26	26·8	·024	2·263	·500
1903	2·93	13·5	100	3·54	28·1	·026	2·860	·532
1904	3·08	15·1	182	3·89	26·6	·028	2·951	·555
1905	3·59	13·6	152	3·57	27·4	·027	2·321	·554
1906	2·55	14·8	142	3·56	29·6	·029	2·492	·596
1907	3·51	14·9	176	3·31	29·0	·029	2·584	·590
1908	4·26	15·2	166	3·44	30·0	·028	2·608	·517
1909	4·17	15·6	148	3·46	28·9	·031	2·737	·586
1910	2·16	15·8	87	3·59	31·0	·031	2·828	·627
1911	3·26	17·5	133	4·04	36·3	·033	2·805	·689
1912	3·69	16·8	168	3·86	32·0	·032	2·810	·679
1913	3·29	16·8	126	3·93	32·4	·030	2·910	·700

TABLE VII

AVERAGE CONSUMPTION OF COMMODITIES IN GERMANY.[1]

		1871–1880.	1881–1890.	1891–1900.	1901–1910.	1911–1913.
Cotton, raw .	kg.	2·85	3·76	5·24	6·39	7·18
Jute . . .	kg.	·235	·935	1·63	2·17	2·2[illegible]5
Rice . . .	kg.	1·60	1·78	2·44	2·45	2·9
Tea . . .	kg.	·025	·035	·05	·055	·06
Coffee. . .	kg.	2·30	2·41	2·55	2·99	2·58
Cocoa. . .	kg.	·05	·08	·22	·475	·78
Groceries. .	kg.	·11	·13	·155	·17	·16
Fruits, tropical	kg.	·64	·895	1·68	2·845	4·35
Sugar. . .	kg.	5·9	7·7	11·05	16·0	16·3
Tobacco .	kg.	1·75	1·45	1·55	1·57	1·60
Beer . . .	L.	88·3	96·7	107·5	108·1	103·5
Spirits . .	L.	4·5	4·97	5·8	6·16	5·3
Wheat . .	lb.	—	134·0[2]	169·0	200·0	—
Rye . . .	lb.	—	307.0[3]	351·0	364·0	—
Wool . . .	lb.	3·75	5·45	7·1	6·2[4]	—

[1] Calculated from *Stat. Jahrbucher*, Stat. Abst. for Foreign Countries.

[2] The periods are 1880–9, 1890–9, and 1900–8 respectively.

[3] According to German official sources the consumption was 118 kgs. from 1881–90, 134 kgs. from 1891–1900, 146 kgs. from 1900–10, and 145·15 kgs. from 1911–13.

[4] 1900–1908.

TABLE VIII

THE GROWTH OF CONSUMPTION OF SOME COMMODITIES IN GERMANY FROM 1836–1910, PER HEAD OF POPULATION.[1]

Years.	Cotton, Raw.	Groceries.	Coffee, Raw.	Cocoa, Raw.	Rice.	Tropical. Fruits.	Tea.	Jute.	Sugar.
	Kg.	Kg.	Kg.	Kg.	Kg.	Kg.	Kg.	Kg.	Kg.
1836–40	·34	·05	1·01	·01	·18	·06	·004	—	—
1841–5	·47	·07	1·25	·01	·33	·07	·004	—	—
1846–50	·53	·07	1·34	·02	·43	·06	·01	—	—
1851–5	·85	·07	1·57	·02	·87	·06	·02	—	—
1856–60	1·39	·08	1·79	·02	·99	·07	·02	—	—
1861–5	1·33	·09	1·87	·03	·85	·09	·02	—	—
1866–70	1·81	·09	2·20	·03	1·11	·41	·02	·06	—
1871–5	2·84	·10	2·27	·05	1·55	·57	·02	·15	6·0
1876–80	2·86	·12	2·33	·05	1·66	·61	·03	·32	5·8
1881–5	3·34	·12	2·44	·06	1·81	·75	·03	·66	7·0
1886–90	4·19	·14	2·38	·10	1·76	1·04	·04	1·21	8·4
1891–5	4·95	·15	2·41	·16	2·49	1·39	·05	1·56	10·6
1896–00	5·54	·16	2·69	·28	2·39	1·98	·05	1·71	11·5
1901–5	6·15	·16	3·00	·38	2·33	2·54	·05	2·04	14·4
1906–10	6·64	·18	2·99	·57	2·58	3·15	·06	2·31	17·6

[1] *Stat. Jahrbuch. für d. Deutsch. Reich.* 1914.

TABLE IX

PER CAPITA AVERAGE CONSUMPTION OF COMMODITIES IN U.S.A.

	1871–1880.	1881–1890.	1891–1900.	1901–1910.	1911–1916.
Wheat . bush.	5·20	5·43	4·67	6·41	—
Coffee . . lb.	7·25	8·59	9·41	10·98 (1900-1908)	9·82
Cotton . lb.	14·45	18·3	21·4	26·3	—
Rice . . lb.	1·67	2·53	2·30	6·19	7·96
Sugar . . lb.	39·17	48·59	63·15	74·59	83·44 [1]
Tea . . lb.	1·33	1·35	1·265	1·009	·99
Wool . . lb.	5·45	6·6	6·4	—	—
Wine . . galls.	·47	·48	·40	·555	·52
Spirits . . galls.	1·39	1·34	1·38	1·41	1·40
Beer . . galls.	6·93	11·38	15·34	18·63	10·60
Indian corn .	25·61	27·99	24·89	28·62	—

[1] Four years only: 1911, 1912, 1913, 1914.

TABLE X

CONSUMPTION OF COMMODITIES IN U.S.A.

Sugar *per Capita*, lb.

Year	lb.	Year	lb.	Year	lb.
1865 . .	18·17 lb.	1882 . .	40·82 lb.	1899 . .	61·98 lb.
1866 . .	28·45 lb.	1883 . .	45·20 lb.	**1900** . .	58·91 lb.
1867 . .	24·30 lb.	1884 . .	54·18 lb.	1901 . .	71·96 lb.
1868 . .	31·24 lb.	1885 . .	47·87 lb.	1902 . .	63·35 lb.
1869 . .	35·19 lb.	1886 . .	49·09 lb.	1903 . .	78·92 lb.
1870 . .	32·73 lb.	1887 . .	53·26 lb.	1904 . .	68·66 lb.
1871 . .	36·47 lb.	1888 . .	50·29 lb.	1905 . .	71·66 lb.
1872 . .	40·64 lb.	1889 . .	50·44 lb.	1906 . .	75·74 lb.
1873 . .	40·08 lb.	**1890** . .	50·72 lb.	1907 . .	81·19 lb.
1874 . .	41·64 lb.	1891 . .	60·70 lb.	1908 . .	74·11 lb.
1875 . .	43·33 lb.	1892 . .	60·22 lb.	1909 . .	80·43 lb.
1876 . .	35·42 lb.	1893 . .	64·24 lb.	**1910** . .	79·90 lb.
1877 . .	39·07 lb.	1894 . .	72·99 lb.	1911 . .	77·15 lb.
1878 . .	34·59 lb.	1895 . .	62·69 lb.	1912 . .	82·43 lb.
1879 . .	40·99 lb.	1896 . .	63·98 lb.	1913 . .	85·04 lb.
1880 . .	39·46 lb.	1897 . .	78·20 lb.	1914 . .	89·14 lb.
1881 . .	42·89 lb.	1898 . .	47·55 lb.		

Stat. Abstr. of U.S.A. 1916. No. 39. 1917.

TABLE XI

GROWTH OF PER CAPITA CONSUMPTION OF COMMODITIES IN U.S.A.

Years.	Wheat.	Sugar.	Coffee.	Tea.	Spirits.	Wines.	Malt, Beer.	All Liquors and Wines.
	Bush.	Lb.	Lb.	Lb.	Proof Galls.	Galls.	Galls.	Galls.
1830	—	—	2·98	·53	—	—	—	—
1840	—	—	5·06	·99	2·52	·29	1·36	4·17
1841–50	—	—	6·49	·86	2·23	·27	1·58	4·08
1851–60	—	—	6·81	·76	2·86	·34	3·22	6·42
1861–70	—	—	4·69	·92	2·07	·32	5·31	7·70
1871–80	5·20	39·17	7·25	1·33	1·39	·47	6·93	8·79
1881–90	5·43	48·59	8·59	1·35	1·34	·48	11·38	13·20
1891-1900	4·67	63·15	9·41	1·26	1·38	·40	15·34	17·12
1901–10	6·41	74·59	10·98	1·10	1·41	·55	18·63	20·59
1911–16	5·93	83·44	9·82	1·0	1·40	·52	19·60	21·52

TABLE XII

SHOWING INDEX NUMBERS [1]

Quinquennial Average Level of the Consumption of Commodities, 1870–9 = 100.

	1860–1864.	1865–1869.	1870–1874.	1875–1879.	1880–1884.	1885–1889.	1890–1894.	1895–1899.	1900–1904.	1905–1909.
Wheat	101	96	97	103	104	104	111	107	108	111
Cocoa	44	97	87	113	126	167	206	264	375	397
Coffee	118	110	100	100	92	85	75	71	72	68
Currants, raisins .	85	93	100	100	98	96	109	111	98	109
Cotton	61	73	102	98	109	105	105	104	98	112
Meat	—	91	99	101	100	100	110	119	119	118
Rice	56	56	98	102	130	90	86	77	74	84
Sugar	63	75	89	111	122	129	138	148	150	148
Tea	65	82	93	107	109	116	125	135	142	145
Tobacco	87	95	97	103	100	103	114	121	131	136
Wool	86	92	100	100	95	108	114	120	103	106
Wine	61	89	102	98	82	72	74	77	66	52
Spirits	76	83	96	104	89	81	86	83	88	73
Malt and beer .	83	92	100	100	99	98	107	112	109	98
Average unweighted	·76	84·5	97	103	104	104	111	118·5	122	126
Increase p.c. over 1860–4	—	11	27	35	37	37	46	58	60	66

[1] G. H. Wood, "Some Statistics Relating to Working Class Progress since 1860." *Journal of Royal Statistical Society*, vol. 62, 1899, p. 663.

TABLE XIII

CONSUMPTION OF COMMODITIES IN ITALY PER HEAD OF POPULATION.[1]

	Wheat.	Maize.	Wine.	Spirits.	Beer.	Sugar.	Coffee.	Tobacco.
	Kg.	Kg.	L.	L.	L.	Kg.	Kg.	Kg.
1881–1885	123	76	72	1·13	·69	3·17	·58	·59
1886–1890	122	67	98	·61	·82	2·47	·45	·53
1891–1895	120	58	91	·62	·58	2·37	·42	·51
1896–1900	117	68	91	·58	·55	2·43	·42	·47
1901–1905	152	74	111	·68	·79[2]	2·98[3]	·54[3]	·49
1906–1910	155	75	127	·51	1·63	3·92	·67	·53
1911–1913	171	80	127	·65	2·13	4·77	·77	·54

[1] Annuar. Stat. different years; wheat, maize, wine, and tobacco only from 1884–5 as first period.
[2] Only approximately.
[3] 1901–1906.

TABLE XIV

ESTIMATED TOTAL CONSUMPTION OF COMMODITIES IN THE UNITED KINGDOM FROM 1893–1904, ACCORDING TO G. H. WOOD. PER HEAD OF POPULATION.[1]

	1893.	1894.	1895.	1896.	1897.	1898.	1899.	1900.	1901.	1902.	1903.
Corn (wheat, flour). bush.	6·08	5·82	6·53	5·14	5·53	6·11	6·10	5·76	5·80	6·11	6·30
Cocoa . . lb.	·54	·58	·63	·62	·7	·79	·83	·92	1·02	1·09	·97
Coffee . . lb.	·69	·69	·70	·69	·68	·68	·71	·71	·76	·68	·71
Cotton . . lb.	31·02	39·89	39·72	39·81	37·5	47·6	32·4	37·5	39·0	36·7	35·1
Currants, raisins lb.	5·02	4·90	4·97	4·95	4·78	4·81	4·81	3·70	4·09	4·78	4·53
Meat . . lb.	114·23	119·77	123·73	130·39	129·79	132·22	138·49	133·59	133·62	126·44	129·9
Rice . . lb.	8·54	7·26	8·09	6·49	8·59	7·52	8·76	10·14	11·43	17·14	12·18
Sugar . . lb.	78·85	80·06	88·13	85·29	78·12	82·73	82·08	85·53	91·39	82·17	79·82
Tea . . lb.	5·41	5·52	5·67	5·77	5·79	5·83	5·95	6·07	6·10	6·07	6·04
Tobacco . lb.	1·63	1·66	1·67	1·73	1·66	1·74	1·79	1·87	1·81	1·85	1·87
Wool . . lb.	12·30	12·93	13·15	13·40	11·70	13·44	12·09	11·62	12·40	10·90	9·85
Wine . .galls.	·37	·36	·37	·40	·39	·41	·41	·38	·37	·36	·33
Spirits . .galls.	·98	·97	1·0	1·02	1·02	1·03	1·09	1·12	1·09	1·05	·99
Beer . .galls.	29·59	29·47	29·65	30·89	31·29	31·76	32·13	31·56	30·75	30·29	29·78

[1] "Some Statistics Relating to Working Class Progress." *Journal R. Stat. Soc.*, 1899, vol. 62, p. 650. Wool according to Wood's estimate.

TABLE XV

ANNUAL CONSUMPTION OF COMMODITIES IN THE UNITED KINGDOM PER HEAD OF POPULATION.[1]

Article.	1897.	1898.	1899.	1900.	1901.	1902.	1903.	1904.	1905.	1906.	1907.	1908.	1909.	1910.	1911.	1912.	1913.
Corn (wheat, flour) bush.	5·53	6·11	6·10	5·76	5·80	6·11	6.30	6·04	6·34	6·22	6·20	5·78	6·15	6·20	6·02	6·28	6·17
Cocoa . . lb.	·70	·79	·83	·92	1·02	1·09	·97	1·06	1·08	1·02	1·01	1·05	1·20	1·18	1·23	1·73	1·70
Coffee . . lb.	·68	·68	·71	·71	·76	·68	·71	·68	·67	·66	·67	·66	·67	·65	·62	·61	·61
Cotton. . lb.	37·5	47·6	32·4	37·6	39·0	36·7	35·1	39·8	44·4	40·4	46·7	39·9	42·8	37·9	41·9	54·36	41·21
Currants, raisins . . lb.	4·78	4·81	4·81	3·70	4·09	4·78	4·53	4·50	4·59	4·86	4·91	4·62	4·88	4·64	4·89	4·66	4·79
Meat . . lb.	129·79	132·22	138·49	133·59	133·62	126·44	129·90	130·33	130·45	130·72	130·18	129·44	125·41	123·66	128·41	122·92	123·65
Rice (meal, 1900) lb.	8·59	7·52	8·76	10·14	11·43	17·14	12·18	12·15	13·98	15·15	13·21	15·67	14·06	20·35	15·08	14·81	15·01
Sugar . . lb.	78·12	82·73	82·08	85·53	91·39	82·17	79·82	83·0	74·45	83·33	86·75	82·71	86·71	83·45	80·22	79·13	82·54
Tea . . lb.	5·79	5·83	5·95	6·07	6·16	6·07	6·04	6·02	6·02	6·22	6·26	6·24	6·36	6·39	6·47	6·46	6·64
Tobacco . lb.	1·66	1·74	1·79	1·87	1·31	1·85	1·87	1·90	1·92	1·93	2·0	1·99	1·92	1·96	2·05	2·06	2·08
Wool . . lb.	11·70	13·44	12·09	11·62	12·40	10·90	9·85	9·56	10·19	10·95	12·56	11·14	11·18	13·00	13·80	14·13	14·53
Wine . .galls.	·39	·41	·41	·38	·37	·36	·33	·28	·28	·28	·28	·26	·26	·28	·25	·25	·25
Spirits. .galls.	1·02	1·03	1·09	1·12	1·09	1·05	·99	·96	·92	·91	·91	·86	·70	·65	·68	·67	·69
Beer . .galls.	31·29	31·76	32·53	31·56	30·78	30·29	29·78	28·92	27·85	28·16	27·81	26·88	26·12	26·32	27·22	26·74	27·31

[1] Published by the permission of Professor Bowley.

TABLE XVI

CONSUMPTION

Index Numbers of Commodities in the United Kingdom (1870–9) = 100.[1]

Article.	1897.	1898.	1899.	1900.	1901.	1902.	1903.	1904.	1905.	1906.	1907.	1908.	1909.	1910.	1911.	1912.	1913.
Corn (wheat, flour)	100	110	110	104	105	110	114	109	114	112	112	104	111	112	109	113	111
Cocoa	259	293	307	341	378	404	359	393	400	378	374	389	444	437	456	641	630
Coffee	69	69	72	72	78	69	72	69	68	67	68	67	68	66	63	62	62
Cotton	101	125	85	98	102	96	92	104	116	106	122	105	112	99	110	143	108
Currants, raisins	109	109	109	84	93	109	103	102	105	111	112	105	111	106	111	106	109
Rice[2] meal from 1900	83	73	85	59	67	100	71	71	82	88	77	91	82	119	88	143	145
Meat	118	120	123	121	122	115	118	119	119	119	118	118	114	113	117	112	112
Sugar	139	147	146	152	163	146	142	148	133	149	155	147	154	149	164	141	147
Tea	135	136	139	142	144	142	141	140	140	145	146	145	148	149	151	151	155
Tobacco	117	123	126	132	128	130	132	134	132	136	141	140	132	138	142	144	146
Wool	110	127	114	110	117	103	93	90	96	103	119	105	106	123	130	132	137
Wine	75	79	79	73	71	69	63	54	54	54	54	50	50	54	48	49	49
Spirits	86	67	92	95	92	89	84	81	78	77	77	73	59	55	58	57	59
Beer	113	114	117	114	111	109	107	104	100	101	100	97	94	95	98	96	98
Total	1,614	1,712	1,704	1,697	1,771	1,791	1,691	1,717	1,737	1,746	1,776	1,736	1,785	1,815	1,845	—	—
Unweighted average	115	122	122	121	127	128	121	123	124	125	127	124	127	130	132	—	—
Do., excluding cocoa	104	109	107	104	107	107	102	102	103	105	108	104	103	106	107	—	—
Weighted average:																	
System 1	116	123	119	117	121	118	116	117	118	120	125	118	120	120	126	—	—
,, 2	115	123	121	120	124	122	120	121	123	123	126	121	124	125	128	—	—
,, 3	116	124	122	121	125	123	120	122	124	129	127	122	125	126	130	—	—
,, 4	112	120	117	116	119	116	115	115	117	118	121	116	118	118	121	—	—
,, 5	114	122	119	118	121	117	116	117	118	119	122	117	119	119	123	126	124

[1] Rice incorrect, but the weight is so small except for unweighted average as to be negligible.

TABLE XVII

CONSUMPTION OF COMMODITIES IN FRANCE PER HEAD, FROM 1864–74.[1]

Year.	Wheat, Flour.	Potatoes.	Sugar.	Wine.	Spirits, Alcohol	Beer.	Tea.	Coffee.	Cocoa.
	Hect.	Quint.	Kg.	L.	L.	L.	Kg.	Kg.	Kg.
1864	2·90	2·22	5·5	61	2·33	19·1	·008	1·067	·142
1865	2·40	2·40	6·2	68	3·34	20·2	·008	1·143	·150
1866	2·08	1·92	7·1	75	2·53	21·2	·010	1·176	·165
1867	2·40	2·07	7·1	68	2·47	18·4	·008	1·235	·172
1868	3·32	2·79	6·1	71	2·55	19·2	·008	1·364	·191
1869	2·84	2·44	7·3	72	2·63	19·7	·008	1·310	·207
1870	2·84	2·44	5·8	65	2·32	17·8	·010	1·977	·308
1871	2·30	2·33	7·8	66	2·81	19·1	·007	1·109	·221
1872	3·38	2·28	5·1	77	2·09	20·5	·006	·462	·92
1873	2·36	2·48	6·9	76	2·59	21·1	·007	1·233	·203
1874	3·88	3·00	6·3	66	2·69	20·7	·008	1·059	·205

[1] *Annuaire Statistique*, vol. 33, 1913, pp. 106–118. Résumé rétrospectif.

TABLE XVIII

CONSUMPTION OF COMMODITIES IN RUSSIA, INCLUDING POLAND (SIXTY GOVERNMENTS), PER HEAD OF POPULATION.[1]

Period.	Wheat.	Rye.	Barley.	Oats.
	Kg.	Kg.	Kg.	Kg.
1896–1900 . . .	40·45	138·36	25·47	67·54
1901–1905 . . .	58·82	137·63	27·77	67·15
1901	43·67	118·81	21·39	39·30
1902	72·07	149·01	34·01	78·69
1903	57·71	145·13	29·61	57·18
1904	72·51	167·42	27·41	99·61
1905	47·99	107·91	26·36	59·93
1906	33·29	90·33	19·75	40·61
1907	44·97	147·97	27·83	69·97

[1] *Das Getreide im Weltverkehre*. IV Folge. 1909. Vienna.

TABLE XIX

CONSUMPTION OF COMMODITIES IN GERMANY PER HEAD OF POPULATION.[1]

Period.	Rye.	Wheat. Spelz.	Potatoes.	Spirits.[2]	Beer.[3]	Tobacco.	Sugar.	Salt (eating)
	Kg.	Kg.	Kg.	L.	L.	Kg.	Kg.	Kg.
1900–1	147·6	91·0	604·6	6·3	118	—	—	—
1901–2	137·7	85·0	732·4	6·1	117	—	—	—
1902–3	158·3	100·1	636·1	6·2	110	—	—	—
1903–4	154·8	93·2	614·1	6·3	110	—	17·2	7·9
1904–5	147·0	93·4	502·8	6·0	110	—	14·4	7·5
1905–6	149·0	99·8	687·0	6·2	112	—	16·6	7·8
1906–7	143·5	94·4	592·6	6·1	112	(1906) 1·5	16·8	7·8
1907–8	142·4	90·7	625·3	6·3	111	(1907) 1·6	17·1	7·9
1908–9	141·3	83·6	631·4	6·5	105	(1908) 1·7	17·6	7·7
1909–10	152·0	93·3	624·9	5·7	99	1·4	17·5	7·8
1910–11	139·3	87·6	565·8	5·2	99	1·5	19·0	8·0
1911–12	140·1	87·6	438·8	5·3	106	1·5	16·9	7·6
1912–13	145·2	93·6	656·1	5·4	101	1·7	19·2	7·9

[1] *Stat. Jahrbuch für das Deutsche Reich.*, 35 Jrg., 1914; as human and animal food and in technical use.

[2] For all purposes.

[3] The years are: 1900, 1901, etc.

TABLE XX

CONSUMPTION OF SOME COMMODITIES IN GERMANY PER HEAD OF POPULATION.[1]

Year.	Cotton	Groceries.	Coffee.	Cocoa.[2]	Rice.	Tea.	Jute.	Trop. Fruits.	Herrings.
	Kg.	Kg.	Kg.	Kg.	Kg.	Kg.	Kg.	Kg.	
1901	5·73	·16	3·59	·30	2·13	·05	1·94	2·15	—
1902	5·79	·15	4·06	·34	2·23	05	2·31	2·51	—
1903	6·28	·15	3·69	·35	2·25	·05	1·73	2·69	—
1904	6·41	·17	3·68	·44	2·61	·05	2·22	2·82	—
1905	6·52	·17	3·53	·47	2·41	·05	2·00	2·54	—
1906	6·28	·17	3·02	·55	2·73	·06	2·30	2·71	2·95
1907	7·29	·17	3·02	·52	2·51	·06	2·39	2·96	3·12
1908	6·79	·20	3·03	·52	2·53	·06	2·33	3·07	2·85
1909	6·98	·19	3·30	·61	2·54	·08	2·64	3·05	2·93
1910	5·87	·15	2·60	·64	2·68	·05	1·89	3·94	2·93
1911	6·70	·16	2·79	·75	2·71	·06	2·08	4·09	2·71
1912	7·56	·16	2·53	·81	2·43	·06	2·28	4·52	2·71
1913	7·23	·16	2·44	·77	3·56	·06	2·29	4·44	2·89

[1] *Stat. Jahrbuch. f. d. Deutsche Reich,* 1914, 28 Jrg.

[2] Cocoa in grain.

TABLE XXI

WAR CONSUMPTION OF COMMODITIES IN FRANCE PER HEAD OF POPULATION, FROM 1913 ONWARDS.[1]

Article.		1913.	1914.	1915.	1916.
Wheat . . .	Hect.	3·38	3·08	2·66	2·86
Potatoes . . .	Qnt.	3·43	3·05	2·35	2·30
Sugar	Kg.	18·1	—	—	—
Wine	L.	126·0	165·0	70·0	112·0
Spirits . . .	L.	3·96	3·35	3·04	3·04
Beer	L.	32·4	23·4	15·0	15·0
Cotton . . .	Kg.	6·8	1·5	5·5	5·9
Wool	Kg.	6·8	6·8	6·8	6·8
Tea	Kg.	·030	·048	·070	·064
Coffee . . .	Kg.	2·904	2·931	3·488	3·853
Cocoa . . .	Kg.	·695	·658	·881	·926

[1] *Annuaire Stat.*, vol. 34, 1914 et 1915.

TABLE XXII[1]

Period.	Area. Sown with Wheat. Million Acres.	Produce. Per Acre. Bush.	Produce. Total. Million Bush.	Net Imports. Wheat and Wheat-flour. Million Bush.	Per cent. of Supplies Imported.
		UNITED KINGDOM.			
1881–90	2·7	26	76	144	67
1891–1900	2·0	30	60	177	76
1901–10	1·7	32	55	209	80
		FRANCE.			
1881–90	17·2	17	301	39	12
1891–1900	17·1	18	305	36	11
1901–10	16·2	20	319	10	3
		GERMANY, CORRECTED TABLE.			
1881–90	4·7	22	104	18	16
1891–1900	4·9	25	125	41	27
1901–10	4·6	29	133	70	36
		AUSTRIA-HUNGARY.			
1881–90	9·5	17	161	Export : 11	—
1891–1900	10·9	17	186	„ 1	—
1901–10	11·9	18	213	Import : 3	—

[1] J. F. Unstead, *The Geographical Journal*, 1913.

TABLE XXII—*continued.*

Period.	Area. Sown with Wheat. Million Acres.	Produce. Per Acre. Bush.	Produce. Total. Million Bush.	Net Imports. Wheat and Wheat-flour. Million Bush.	Per Cent. of Supplies Imported.
			RUSSIAN EMPIRE (WHOLE).		
1881–90	38·6	8·2	318	Export : 87 (27% of harvest exported)	
1891–1900	46·8	8·5	400	,, 104 (26% ,,)	
1901–10	61·7	10	616	,, 142 (23% ,,)	
			ITALY.		
1881–90	11·3	10	118	Import : 23	18
1891–1900	11·3	11	123	,, 22	17
1901–10	12·2	13	163	,, 38	21

TABLE XXIII

AVERAGE PRODUCTION IN THE WORLD.[1]

Period.	Population. Millions.	Gold Total. £000,000.	Pig-iron. Metric Tons, 000,000.	Wheat. Quarters, 000,000.
1881–1890	1369	22·10	22·45	269·9
1891–1900	1488	43·16	31·50	312·3
1901–1910	1609	77·69	53·83	403·1

[1] J. Kitchin, *Trade-Cycles Chart.* 3rd edition.

TABLE XXIV

World Production.[1]

Year.	Pig-lead. Metric Tons, 000.	Pig-iron. Metric Tons, 000,000.	Copper. Metric Tons, 000.	Spelter, English Tons, 000.	Raw Tin. Metric Tons, 000.	Gold. £000,000.
1901	846=10	40·95	525	507	87	54·0
1902	873	44·34	550	545	89	61·0
1903	873	47·11	584	571	91	67·3
1904	970	46·07	648	625	103	71·2
1905	968	54·05	693	659	102	78·1
1906	984	59·07	720	702	104	82·9
1907	1015	60·68	712	738	102	85·0
1908	1054	48·64	764	722	113	90·9
1909	1087	61·22	854	783	113	93·2
1910	1127	66·21	891	816	115	93·5
1911	1136	63·21	894	902	118	94·8
1912	1182	73·53	1,019	978	125	97·4
1913	1187	79·40	1,006	998	129	95·0

[1] H. R. Merton and Co., *Comparative Statistics of Lead, Copper, Spelter, Tin, etc.* London, 1914, and Metalgesellschaft, 1905.

TABLE XXV

Index Numbers of World Production of Cereals and some other Commodities.[1]

Year.	Wheat.	Rye.	Barley.	Oats.	Maize.	Rice.	To-bacco.	Su-gar.[3]	Cotton.
1901 [2]	100	100	100	100	100	100	100	100	100
1902	107·6	115·7	113·5	125·0	143·2	112·1	105·3	108·7	111·7
1903	113·4	116·6	113·0	117·5	134·9	111·2	107·9	97·9	105·4
1904	108·3	122·7	107·4	124·6	134·6	115·3	91·4	101·0	136·3
1905	114·7	105·0	107·9	121·6	154·4	105·7	91·3	96·2	111·6
1906	119·5	100·5	119·4	123·8	166·7	108·6	95·3	114·8	143·4
1907	108·8	108·5	117·7	125·4	148·9	100·5	99·4	120·7	115·7
1908	108·5	111·7	117·3	124 6	155·9	104·2	102·8	114·0	134·8
1909	124·2	122·6	136·6	149·9	150·9	137·3	127·0	118·5	113·8
1910	123·4	117·2	127·3	145·1	164·4	134·0	128·5	121·6	126·3
1911	132·5	112·3	132·0	136·8	170·5	147·0	—	—	—
1912	143·4	135·5	140·7	163·6	194·0	145·5	—	—	—
1913	152·7	133·8	151·9	164·8	167·2	141·0	—	—	—

[1] From *Ann. Int. de Stat. Agricole*, 1910. Inst. Int. d'Agriculture, Rome, 1912. The years 1911–13 calculated on the basis of figures given by the same Institute, *Stat. Notes on the Yield, etc.*, 1916.

[2] For cereals, 1901 and 1901–2, 1902 and 1902–3, etc.

[3] Cane and beet.

TABLE XXVI

Average Population in the Decades.[1]

Period.	United Kingdom.	France.	Germany.	U.S.A.
		0,000 omitted.		
1880–9	35·90	37·99	46·65	55·60
1890–9	39·07	38·50	51·93	68·36
1900–9	43·08	39·19	60·24	92·32
		Cattle.		
		000,000.		
1880–9	10·30	12·51	16·67 [2]	44·43
1890–9	10·97	13·27	18·25	49·10
1900–9	11·56	13·53	18·78	66·50
		Sheep.		
		000,000.		
1880–9	29·01	22·28	19·26 [2]	46·22
1890–9	31·52	22·24	14·82	41·67
1900–9	30·23	18·41	12·10	56·04
		Pigs.		
		000,000.		
1880–9	—	—	10·68 [2]	—
1890–9	—	—	14·48	—
1900–9	—	—	19·48	—

[1] Official statistics.

[2] The average of years 1880 and 1890, 1890 and 1900, and 1900 and 1910 taken as representing the average of the decade.

TABLE XXVII

Index Numbers of Wholesale Prices, 1871–1912.[1]

Prices in 1900 = 100.

Groups of Commodities.	1900–4.	1905–9.	1910–12.
Group I. Coal and metals . . .	80·7	77·9	78·7
Group II. Textiles (raw materials) .	102·0	115·5	128·2
Group III. Food, drink, tobacco—			
A. Corn, etc.	102·2	108·9	114·7
B. Meat, fish, dairy produce .	100·8	102·8	112·5
Whole	100·7	104·7	113·6
Group IV. Miscellaneous. . . .	93·8	95·5	106·6
All forty-seven articles	97·7	102·3	111·0

[1] *Cost of Living of the Working Classes.* Report of an inquiry by the Board of Trade into working-class rents and retail prices, 1912. Cd. 6955, 1913. Averages calculated from the figures given in Cd. 6955.

TABLE XXVIII

GERMANY.

Index Numbers of Wholesale Prices of some Commodities, based on the Figures of the Imperial Statistical Office, with the base 1900 = 100.[1]

Period.	Rye and Wheat, Potatoes.	Oxen, Pigs, Calves, Sheep.	Wool, Cotton.	Copper,[2] Pig-iron.	Coal [2] and Petroleum[3]
1900–4	100	106	97	78	91
1905–9	118	125	109	77	89
1910–12	138	139	120	77	97

[1] Cd. 6955.
[2] English and German.
[3] American and Russian.

TABLE XXIX

INDEX NUMBERS OF WHOLESALE PRICES IN RUSSIA.

Average 1890–99 = 100.[1]

Article.	1900–1904.	1905–1909.	1910–1911.
Cereals [2]	104·5	132·2	121·3
Animal [3]	119·9	142·9	149·2
Oleaginous [4]	108·9	112·8	137·8
Textile [5]	128·9	137·3	153·1
Mineral [6]	108·4	128·9	123·3
Dyes and chemicals [7]	101·1	113·3	115·7
Colonial [8].	104·4	107·0	108·1
General index number . .	110·9	124·9	129·7

[1] Cd. 6955.
[2] Cereals = rye, wheat, oats, barley, maize, peas, buckwheat, buckwheat-meal, millet, wheat-flour, rye-flour, bran, malt.
[3] Animal products : Horned cattle, live sheep and pigs, beef, pork, hides, tallow, butter, herrings.
[4] Oleaginous products : Linseed, hempseed, sunflower seed, linseed oil, hempseed oil, sunflower seed oil, rapeseed oil, olive oil, oilcake.
[5] Textiles : Flax, hemp, cotton, cotton yarn, calico, wool.
[6] Mineral products : Coal, naphtha, waste, kerosine, pig-iron, manufactured iron, copper, tin, zinc, lead.
[7] Dyes, chemicals : Whitelead, indigo, dye extracts, white resin, tragacanth, borax, coppers, potash, soda, saltpetre, sulphur.
[8] Colonial : Salt, sugar, coffee beans, tea, rice, pepper, currants, almonds, hops.

TABLE XXX

UNITED STATES OF AMERICA.

Index Numbers of Wholesale Prices of Commodities in the United States by Groups and for all Articles.[1]
Wholesale Prices, Official Index Numbers Recalculated by Board of Trade, 1900 = 100.

Groups of Commodities.	1900–1908.	1905–1909.	1910–1911.
Farm products	109·9	122·5	149·1
Food	102·4	112·2	124·7
Cloth and clothing	98·5	111·5	113·8
Fuel and lighting	108·6	108·5	102·5
Metals and implements . .	95·7	108·1	102·8
Lumber and building materials	102·9	118·6	131·8
Drugs and chemicals . . .	98·1	95·8	102·5
House furnishing goods . .	104·4	106·4	105·0
Miscellaneous	101·4	110·5	120·3
All commodities	101·1	110·5	115·8

[1] Cd. 6955.

TABLE XXXI

INDEX NUMBERS OF RETAIL PRICES OF FOOD AND FUEL IN VIENNA.[1]

1900 = 100.

Groups of Commodities.	1900–1904.	1905–1909.	1910–1912.
Flour, bread, and potatoes .	95·6	114·4	132·1
Beef, veal, pork, and lard .	103·1	118·8	140·7
General index numbers, including petroleum and coal (sixteen articles)[2]	100·7	112·1	125·6
General index numbers, excluding petroleum and coal. .	101·1	114·1	129·4

[1] Cd. 6955.

[2] Articles included: Flour, bread, peas, lentils, potatoes, sauerkraut, milk, sugar, butter, beef, veal, pork, lard, bacon, petroleum, coal.

TABLE XXXII

INDEX NUMBERS OF RETAIL PRICES OF FOOD, DRINK,[1] FUEL AND LIGHTING MATERIALS IN HUNGARY, 1900–11.

1900 = 100.

Period.	Average Food, Drink, Fuel and Lighting Material.	Food only.
1900–1904	103	103·4
1905–1909	122·5	124·2
1910–1911	130·1	133

[1] Cd. 6955.

TABLE XXXIII

INDEX NUMBERS OF WHOLESALE PRICES IN JAPAN.[1]

1900 = 100.

Groups of Commodities.	1900–1904.	1905–1909.	1910–1911.
Food, drink, tobacco . . .	107	134	135
Clothing and textiles . . .	102	122	128
Minerals, fuel, timber, manufactured articles	95	106	112
General average	101	121	125

[1] Cd. 6955.

TABLE XXXIV

COURSE OF WHOLESALE PRICES IN CANADA.[1]

Average Prices 1890–1899 = 100.

Groups of Commodities.	1900–1904.	1905–1909.	1910–1912.
Grain and fodder	109·1	134·7	152·1
Animals and meat	113·2	132·6	157·0
Textiles	104·2	116·7	118·1
Metals and implements . .	106·2	111·9	106·9
Fuel and lighting	103·6	105·1	105·6
Drugs and chemicals . . .	103·7	106·0	112·4
General index numbers [2] . .	109·2	120·4	128·7

[1] Cd. 6955.

[2] Including: Grains and fodder, animals and meat, dairy products, fish, other foods, textiles, hides, tallow, leather, boots and shoes, metals and implements, fuel and lighting, building materials, house furnishings, drugs and chemicals, miscellaneous.

TABLE XXXV

WHEAT AREA.[1]

Country.	1909–13.	1913.	1914.	1915.	1916.
	000 Hect.				
Germany	1,930	1,974	1,996	—	—
Austria	1,219	1,213	670	—	—
Hungary	3,674	3,433	3,790	3,320	—
Bulgaria	1,074	1,016	1,068	1,086	1,086
France	6,540	6,542	6,060	5,967	—
U.K.	764	725	771	944	830
Italy	4·744	4,744	4,768	5,059	4,726
Rumania	1·852	1,623	2,112	1,904	1,960
Russian Emp.	24,772 (1910–13)	25,118	25,392	24,487	20,542
Canada	4,262	4,518	4,166	5,255	4,081
U.S.	19,059	20,309	21,668	24,871	20,587
British India	11,824	12,158	11,519	13,142	12,198
Russia, As.	3,853	5,002	5,511	5,881 (10 gov.)	—
Algeria	1,414 (1909–10, 13–14)	1,395 (13–14)	1,363 (14–15)	1,299 (15–16)	— (16–17)
Argentine	6,496	6,574	6,621	6,450	6,511
Australia	3,077	3,758	4,777	4,654	4,541
New Zealand	98	67	93	135	—
Total.	106,188	110,350	111,778	117,703	104,481

[1] *Notes of Int. Agricult. Inst.*, 1917.

TABLE XXXVI

WORLD PRODUCTION OF COAL AND STEEL.

Period.	Coal.[1] 000,000 Metric Tons.	Steel.[2] 000,000 Metric Tons.
1901	79·2	31·4
1902–4	85·9	35·8
1905–7	102·4	48·3
1908–10	110·1	52·2
1911–12	127·1	64·0 (approx.)

[1] *Stat. Abst. for Foreign Countries.* No. 39. 1901–12. 1914.
[2] *The Mineral Industry*, 1911, vol. 20, 1912, p. 435. The year 1911–12 approximately.

TABLE XXXVII

WHEAT YIELD PER ACRE.[1]

Country.	1881–1890.	1891–1900.	1901–1910.
	Bushels per Acre.		
United Kingdom	28	30	32
France	17	18	20
Germany	19	25	29
Austria-Hungary	17	17	18
Russia (European)	8	8	10
Scandinavia	22	24	27
Iberian Peninsula	11	10	13
Italy	10	11	13
Balkan Peninsula	13	13	13
Rumania	12	14	17
Belgium	30	33	35
Holland	27	28	33
Switzerland	29	31	33
Denmark	27	30	35
Europe	13	13	14
Asia	10	10	11
Canada	16	18	19
United States	12	13	14
North America, including Mexico	12	14	15
Argentine	12	11	11
South America	12	12	11
Australasia	10	8	11
Africa	8	8	10
WORLD	12	12	13

[1] J. F. Unstead, "Stat. Study of Wheat Cultivation and Trade," 1881–1910. *The Geographical Journal*, vol. 42. 1913. August–September.

TABLE XXXVIII

PRODUCTIVE AND UNPRODUCTIVE AREAS AS PERCENTAGES OF TOTAL AREA.[1]

Countries.	Productive Area.	Per cent.	Unproductive Area.	Per cent.	Total Area.
	Hectares.		Hectares.		Hectares.
Germany . .	51,153,756	94·6	2,911,029	5·4	54,064,785
Austria. . .	28,204,456	94·0	1,796,337	6·0	30,000,793
Belgium . .	2,607,514	88·5	338,043	11·5	2,945,557
Bulgaria . .	7,119,352	73·9	2,515,198	26·1	9,634,550
France . . .	49,737,185	93·9	3,218,579	5·1	52,955,764
U. Kingdom .	26,927,308	86·2	4,295,612	13·8	31,222,920
Gt. Britain .	19,326,870	84·1	3,660,519	15·9	22,987,389
Ireland . .	7,600,438	92·3	635,095	7·7	8,235,531
Hungary . .	31,252,671	96·2	1,223,029	3·8	32,475,700
Italy . . .	26,371,607	92·0	2,296,615	8·0	28,668,222
Rumania . .	9,973,663	76·6	3,044,037	23·4	3,017,700
Canada . .	25,665,752	2·7	940,311,366	97·3	965,977,118
Central India .	187,813,168	74·6	63,788,023	25·4	251,601,191
Argentine . .	217,647,000	73·7	77,608,100	26·3	295,255,100

[1] Annuaire Inst. Inter. Agricult. Rome, 1910.

FIG. 2.

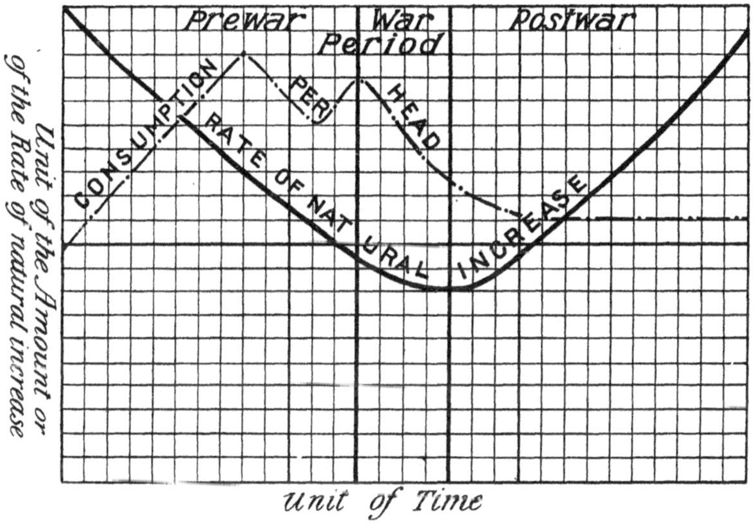

DIAGRAM,
showing the pre-war, war and post-war fluctuation in the rate of natural increase and in the consumption per head. The pre-war period of the consumption is in ascending phase, while the war and post-war period is in declining or stationary. The pre-war period of the rate of natural increase is in declining, while the post-war is in ascending.

FIG. 3.

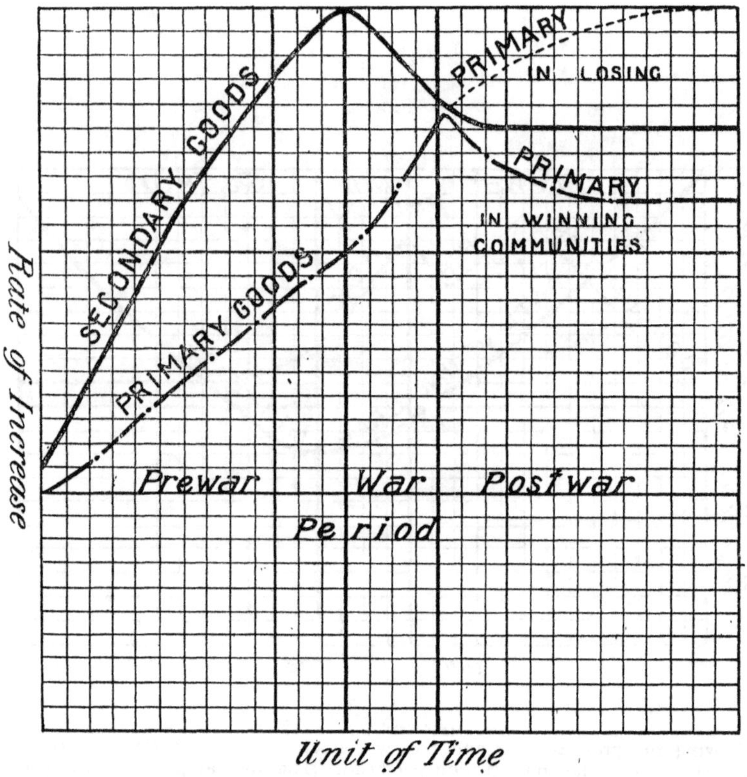

DIAGRAM,

showing the pre-war, war and post-war production of primary and secondary goods. The rate of increase in the production of secondary goods is twice as great as that in the production of primary ones in the pre-war period. During the war the production of secondary goods is declining, while that of prmary goods is ascending. In the post-war period is increasing in the countries losing the war, and declining in the war-winning communities, while the production of secondary goods is in stable condition.

FIG 4.

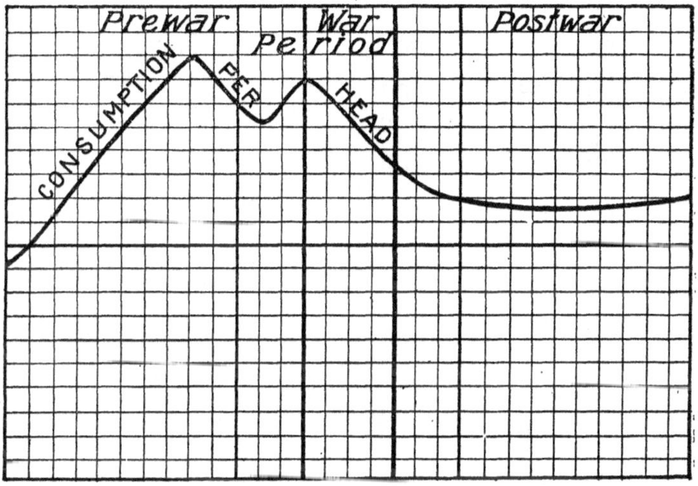

DIAGRAM,

showing the general pre-war ascending phase in the consumption with "the pressure on consumption" in the same period.

FIG. 5.

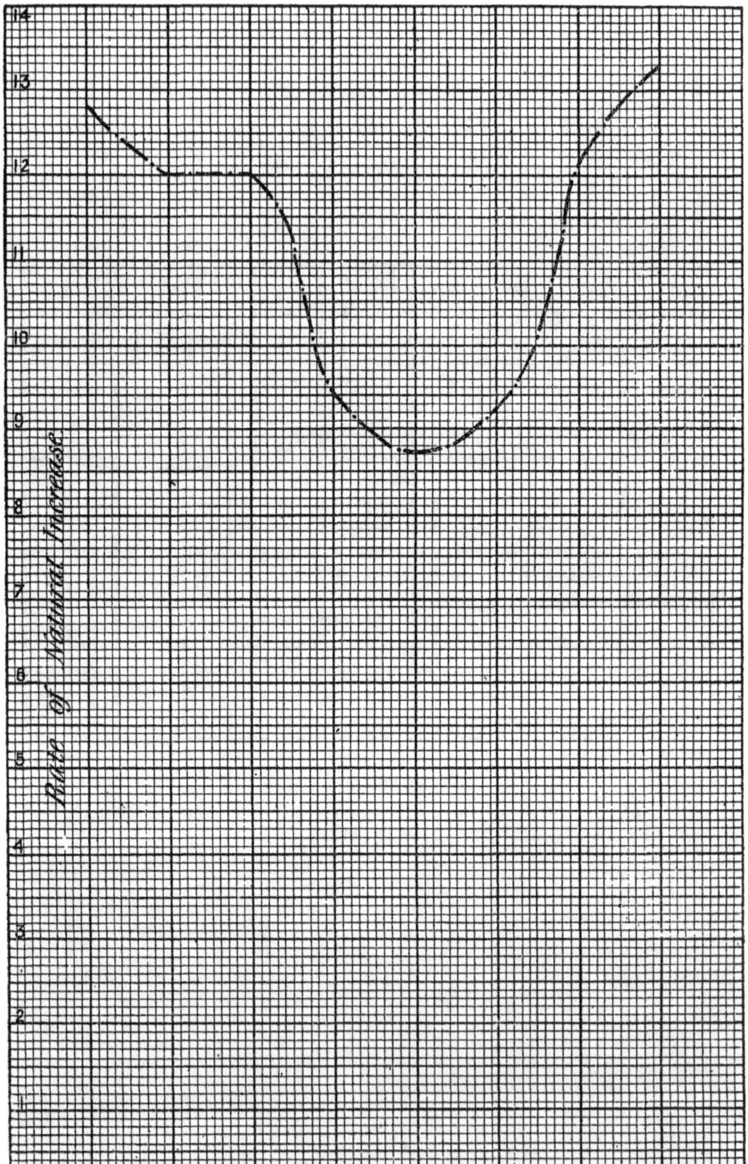

DIAGRAM,
showing the balancing action of Russo-Japanese War, 1904–5, on the rate of natural increase in Japan rate per 1,000 inhabitants.

For Product Safety Concerns and Information please contact our EU
representative GPSR@taylorandfrancis.com
Taylor & Francis Verlag GmbH, Kaufingerstraße 24, 80331 München, Germany

www.ingramcontent.com/pod-product-compliance
Lightning Source LLC
LaVergne TN
LVHW011127300926
849160LV00008B/543
* 9 7 8 0 4 1 5 6 0 7 0 6 3 *